# THE ROMAN REPUBLIC

BOOKS ON HISTORY BY

ISAAC ASIMOV

THE KITE THAT WON THE REVOLUTION

A SHORT HISTORY OF BIOLOGY

A SHORT HISTORY OF CHEMISTRY

ASIMOV'S BIOGRAPHICAL ENCYCLOPEDIA OF SCIENCE AND TECHNOLOGY

THE GREEKS

THE ROMAN REPUBLIC

# THE ROMAN REPUBLIC

BY ISAAC ASIMOV

HOUGHTON MIFFLIN COMPANY BOSTON

THE RIVERSIDE PRESS CAMBRIDGE

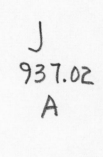

J
937.02
A

To Mary K.

for increasing the

pleasantness of life

# CONTENTS

**1 THE SEVEN KINGS**     **1**

ITALY IN THE BEGINNING     2

THE FOUNDING OF ROME     7

THE FIRST CENTURY AND A HALF     12

ETRUSCAN DOMINATION     17

**2 THE REPUBLIC SURVIVES**     **24**

FIGHTING OFF THE ETRUSCANS     24

THE PATRICIANS AND PLEBEIANS     28

THE DECLINE OF THE ETRUSCANS     34

THE GAULS     37

**3 THE CONQUEST OF ITALY**     **44**

LATIUM AND BEYOND     44

THE SAMNITES     49

ROADS AND LEGIONS     53

SAMNIUM AND BEYOND     58

**4 THE CONQUEST OF SICILY**     **65**

PYRRHUS     65

CARTHAGE 72

THE ROMANS AT SEA 77

THE FIRST PROVINCES 82

5   HANNIBAL 87

FROM SPAIN TO ITALY 87

THE ROMAN DISASTERS 93

THE TURN OF THE TIDE 99

VICTORY IN AFRICA 105

6   THE CONQUEST OF THE EAST 112

SETTLEMENT WITH PHILIP 112

SETTLEMENT WITH ANTIOCHUS 119

SHADOW OVER GREECE 122

THE END OF CARTHAGE 127

7   INTERNAL TROUBLES 134

WEALTH AND SLAVERY 134

THE GRACCHI 138

MARIUS 143

THE SOCIAL WAR 150

8   SULLA AND POMPEY 158

PONTUS 158

SULLA IN CONTROL 162

NEW MEN 169

POMPEY CLEARS THE EAST 176

9  THE TRIUMVIRATE                    182

    THE CONSPIRACY OF CATILINE      182

    THREE-MAN RULE                  187

    GAUL                            191

    PARTHIA                         194

10  CAESAR                            201

    THE SECOND CIVIL WAR            201

    EGYPT                           206

    THE DICTATOR                    211

    THE ASSASSINATION               217

11  THE END OF THE REPUBLIC           223

    CAESAR'S HEIR                   223

    THE SECOND TRIUMVIRATE          227

    ANTONY AND CLEOPATRA            232

    PEACE AT LAST                   237

A TABLE OF DATES                     242

# THE ROMAN REPUBLIC

1

# THE SEVEN KINGS

Extending southward from the continent of Europe into the Mediterranean Sea is a peninsula about five hundred miles long and shaped very much like a boot. It has a well-formed toe and a high heel. It even has a small spur above the heel. It is known to its inhabitants as *Italia* and to us as Italy.

On that peninsula there arose what was to become the largest, the most powerful and most respected government of ancient times. Beginning as a small town, it gained strength over the centuries until it ruled over all the territory from the Atlantic Ocean to the Caspian Sea, and from the island of Britain to the upper Nile.

Its system of government had many failings, but it was better than any that had gone before. It eventually brought peace and prosperity for centuries to a world that had been racked by continuous war. And when it finally collapsed, what followed was so hard and miserable that for a thousand years men looked back upon it as a time of greatness and happiness.

In one respect certainly it was unique. It marked the only time in history, either before or since, that all the civilized West was under a single rule. Its laws and traditions have therefore influenced all the lands of the West today, including our own.

In this book I intend to tell, briefly, the first part of the Roman story — the tale of its rise to power. That tale involves an extraordinary series of both triumphs and disasters; it involves great bravery in time of battle, and sometimes stupidity; sordid intrigue at home, and sometimes glowing idealism. In this book I will therefore concentrate on the excitement of war and politics.

It must be remembered, of course, that history is more than that. It is also the record of the ideas and customs a people evolve, the engineering feats they carry through, the books they write, the art they create, the games they amuse themselves with, the life they live.

I will say what I can about Roman life and thought, but just the same, soldiers and politicians will have to take up most of the room in the history I am about to begin.

## ITALY IN THE BEGINNING

To start with, there was absolutely no reason to suspect that it would be in Italy that the ancient world would reach its climax. About 1000 B.C. Italy was a backward land, thinly populated by uncivilized tribes.

Elsewhere, civilization had already been long established. In Egypt, the pyramids had been built over fifteen centuries earlier. In the Near East, cities had flourished during those centuries, and an advanced civilization, with a navy and internal plumbing, had been in existence on the island of Crete.

Then, between 1200 B.C. and 1000 B.C. there came an upheaval. People were on the move and old civilizations tottered. The tribes flooding down from the north had iron weapons; hard, sharp swords that could hack their way right through the softer, bronze shields of the civilized armies. Some of the civilizations were destroyed, others badly weakened and shaken.

Iron-using tribes spread southward into Italy, too, about 1000 B.C. Here there were no civilizations to destroy, however. Indeed, the newcomers represented an advance in culture. Their remains have been found by modern archaeologists and particularly rich pickings were discovered in Villanova, a suburb of the city of Bologna, in north central Italy. For that reason, the iron-using tribes are referred to as the Villanovans.

Some time after the coming of the Villanovans, the first real civilization arose in Italy. The people making up that civilization called themselves the Rasena and the Greeks called them Tyrrhenoi. The portion of the Mediterranean Sea just southwest of Italy is still called the Tyrrhenian Sea (tih-ree'nee-an).

The people are best known to us, however, as the Etruscans (ee-trus'kanz), and the land they inhabited was called Etruria (ee-troor'ee-uh).

Etruria occupied the west coast of Italy from its center at the Tiber River to the Arno River some 200 miles farther to the northwest. In modern times, much of this area makes up the portion of modern Italy called Tuscany, a name which obviously harks back to the Etruscans.

Who were the Etruscans? Were they the Villanovans who slowly became civilized? Or were they new tribes reaching Italy from regions that were already civilized? It is hard to tell. The Etruscan language has never been deciphered, so that their inscriptions are still mysteries to us. Furthermore, in later centuries, their culture and way of life were so well absorbed by the civilizations that followed that little remains from which we can judge their early history. The Etruscans live on chiefly as a set of question marks.

The ancients thought, however — and in this they may be right — that the Etruscans came to Italy from Asia Minor shortly after 1000 B.C. Perhaps the Etruscans were driven out of Asia Minor by the same chain of barbarian invasions and migrations that brought the Villanovans into Italy.

The Etruscan cities formed a loose union among themselves, and between 700 B.C. and 500 B.C. their power was at its height. They then controlled almost all of central Italy, penetrating the valley of the Po River in the north and reaching the Adriatic Sea.

Because so little is known about the Etruscans, it is easy to underestimate them and their contribution to the history of mankind. Early Rome was almost an Etruscan city and much of its basic traditions and culture were borrowed. The religion of Rome had a strong Etruscan tinge, as did the ritual surrounding the city's government, its games, its "triumph" rites, even some of its vocabulary.

Etruscan art was, in later centuries, very much influenced by the Greeks, but there was always much that was purely Etruscan and that was attractive in its own right. Etruscan statues often possess lips that curve sharply upward in what is sometimes known as the "archaic smile," and this introduces an oddly comic note.

Etruscan art shows a strong Oriental influence. This may indicate the Asian origin of the people or merely show the extent of their trade with the East; though the latter case could also bespeak their origin in that corner of the world.

The language, though undeciphered, has been probed relentlessly for any hints as to the origin of the Etruscans. Most of it consists of short inscriptions gathered from tombs, and there the work of experts just adds to the confusion. Some find indications that the language is Indo-European, others that it is Semitic. It is sometimes suggested that there may be both influences present and that the language is a fusion of an Indo-European peasantry dominated by an aristocracy that came from Asia with its own Semitic language. Another suggestion is that the language has no relatives at all but, like the Basque language, is a relic from the times before the Indo-European peoples invaded and occupied Europe.

The Etruscan religion, like that of the Egyptians, was strongly death-centered. Tombs were elaborate; most surviving statues were designed to memorialize the recently dead; a favorite subject for art is the funeral feast. The religious ritual was gloomy and there was a great interest in attempts to foretell the future by studying entrails of sacrificed beasts, the flights of birds, or thunder and lightning. The Romans inherited much of this and throughout the history of the republic often let superstition guide their behavior.

Etruscan engineering and technology seems to have been first class for its time. Their cities were broad and well built with massive walls solidly constructed of large rocks joined without cement. They had good roads and tunnels; temples that were larger than those of the Greeks and that made use of the arch, which Greek temples did not use.

At home their women occupied a position of considerable social prestige. This is not always so in ancient societies and, when it *is* so, it is usually taken as the sign that the culture is enlightened and "modern" in its outlook on life.

In short, the Etruscan realm was a kind of Rome before Rome; but one that took a wrong turning, because its cities never succeeded in uniting in a centrally controlled government. Because of this, a city just outside Etruria, which did centralize the regions round about and which had always a firm goal in mind, defeated the numerous Etruscan cities (each originally stronger than itself) one by one and little by little and wiped them out — leaving for us only a mystery that may never be solved.

But while the Etruscans were establishing themselves in Italy, other eastern peoples were also penetrating the western Mediterranean. The Phoenicians, from the eastern rim of the Mediterranean were proficient in colonizing and founded numerous cities in northern Africa. Of these, the one that was later to become most famous and powerful was Carthage (kahr'thij), which existed near the site of the modern city of Tunis. The traditional date of the founding of Carthage is 814 B.C.

Carthage was only 250 miles southwest of the toe of Italy, and between Italy and Carthage lay the large triangular island of Sicily, looking for all the world like a three-cornered football about to be kicked by the Italian boot. Because of its triangular shape, the Greeks called it Trinacria (trih-nak'ree-uh) meaning "three-cornered." The far better known "Sicily" is derived from the tribal name of its earliest known inhabitants, the Sicels.

Carthage was only ninety miles southwest of the western end of Sicily.

The Greeks, also, came to move westward from their own centers of population, which lay some 200 miles southeast of the Italian heel. In the eighth century B.C., the Greeks founded numerous flourishing cities in southern Italy; cities that grew so prosperous that the region came to be called Magna Graecia (mag'nuh gree'shuh)* in later times.

The Magna Graecian city which was eventually to become most famous was known as Taras to the Greeks, but as Tarentum (tuh-ren'tum) to the Romans. It was founded about 707 B.C. and was located on the seacoast of the inner section of the Italian heel, just where the coast turns to form the instep.

The island of Sicily was colonized both by Greeks, in its east-

---

* In this book, I will give the pronunciation of the less familiar names of people and places. When I do so, however, I will give the English pronunciation and not the Latin or Greek pronunciation that is usually quite different. The Latin pronunciation of "Magna Graecia," for instance, would be "mag'nah gry'kee-uh."

ern reaches, and by Carthaginians in the west. The largest and most famous of the Greek cities in Sicily was Syracuse, founded about 734 B.C. It was located on the southeastern shore of the island.

This, then, was the situation in the middle of the eighth century B.C. The Etruscans ruled the middle and the Greeks the south of Italy, while the Carthaginians were just over the horizon to the southwest. And it was at this time that a small village named Rome was founded on the southern shores of the Tiber River, just on the Etruscan boundary.

Rome was part of an Italian district named Latium (lay'-shee-um), which extends along the coast for about a hundred miles southwestward of Etruria. Latium, like Etruria, did not consist of a centralized government. Rather, each district consisted of a number of *city-states;* small areas that included farming regions plus a central town. Each city-state governed itself, but formed alliances with neighboring towns for self-defense against a common enemy.

Some thirty towns of Latium, with a common language (Latin) and similar customs, combined to form a Latin League about 900 B.C., probably as a defense against the Etruscans who were then beginning to establish themselves firmly to the northwest. The most important and dominating town of the Latin League of those early days was Alba Longa, which was located about twelve miles southeast of the site on which Rome was eventually established.

It is to Rome itself, then, that we must now turn.

## THE FOUNDING OF ROME

The actual details of the founding of Rome and of its early

history are shrouded in a darkness that will probably never be penetrated.

In later years, however, when Rome had become the greatest city of the world, Roman historians wove fanciful tales of the founding of the city and of the events that followed. The tales are pure myth and have no historical value whatever. Still, they are so famous and so well known that I will repeat them, reminding you every once in a while, however, that it is all myth.

When the Romans were polishing their myths into final form, the Greek civilization was long past its prime, but it was still greatly admired for its past achievements. The greatest event in the early history of Greece had been the Trojan War, and it was to that war that the Roman legend-makers strove to trace the beginning of their own history.

In the Trojan War, a Greek army crossed the Aegean Sea to the northwestern shore of Asia Minor where stood the city of Troy. After a long siege, the Greeks took the city and burned it.

Escaping from the burning city (so went the tale) was one of the bravest of the Trojan heroes, Aeneas (ee-nee'as). With some other refugees, he sailed away in twenty ships, searching for a place to build a new city in place of the one the Greeks had destroyed.

After numerous adventures he landed on the northern coast of Africa where the city of Carthage had just been founded under the leadership of Queen Dido (digh'doh). Dido fell in love with the handsome Aeneas and, for a while, the Trojan considered remaining in Africa, marrying Dido, and ruling Carthage as its king.

However, according to the story, the gods knew that this was not to be his fate. They sent a messenger to order him to leave, and Aeneas (who always obeyed the gods) left hastily, without warning Dido. The poor queen, upon finding herself deserted, killed herself in despair.

This was the romantic high spot of the legend of Aeneas, and the Romans must have loved the way in which it connected the early histories of Rome and Carthage. Centuries after the time of Dido, Rome and Carthage engaged in gigantic wars and Carthage lost in the end, so it seemed fitting that the first Carthaginian ruler had died for love of the ancestor of the Roman people. Carthage lost in both love and war.

However, it is easy to see that none of this could have happened even if Aeneas and Dido had been real people who had truly lived. The Trojan War was fought about 1200 B.C. and Carthage was not founded until nearly four centuries later. It is as though we were asked to believe that Columbus in his voyage across the Atlantic had stopped off in England and fallen in love with Queen Victoria.

But let's go on with the legend anyway. Aeneas, after leaving Carthage, eventually made his way to the southwest coast of Italy where a king named Latinus (luh-tigh′nus) ruled and, supposedly, gave his name to the region, the people, and their language.

Aeneas married Latinus's daughter (he had lost his first wife in Troy) and, after a short war with neighboring towns, established himself as ruler of Latium. Aeneas's son, Ascanius (as-kay′nee-us) founded Alba Longa thirty years later, and his descendants ruled over it as kings.

The legend does not stop there. A later king of Alba Longa is described as having been cast off the throne by his younger brother. The daughter of the true king had given birth to twin sons whom the usurper ordered killed lest they grow up to dispute the rule of the city. The infants were therefore placed in a basket and set afloat on the Tiber. The usurper assumed they would die without his having actually to kill them.

But the basket drifted ashore fourteen miles short of the mouth of the river, at the foot of what later came to be known as the Palatine Hill. There a she-wolf found them and took care of them. (This is one of the more ridiculous portions of the story, but one of the most popular ones. It pleased the later Romans because it showed them that these ancestors of theirs had absorbed wolflike courage and bravery while still infants.)

A herdsman found the twins some time later, drove off the wolf, brought them home and reared them as his own, naming them Romulus and Remus.

Once grown, the twins led a revolt that drove the usurper from the throne and reinstated their grandfather, the rightful king, as ruler of Alba Longa. The twins then decided to build a city of their own on the banks of the Tiber. Romulus wanted to place it on the Palatine Hill where they had been found by the wolf. Remus suggested the Aventine Hill about half a mile to the south.

They decided to consult the gods. At night, each took his place on the hill he favored and waited to see what omen the dawn would bring. As soon as dawn lit the sky, Remus spied six eagles (or vultures) winging past. At sunrise, however, Romulus saw twelve.

Remus claimed he had won because his birds had appeared first; Romulus, on the other hand, pointed out that his birds had been more numerous. In the quarrel that followed Romulus killed Remus and then, on the Palatine, began to lay out the walls of his new city, over which he was to rule and which he named Rome in his own honor. (Of course, the name "Romulus" may simply have been invented in later times to symbolize the founding of the city, for "Romulus" means "little Rome.")

The traditional date of the founding of Rome was 753 B.C., and we will stop for just a moment to deal with this matter of dates.

In ancient times, there was no set system for numbering years. Each region had its own custom in this respect. Sometimes the year was identified simply by the name of the ruler: "In the year when Cyrenius was governor," or "In the tenth year of the reign of Darius."

Eventually, the more important nations found it convenient

to pick some important date in their early history and count the years from that. The Romans chose the time of the founding of their city and eventually numbered their years from that date. They would speak of a particular year as, let us say, 205 years "Ab Urbe Condite," meaning "from the founding of the city." We would write such a date as 205 A.U.C. (and the Romans wrote it CCV A.U.C.).

Other cities and nations used other systems of counting, and this makes for considerable confusion in trying to date events in ancient times. Still, when some particular event is recorded in the annals of two different regions under two different systems of dates, we can tie those two systems together.

The civilized world today counts the years from the birth of Jesus Christ, and when we speak of the year A.D. 1863, for instance, "A.D." stands for "Anno Domini" ("in the year of the Lord").

About A.D. 535, a Syrian scholar, Dionysius Exiguus, produced arguments to show that Jesus was born in the year 753 (A.U.C. or 753 years after the founding of Rome). We now know that this date is too late by at least four years, as Jesus was born while Herod was king of Judea and Herod died in 749 A.U.C. Nevertheless, Dionysius's date has been retained.

We say now that Jesus was born in 753 A.U.C. and call that year A.D. 1. This means that Rome was founded 753 years "before Christ," or 753 B.C.

All other dates before the birth of Jesus are written in this fashion, and that includes the dates used in this book.* The important thing to remember about such dates is that they run backward. That is, the smaller the number, the later the year. Thus, 752 B.C. comes a year *after* 753 B.C., and 200 B.C. is one century *later* than 300 B.C.

With that straightened out, let's look more closely at 753 B.C.

* A few key dates will be given in A.U.C., and in the "Table of Dates" at the end of the book all dates will be given in both B.C. and A.U.C.

and see what kind of world it was into which Rome had been born.

Twelve hundred miles to the southeast, the kingdom of Israel was flourishing under its king, Jeroboam II, but still further east, the kingdom of Assyria was gathering strength and would soon establish a powerful empire over a large section of western Asia. Egypt was passing through a period of weak government and in less than a century would fall under the control of Assyria.

The Greeks were just emerging from a period of darkness that had followed the barbarian invasions of 1000 B.C. The Olympian Games had been established (according to the later Greek tales) only twenty-three years before the founding of Rome, and now Greece was just beginning to spread out and colonize the coasts of the Mediterranean Sea, including Sicily and southern Italy.

The Israelites, Egyptians, and Greeks were not in the least aware of the founding of a tiny village on an obscure hill in Italy. Yet that village was destined to establish an empire far mightier than that of the Assyrians and to rule for many centuries over the descendants of those Israelites, Egyptians, and Greeks.

## THE FIRST CENTURY
## AND A HALF

Romulus, according to the ancient Roman tales, ruled till 716 B.C. He then disappeared in a thunderstorm and was supposed to have been taken up to heaven to become the war god Quirinus (kwih-righ′nus). By the time of his death, the city of Rome had spread out from the Palatine to the Capitoline and Quirinal Hills to the north.*

* Eventually, Rome occupied seven hills, and one of her titles came to be "The City of the Seven Hills."

The best known story about the reign of Romulus concerns the dilemma of the early settlers who found that while men flocked to the new town, women did not. The men therefore determined to seize the womenfolk of the Sabines (say'binez), a group of people living to the east of Rome. This was done through a mixture of fraud and force. The Sabines naturally considered this grounds for war, and Rome found herself engaged in the first battle of what was to prove a long history of battles.

The Sabines laid siege to the Capitoline Hill and their chance at victory came through Tarpeia (tahr-pee'uh), the daughter of the Roman commander who was holding out against them.

The Sabines managed to persuade Tarpeia to open the gates for them in return for what they wore on their left arms. (Tarpeia set that condition, meaning the golden bracelets they wore.) That night she secretly opened the gates, and the first few Sabines, as they entered, threw their shields at her, for they wore their shields on their left arms, too. The Sabines, who (like most people) were willing to make use of traitors but didn't like them, thus kept their bargain and killed Tarpeia.

A cliff that formed part of the Capitoline Hill was thereafter known as the Tarpeian Rock. In memory of the treason of Tarpeia, this cliff was used as a place of execution, and criminals were hurled off it to their death.

After the loss of the Capitoline Hill to the Sabines, the fight between them and the Romans continued quite evenly. Finally, the Sabine women, who had come to love their Roman husbands (according to the story) rushed between the armies and brought about a negotiated peace.

The Romans and Sabines agreed to rule together in Rome and to unite their lands. After the Sabine king died, Romulus ruled over both Romans and Sabines.

No doubt this reflects a dim memory of the fact that Rome did not originate through any romantic tales such as those involving Romulus and Remus. Instead, there were already vil-

lages on the seven hills, and eventually several neighboring
villages combined to form Rome. The city may first have
begun through the union of three such villages, each contributing a tribe, one of Latins, one of Sabines and one of Etruscans.
The very word "tribe" comes from the Latin word for "three."

After the death of Romulus a Sabine named Numa Pompilius
was elected to the throne and ruled for over forty years to 673
B.C.

It was Numa Pompilius who was supposed to have founded
the Roman religion, though in actual fact, much of it must have
been borrowed from the Etruscans and the Sabines. Quirinus,
for instance (who was later turned into the deified Romulus)
was originally a Sabine war god who was about the equivalent
of the Latin war god, Mars.

In later years, the Romans, because of their admiration for
the sophisticated Greeks, identified their gods with those in
the Greek myths. Thus, the Roman Jupiter was considered to
be equivalent to the Greek Zeus; Juno was Hera; Mars was
Ares; Minerva was Athene; Venus was Aphrodite; Vulcan was
Hephaestus, and so on.

The combination came to be so firm that nowadays we often
use the Roman names (more familiar to most moderns) in telling the Greek myths, and we almost forget that the Romans
had myths of their own for their gods.

There were some Roman religious beliefs that remained
strictly Roman, because there was no Greek counterpart. One
of these involved the god Janus (jay'nus), whose worship was
supposedly established by Numa Pompilius.

Janus was the god of doors, which is more important than it
sounds, for doors symbolize entrances and exits; therefore beginnings and endings. (The month January, which begins the
year, is named in his honor, and the guardian of the doors of a
building — and of its other portions as well — is a "janitor.")

Janus was usually pictured with two faces, one looking forward toward the end of things and one backward toward the

beginning. His sanctuaries consisted of arches through which one could enter or leave. A particularly important sanctuary consisted of two parallel arches, connected by walls and possessing gates. These gates were supposed to remain open whenever Rome was at war, and closed when Rome was at peace.

They remained closed during Numa's peaceful reign, but Rome's warlike history thereafter is best shown by the fact that in the next seven centuries of the city's existence, the gates of Janus were only closed four times, and then for only short periods.

With the death of Numa Pompilius in 673 B.C., Tullus Hostilius was elected as the third king. Under him, Rome spread out to a fourth hill, the Caelian Hill (see'lee-an) to the southeast of the Palatine. On the Caelian, Tullus built his palace.

By this time, Rome was beginning to be prominent among the cities of Latium. Her position on the Tiber encouraged trade, which in turn led to prosperity. What's more, the higher civilization of the Etruscans was just across the river and Rome benefited by what she borrowed. In addition, the presence of the Etruscans kept the Romans together and helped keep down internal disagreements, for it was not safe to quarrel between themselves with an enemy on their doorstep. Furthermore, out of self-defense, the Romans had to develop a warlike tradition.

Alba Longa, accustomed to dominate Latium, viewed the rise of Rome with disapproval. Warfare sputtered on and off between the two cities, and in 667 B.C. a major battle seemed on the point of taking place.

On the eve of this battle (the Roman legends explain) it was decided to settle the matter by a duel. The Romans were to choose three men from among themselves, and the Albans were to do likewise. These six men were to fight, three against three, and the two cities were to abide by the decision.

The Romans chose three brothers who all bore the same family name of Horatius, and who were together known by the Latin form of the plural of the word as the Horatii (hoh-ray'-

shee-igh).* The Albans also chose three brothers, the Curiatii
(kyoo''ree-ay'shee-igh).

In the fight that followed, two of the Horatii were killed.
However, the Horatius still alive was unwounded, while each
of the Curiatii was cut and bleeding. Horatius then employed
strategy. He fled, while the Curiatii, seeing victory at hand,
pursued furiously; the most lightly wounded in advance and
the most seriously wounded limping along in the rear.

Horatius then turned and was able to fight with each
wounded man separately as he came up. He killed each and,
in his person, Rome was victor over Alba Longa.

There is a rather gruesome postscript to the tale of the Horatii. The victorious Horatius, returning to Rome in triumph, was
greeted by his sister, Horatia. She had been engaged to be married to one of the Curiatii and she was not in the least pleased
at the death of her betrothed. She expressed her sorrow loudly.

In anger, Horatius stabbed his sister to death, crying, "So
perish every Roman woman who bewails a foe."

The Romans like to tell stories like this in order to show how
their heroes always placed the good of the city ahead of the
love of their family and of their personal welfare. In actual
fact, however, such "Roman virtue" appeared much more often
in Roman legends than in Roman reality.

Alba Longa submitted after the duel but apparently seized
its first chance to rebel, and in 665 B.C. it was taken by Rome
and destroyed.

When Tullus Hostilius died in 641 B.C., the Romans selected
a grandson of Numa Pompilius (who throughout their history
was looked upon as a particularly pious and virtuous king) to
rule over them. This new king, the fourth, was Ancus Martius
(ang'kus mahr'shee-us).

The rule of these Roman kings in the first century and a half

---

* Romans bore two names, as we do, the first being a personal
name and the second a family or tribal name. Additional names
were sometimes used to indicate some accomplishment of the
individual or some personal characteristic.

of Rome's existence was not absolute. The king was advised by a gathering of one hundred of the older representatives of the various clans that made up the city's people; representatives who, because of their age and experience, might be expected to advise the king well. This group of older men was the *senate*, so called from the Latin word for "old men."

The senate stood to the rest of the Romans as a father stood to his family. The senate, like a father, was older and wiser and its commands were expected to be obeyed. The senators were therefore *patricians*, from the Latin word for "father." This term was extended to their families as well, for future senators were chosen from these families.

According to tradition, Ancus Martius brought in new colonists from among conquered tribes outside Rome, since the growing city could use the extra hands. These were settled on the Aventine Hill, which Remus had wanted to use as the site of Rome a century and a quarter before. Now it became the fifth hill of Rome.

These newcomers on the Aventine were, of course, not allowed to become the social equals of the old families, since the latter were not anxious to share their power. The new families could not qualify for the senate or for other government positions. They were the *plebeians*, from a Latin word meaning "common people."

## ETRUSCAN DOMINATION

During this early period of Roman history, the Etruscans were also gaining in strength. The Etruscan cities were far more powerful and civilized than the rough little town on the Tiber. If Etruria were under the rule of a single powerful city, no doubt Rome would have been occupied and absorbed and no more would have been heard of it. However, the Etruscan realm consisted of numerous cities only loosely combined and jealous of each other, so that Rome could quietly maintain her existence amid the Etruscan quarrels.

Even so, it was a near thing. The Etruscans were expanding north and south and their grip closed about Rome, to some extent at least. The Roman legends do not say flatly that Rome went through a period when she was under Etruscan domination, for the historians never liked to admit anything that was humiliating to the great city of later times. Still, the fifth king of Rome was an Etruscan, as even the legends admit.

The legends do their best to soften matters by making the fifth king the son of a Greek refugee who migrated to Etruria and married a native woman there, but this is not very likely. His native town was Tarquinii (tahr-kwin′ee-igh) on the Etrurian seacoast about fifty miles northwest of Rome. He was named Lucius Tarquinius Priscus.

"Lucius" is his first name,* "Tarquinius" is his family name, given him by the Romans after his place of birth (in English, it is usually shortened to "Tarquin"). "Priscus" is the name added to describe the particular individual. It means "elder" or "first" and indicates that he was the first of his family to play a part in Roman history.

Tarquinius Priscus was supposed to have come to Rome as an immigrant and to have distinguished himself in war and in council so well that the king, Ancus Martius, made him regent of the kingdom and guardian of his sons. Ancus Martius′ sons might have been expected to inherit the kingdom when they gained adulthood, but the Romans were so pleased with Tarquinius Priscus that they chose him king instead.

(This seems extremely unlikely. It is much more probable that Tarquinius Priscus was the governor set over Rome by the Etruscans; that he ruled from behind the scenes while Ancus

---

* The Romans had a very small supply of first names. Among those most frequently used were Lucius, Marcus, Gaius and Titus.

Martius was king; and that he took over openly after the king's death in 616 B.C.)

Under Tarquinius Priscus, Rome prospered as Etruscan civilization and fashions flooded into the town. He built the Circus Maximus ("large ring"), a long oval in which chariot races could be run before spectators seated on numerous tiers of seats.

He also introduced athletic games after the Etruscan fashion. These eventually came to feature combats between armed men who were called *gladiators*, from the sword ("gladius") with which they fought.

Then, too, he brought in Etruscan religious customs and began to build a great temple to Jupiter on the Capitoline Hill. This temple, which also served as the fortress of the city, was called the *Capitol*, from the Latin word for "head." (Since the Capitol was felt to be the very heart and center of the Roman city and government, the same name was given to the Capitol in Washington, D.C., where the Congress of the United States holds its sessions.)

In the valley between the two oldest hills of Rome, the Palatine and the Capitoline, was the *forum* ("marketplace"), an open place where people met for trade and to perform public business.

In order to make the forum usable, Tarquinius Priscus had a sewer built to drain off the marshy areas of the valley. This eventually became the *Cloaca Maxima* ("Greatest Sewer"). Rome, even in her greatest days, was never to develop pure science and mathematics as the Greeks did; however, the Romans were always very proud of their great engineering achievements and their practical works of architecture. These early sewers and buildings began that tradition.

In later Roman history, every city had its forum, and Rome itself had a number. This first one, though, between the Palatine and the Capitoline, was the *Roman Forum*, where the

Roman senate met and debated its business. (The word has therefore come to mean any meeting place where open discussion goes on.)

Tarquinius was victorious in wars against the neighboring tribes, and he introduced the Etruscan custom of the *triumph*. A victorious general enters the city in state, preceded by government officials, and followed by his army and by captured prisoners. The procession moved along decorated streets and between lines of cheering spectators to the Capitol. (It was rather like a ticker-tape parade down Fifth Avenue.) At the Capitol, religious services were held and the day ended with a great feast. The triumph was the greatest honor Rome could bestow on her generals. In order to be offered one, a general had to be a high official, he had to fight against a foreign enemy, and he had to win a complete victory that extended Roman territory.

In 578 B.C. Tarquinius Priscus was assassinated by men hired by the sons of the old king, Ancus Martius. However, a son-in-law of Tarquinius Priscus acted quickly and assumed the kingship. The sons of Ancus Martius were forced to flee.

The new ruler was Servius Tullius, the sixth king of Rome. He may have been an Etruscan, too, and behind the story of the assassination of Tarquinius Priscus may be an attempt at rebellion by the native Latins against the Etruscan overlordship. If so, it was a rebellion that failed.

If Servius Tullius were an Etruscan, he nevertheless proved devoted to Rome and under him she continued to flourish. The city expanded over a sixth and seventh hill, the Esquiline and Viminal in the northeast. Servius Tullius built a wall about all seven hills (the Servian Wall) and this marked the "city limits" of Rome for the next 500 years, although the population of the city eventually spread out beyond the walls in all directions.

Servius Tullius also arranged an alliance with the other cities of Latium and formed a new Latin League, dominated by Rome. The Etruscan cities to the north must surely have viewed this with suspicion and must have wondered how far they could trust this new king.

Servius Tullius also tried to weaken the power of the ruling families of the city by extending some political privileges to the plebeians. This angered the patricians, of course, and they conspired against Servius Tullius, perhaps with Etruscan help.

In 534 B.C., Servius Tullius was assassinated. The leading spirit within the conspiracy was a son of the old king Tarquinius Priscus. This son had married Servius Tullius' daughter, and when Servius Tullius was killed, he made himself the seventh king of Rome.

The seventh king was Lucius Tarquinius Superbus ("Tarquin, the Proud") and the third — if Servius Tullius is counted — of the Etruscan rulers of Rome.

The Etruscans were now at the height of their power. Virtually all of central Italy was in their grip. Their navy was powerful in the waters west of Italy. They made this power felt when Greek colonists attempted to settle on the islands of Sardinia and Corsica west of Italy.

The Etruscans formed an alliance with Carthage and their combined fleets sailed against the Greeks in Corsica. About 540 B.C., a naval battle was fought off the Greek colony of Alalia (uh-lay'lee-uh) on the east-central coast of Corsica. The Greeks were defeated and had to abandon both islands. Sardinia, the more southern of the two islands, was taken over by the Carthaginians, while Corsica, just sixty miles west of the Etruscan coast, came under the Etruscan power.

This may explain why it was that the new Tarquin could tyrannize over Rome. Legend retains the picture of Tarquinius Superbus as a cruel ruler who repealed the laws of Servius Tullius that had been meant to help the plebeians. He even tried to reduce the senate to helplessness by having some senators executed and by refusing to replace those who died a natural death.

He gathered an armed guard about himself and apparently

intended to rule as a despot, with his own will the entire law. Nevertheless, he continued to enlarge Rome, completing the great building projects his father had begun.

One famous story about Tarquinius Superbus deals with a *sibyl*, or witch. These were priestesses of Apollo, usually living in caves and supposed to be endowed with the gift of prophecy. Ancient writers speak of a number of these, but the most famous is one who dwelt in the neighborhood of Cumae (a Greek city near the site of the modern Naples) and who was therefore called the Cumaean sibyl. Aeneas was supposed to have consulted her for advice in the course of his wanderings.

The Cumaean sibyl was said to have in her charge the *Sibylline Books*, nine volumes of prophecies supposed to have been made at various times by various sibyls. She met Tarquinius Superbus and offered to sell him the nine volumes for three hundred pieces of gold. Tarquinius refused such an exorbitant price, whereupon the sibyl burned three of the books and asked three hundred pieces of gold for the six that remained. Again Tarquinius refused and again the sibyl burned three of the books, and asked for three hundred pieces of gold for the final three.

This time, Tarquinius, not daring to allow the final prophecies to be destroyed, paid what was requested. The Sibylline Books were thereafter carefully cherished by the Romans. The books were kept in the Capitol, and at time of great crises were consulted by the priests in order that they might learn the proper rites with which to calm the angry gods.

Tarquinius Superbus' arrogance and the even greater pride of his son, Tarquinius Sextus, ended, finally, by making enemies of all the powerful men in Rome, who waited angrily for a chance to rebel.

That chance came in the midst of war. Tarquinius Superbus had abandoned Servius Tullius' policy of peaceful alliance with the other Latin cities. Instead, he forced the nearer ones into subservience and made war on the Volscians (vol'shanz), a tribe that inhabited the southeastern section of Latium.

While the war was going on, Tarquin's son (according to the story) brutally outraged the wife of a cousin, Tarquinius Collatinus. That proved to be the last straw. When news of what had happened spread through the city, a revolt broke out at once under the leadership of Collatinus and a patrician, Lucius Junius Brutus.

Brutus had ample reason to be hostile to the Tarquins, for his father and older brother had been put to death by them. Indeed, the legend relates that Brutus himself would have been executed if he had not pretended to be a moron and therefore harmless. ("Brutus" means "stupid," and this name was given him because of his successful playacting.)

By the time Tarquin could get back to Rome, it was too late. The city's gates were closed to him and he was forced into exile. He was the seventh and last king of Rome. Never again in her long history was Rome to have a king; at least she was never to have a ruler that dared bear that particular title.

Tarquin was exiled in 509 B.C. (244 A.U.C.); thus Rome had spent two and a half centuries under its seven kings. Now we enter a five-century-long period during which the Roman Republic managed first to survive and then to grow mighty.

# 2

## THE REPUBLIC SURVIVES

### FIGHTING OFF THE ETRUSCANS

Of course, the Romans, even under a republic, had to have someone ruling over them. To avoid giving this ruler too much power (no more Tarquins, the Romans decided) he was elected for one year only and could not succeed himself. Furthermore, to make doubly sure, two rulers were elected, and no decision held good unless both were agreed. In this way, even if one of the annual rulers were to attempt some device for increasing his power, the other, in natural jealousy, would stop him. And both, in certain important ways, had to bow to the will of the senate.

This system worked well for several centuries.

At first, these elected Roman rulers were called *praetors* (pree′torz), from words meaning "to lead the way." Later on, however, the fact that there were two of them seemed the most important part of the office and they came to be called *consuls*, meaning "partners." They were men, in other words, who had to "consult" each other and come to mutual agreement before action could be taken.

It is as consuls that these chief rulers are best known to us. Indeed secondary magistrates who served under the consuls eventually came to be called praetors.

The consuls were in charge of the armed forces of Rome and it was their particular job to lead those armies in warfare. Within the city, a lower form of magistrate, the *quaestors* (kwes'torz), also selected two at a time for a year's term of office, served as judges and supervised at criminal trials. (The word "quaestor" means "to seek why.") In later years, their function shifted and came to involve serving as financial officers in charge of the treasury.

The early years of the Roman Republic were hard indeed. To begin with, the city had to face the hostility of the powerful Etruscan cities whom the exiled Tarquins begged for assistance in their efforts to regain the throne. No doubt the Etruscans were made to feel that Rome would become dangerous to them if she were not safely under kings of Etruscan descent and sympathies. The task of fighting off the Etruscans was the chief task of the first two consuls who, naturally, were Collatinus and Brutus.

Even within Rome there were those who, for one reason or another, favored the return of the Tarquins. Among these were two sons of Brutus himself. When the conspiracy of his sons was uncovered, it fell to Brutus, as consul, to sit in judgement upon them. Brutus placed the needs of the Republic above his feelings as a father and joined Collatinus in directing their execution. From that time on, however, according to the story, Brutus felt life to hold nothing of value for him and he sought for death in battle. Finally, in a skirmish with Tarquin's forces, Brutus got his wish, dying in single combat with one of Tarquin's sons.

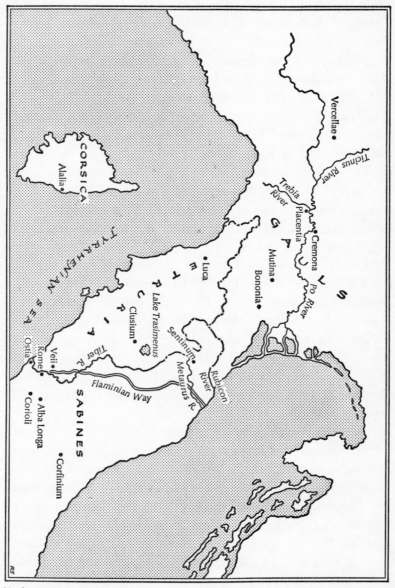

**Northern Italy**

Rome's danger grew acute when Tarquinius Superbus finally managed to enlist the aid of Lars Porsenna (pawr'seh-nuh) of Clusium, a city of central Etruria, about seventy-five miles north of Rome.

The Roman legends tell that Porsenna and his Etruscan army came marching southward to the Tiber, driving the Romans out of their positions on the Janiculum Hill, west of the river. Porsenna would have entered Rome and crushed the Republic, were it not that the wooden bridge across the Tiber was cut down in time.

One of the most famous of the stories of early Roman history tells of Publius Horatius Cocles (kok'leez) * who kept the Etruscan army at bay while the bridge was being cut down. First with two companions and then alone, he faced the army, and when the last timber cracked, he flung himself into the Tiber and, in full armor, swam back to safety. Ever since, the phrase "Horatius at the bridge" has been used to signify one man fighting a desperate battle against overwhelming odds.

Porsenna then settled down to a patient siege of Rome, since he had failed to overwhelm the city at a stroke. Another story is told about the events that led to his giving up the siege. A young Roman patrician, Gaius Mucius, volunteered to make his way into the Etruscan camp and assassinate Porsenna. He was caught and was threatened with being burnt alive if he did not give all the details of what was going on in Rome. The young Roman, to show how little afraid he was of being burnt, placed his right hand in a nearby fire and stood there patiently while allowing it to be completely consumed. Thereafter he received the additional name of Scaevola (see'voh-luh) meaning "left-handed."

Porsenna, the tale goes, was so impressed with this incredible heroism that he despaired of taking a city populated by such

* Cocles means "one-eyed," for Horatius had lost an eye in battle.

men. He therefore negotiated a peace and left for home without replacing Tarquinius Superbus on the throne.

(Modern historians, alas, feel quite certain that these stories about Horatius and Mucius are nothing more than legends and that they were invented by later Romans to hide the embarrassing fact that the Etruscans actually defeated Rome and forced them to accept Etruscan domination. Roman influence over the rest of Latium was destroyed for a considerable period of time because of this. However, the Roman defeat wasn't total. Porsenna had to agree not to restore the kingship and, in the long run, that was what counted.)

The last appearance of the Tarquins in Roman legend took place in 496 B.C. when the Latin cities, themselves, took advantage of Roman losses at the hands of Porsenna and attempted to finish the job.

The Latin army, with Tarquinius Superbus and his sons riding in the fore, met the Romans at Lake Regillus (ree-jil′us) near the city of Rome itself (the exact site is unidentified). The Romans won a complete victory and the Tarquin family, except for the old king himself, was wiped out. Tarquinius Superbus retired to Cumae and died there.

At this battle, Roman legends say, their army was helped by two horsemen of more than human size and strength. They were supposed to be Castor and Pollux (brothers of Helen of Troy in Greek legend). Thereafter, the Romans built special temples to the divine brothers and paid them much honor.

## THE PATRICIANS AND PLEBEIANS

The ending of the monarchy left Rome ruled by an *oligarchy;* that is by a "few," meaning, in this case, the patricians.

Only the patricians could be senators; only they could be consuls, praetors or quaestors.

In fact, it seemed that the only real Romans were the patricians and that the plebeians, while good enough to work the farms and serve in the ranks of the army, were not good enough to take any share in the government.

After the wars with the Etruscans and Latins, times were hard indeed and the lot of the plebeian became unbearable. The farms had been ravaged, food supplies were low, the poor had gone into debt, and the patricians seemed uncaring.

Why should the patrician care? He was well enough off to survive the hard times. And if a plebeian farmer went into debt, the debt laws were so harsh that the plebeian would have to sell himself and his family into slavery to pay off the debt. It would be the patrician landowner to whom he was in debt and for whom he must then slave.

The leader of the patrician party at the time was Appius Claudius. Appius Claudius was a Sabine by birth, but he was always pro-Roman, and in early life he led a large party into Rome and fought loyally for his adopted city. He was accepted as a patrician and was elected consul in 495 B.C. He ruled with a stern hand and the plebeians may well have been all the more angry that the harshest enforcer of the harsh laws concerning debts was not even a native Roman.

It seemed to the plebeians that Rome was no city of theirs, and in 494 B.C. they decided to leave Rome and found a new city of their own on a hill three miles to the east. A sizable number of them did this, and the patricians, who could ill afford to lose so large a part of the population, had to negotiate with them.

According to legend, the plebeians were won back by the words of a Roman patrician named Menenius Agrippa, who told them the tale of the revolt of the parts of the body against the belly.

It seems that the arms complained that they did all the

lifting, the legs did the walking, the jaws the chewing, the heart the beating and so on, while the belly, which did nothing at all, received all the food. The belly replied that although it received the food it returned it via the blood to every part of the body, which could not survive otherwise.

The analogy was that, although the patricians held all the offices, they used their power to guide the city wisely, thus benefiting all the people.

Menenius' fable doesn't really sound convincing, and it is hard to believe that it would persuade downtrodden men to return and allow themselves to continue to be downtrodden. In actual fact, the patricians were forced to offer the rebels much more than entertaining stories.

An agreement was reached whereby the plebeians were allowed to appoint officials of their own; officials chosen by vote of the plebeians and who represented not the Roman people generally but the plebeians only. These officials were called *tribunes* (a name originally given to the leaders of a tribe).

Their purpose was to safeguard the interests of the plebeians and to keep the patricians from passing laws that would be unfair to the common people. Eventually, indeed, the tribunes gained the power of stopping laws they disapproved of by merely crying out "Veto!" ("I forbid!") Not all the power of the consuls and senate could pass a law against the tribune's veto.

Naturally, the tribunes would at first be very unpopular with the patricians and might expect violence. It was agreed, therefore, that a tribune might not be harmed in any way. For any disrespect to the office, he could impose a fine.

Assistants to the tribunes were appointed who might collect these fines. They were the *aediles* (ee'dilez). Their role as fine-collectors led to their serving some of the functions of the modern police. Through the use of the money they collected, they came to be in charge of many public affairs, such as the care of the temples (the word "aedile" comes from a Latin word for "temple"), the sewers, the water supply, food distribution, and public games. They regulated commerce, too.

Gradually, the plebeians entered political life and some of the plebeian families grew quite prosperous. The various city offices, even up to the consulate were gradually opened to them.

In the first years of the tribunate, however, the patricians made occasional efforts to restore their position and to retain all power in their own hands. The head of this movement was, according to Roman legend, the patrician Caius Marcius.

In 493 B.C., the year after the plebeian secession, Caius Marcius was supposed to have led an attack against the important Volscian city of Corioli (koh-righ'oh-ligh). Because of his bravery and success in this battle, he was given the added name of Coriolanus (kawr"ee-oh-lay'nus), by which he is best known to history.

The next year there was a famine in Rome and grain was imported from Sicily. Coriolanus suggested to the patricians that the grain be withheld from the people until they agreed to give up the tribunate.

The tribunes at once accused him of attempting harm against them (which he certainly was, and in a particularly despicable way, too — by trading on human starvation). He was exiled and promptly joined the Volscians.

He led a Volscian army against Rome and defeated the armies he had once headed. Five miles from Rome, he paused to make ready for the final assault. Roman legend tells how he refused the pleas of a Roman mission to withdraw his army. He refused the prayers of priests sent out to reason with him. Finally, his mother was sent out to him, and to her he gave in, crying out, "Oh, mother, thou hast saved Rome, but destroyed thy son!"

Coriolanus led the Volscian army away and according to some stories, was killed by them (and rightly so) as a double traitor.

Modern historians dismiss the whole story of Coriolanus as

a fable. They point out, for instance, that at the time that Coriolanus was supposed to be winning his name and fame in the
siege of Corioli, that town was not a Volscian city at all but a
loyal ally of Rome.

However, even if the details are legendary, the nub of the
story is probably true; that a kind of civil war continued between the patricians and plebeians for quite a while after the
plebeian secession, and that, in the end, the plebeians kept the
ground they had won.

Indeed, the plebeians felt that their own safety required that
the laws of the Romans be placed in written form. As long as
they remained unwritten, there was always room for confusion
as to whether the patricians were bending the law in their own
favor or not. With all points in writing, the tribunes would have
ground for argument.

About 450 B.C., according to tradition, the first written codi-
fication of the Roman laws appeared. To form this code, ten
patricians were selected, and these were called *decemvirs* from
words meaning "ten men." They held sway in place of consuls
until the written code was formed.

The laws were supposed to have been engraved on twelve
bronze tablets and were therefore called the Twelve Tables.
For centuries, these Twelve Tables served as the fundamental
basis of Roman law.

The coming of the written law did not mean, however, that
all became sweetness and light. Roman tradition goes on to
tell that the decemvirs kept themselves illegally in power after
the Twelve Tables were published. They also took on more and
more of the trappings of power. For instance, each of them
came to be attended by twelve bodyguards called *lictors*.

The lictors were plebeians who carried a special symbol of
their office in the form of a bundle of rods, bound together with
an axe in the middle. This indicated the power of the ruler
(originally the king, later the consuls and other magistrates)

to inflict punishment with rods, or death with the axe. These symbols were called *fasces* (fas′eez) from a Latin word meaning "bundles."

The leader of the decemvirs was Appius Claudius Crassus, either the son or the grandson of the Claudius who had been the immediate cause of the plebeian secession nearly half a century before.

This new Appius Claudius was firmly anti-plebeian and, according to later stories, attempted to institute a reign of terror. He went too far, however, when he tried to seize a beautiful girl, Virginia, who was the daughter of a plebeian soldier. Appius Claudius planned to make his action legal by bringing in false witnesses to testify that the girl was actually the daughter of one of his slaves and was therefore automatically also his slave.

Virginia's distracted father, seeing that he would be unable to do anything legally to prevent the powerful decemvir from seizing his daughter, took (according to the legend) the dramatic course of suddenly stabbing her to death in the midst of the trial and proclaiming that only through death could he save her honor.

The plebeians, roused to fury by this, threatened to secede once more. In 449 B.C., the decemvirs were forced to give in and resign their post. Appius Claudius either died in prison or committed suicide.

As a result, the power of the tribunes as spokesmen for the plebeians continued to increase. They were allowed to sit inside the senate house, so that they might more easily influence legislation. They also gradually gained the right to interpret omens to decide if senate business might continue. By finding that the omens were unfavorable, they could easily stop all governmental affairs, temporarily, at least.

In 445 B.C. marriage between patricians and plebeians was allowed, and in 421 B.C. quaestorship was opened to plebeians.

## THE DECLINE
## OF THE ETRUSCANS

The internal squabbling in Rome might have meant her end at the hands of some aggressive neighbor, but the good fortune that was to remain on Rome's side for many centuries was there now. The most dangerous neighbors were the Etruscans and they had begun a rapid downhill slide.

Thanks to the work of Porsenna, Rome and the other Latin cities seemed no danger to the Etruscans who now tried to expand into the lush and fertile areas southeast of Latium. This was Campania, in ancient times the most favored part of all Italy.

There seemed nothing to stand in the way of the Etruscans but the Greek cities, and they, as always, were disunited and might be dealt with one by one. In 474 B.C. the Etruscans laid siege to Cumae, the most northwesterly of all the Greek cities in Magna Graecia.

Unfortunately for the Etruscans, however, the siege came at a high point in Greek history. In Greece itself, the mighty Persian Empire had been beaten back; in Sicily, the Carthaginian forces had been dealt a crippling blow. Everywhere Greeks felt exalted. No "barbarian" was too difficult for them to defeat.

Consequently, when Cumae called for help there was someone to answer. To the rescue came Gelon (jee'lon), the ruler of Syracuse. Six years earlier he had beaten the Carthaginians, and he wasn't in the least unwilling to extend his power into Italy. Northward came his ships, and the Etruscans were thoroughly trounced.

It was a final defeat, for the Etruscans fell back and never dared advance into southern Italy again.

In place of the Etruscans, the native Italian tribes in the south moved to the fore. The chief of these were the Samnites.

The center of their power was Samnium (sam'nee-um), which lay to the east and southeast of Latium.

With the Etruscan power battered by the Greeks, the Samnites drove into Campania and took over. By 428 B.C. they had taken Capua, the largest non-Greek town of the area.

But if the Etruscans had to withdraw from the south, worse was in store for them in the north.

At about the time the Villanovans (see page 3) had entered Italy, another group of peoples, the Gauls, had pushed behind them to occupy much of Europe north of the Alps.

After 500 B.C., Gallic tribes made their way through the barrier of the Alps, which enclosed northern Italy in a semicircle, and began to clash with the Etruscan colonists in the fertile Po Valley. Little by little, as the decades passed, the Gauls extended their sway. And as the Gauls steadily advanced, the Etruscans retreated, until the entire Po Valley made up what was called Cisalpine Gaul (sis-al'pine), meaning "Gaul on this side of the Alps" — "this side" from the standpoint of Rome, of course.

(The area west and north of the Alps was sometimes called Transalpine Gaul, or "Gaul across the Alps." However, Transalpine Gaul was so much the larger of the two and, in later centuries, so much the more important, that it became simply Gaul.)

As the fifth century drew to its close, the Etruscans were clearly in a bad way. Beaten and driven out of Campania and out of the Po Valley, they were now fighting desperately and without success to keep the Gauls out of Etruria itself. The Gauls led devastating raids into the heart of the country, and the despairing Etruscans found safety only within the actual walls of their cities.

While disaster kept mounting year by year for the Etruscans, the Romans were left increasingly free to squabble among themselves and to fight against the other towns of Latium.

The fighting was not always easy. The Volscians extended

their control of the southeastern half of Latium (an advance which may form the basis for the legend of Coriolanus) and allied themselves with the Aequians (ee′kwee-anz), who were tribes dwelling in the mountainous regions on the eastern borders of Latium.

In connection with the wars fought by the Romans against the Aequians, there is one legend that has always been popular; that of Lucius Quinctius Cincinnatus (sin″sih-nay′tus, or -nah′tus). He was a patrician of the same stripe as Coriolanus — arguing against the tribunate and against any written law. However, he is also pictured as a model of old-fashioned virtue and integrity. He lived frugally, farmed his own land, and was a complete patriot. Because his son had been exiled for using violent language against the tribunes, Cincinnatus retired in sorrow to his farm, refusing further involvement in politics.

In 458 B.C., however, the Romans were hotly beset by the Aequians, and a consul and his entire army were threatened with disaster. The call, therefore, went out for Cincinnatus. He was appointed *dictator*. In Roman law, this was an official of absolute power, appointed in time of extreme emergency, but only for six months at a time. The term comes from a Latin word meaning "to say," because, while he was in office, whatever a dictator said was law.

When informed of his appointment, Cincinnatus was plowing his field. Leaving his plow where it was, he left for the Forum, gathered a new army, marched quickly to the site of battle, attacked the Aequians impetuously, defeated them, rescued the consul and his army, and marched back to Rome, all in one day. (This is much too good to be true.)

Back in Rome, Cincinnatus gave up the dictatorial dignity at once, making no attempt to use his absolute power a moment longer than necessary, and returned to his farm.

(This example of virtue, of the use of power but not its abuse, impressed later generations very much. At the end of the American Revolutionary War, George Washington seemed a new Cincinnatus. Officers of the Revolutionary Army, therefore, formed "The Society of the Cincinnati" — using the Latin plural of the name — after the war was over. In 1790, a city on the Ohio River was reorganized and enlarged by a member of the Society, and was named Cincinnati in its honor.)

As Etruria was laid waste by the Gauls, Roman armies even turned triumphantly against the old oppressors. The southernmost of the Etruscan cities was Veii (vee'igh) only twelve miles north of Rome. It was certainly larger than Rome and may even have been the largest of all the Etruscan cities.

The Roman legends make Veii a persistent enemy of Rome and have the two cities almost constantly at odds, with no less than fourteen distinct wars between the two. There may have been exaggeration here, for through most of the first three and a half centuries of Roman history, Veii must have been much the stronger of the two cities and Rome must have had to treat her with caution indeed.

But now with Etruria fully occupied in fighting the Gauls, Rome advanced to the attack. In 406 B.C., the Romans laid siege to the city and, according to the story, kept at it for ten years under the leadership of Marcus Furius Camillus. Finally, in 396 B.C. it was taken and destroyed and its territory was annexed to Rome.

After the victory, the story continues, Camillus was accused of having distributed the spoils unfairly. Filled with anger, he left his ungrateful city in 391 B.C. and went into voluntary exile.

## THE GAULS

The victory over Veii, however, was at first only an empty

one. The Gauls, penetrating deeper into Etruria each year, were not likely to stop there, and the Romans, fishing happily in the troubled Etruscan waters, were to find that their own waters were to be troubled as well.

Soon after the capture of Veii, it began to seem quite plain that the Gallic raiding parties would threaten the new Roman territory northwest of the Tiber and even Rome itself. Romans were going to have to fight the Gauls.

On July 16, 390 B.C. (363 A.U.C.), a Gallic army under the leadership of a tribal chieftain named Brennus met the Romans on the banks of the small Allia River (al'ee-uh) at a point ten miles north of Rome and defeated them completely. (Ever afterward, July 16 was considered an unlucky day by the Romans.)

(This date was not known as July 16 to the Romans, of course. The names of their months have been adopted by us, so these are familiar to us with two exceptions. In the time of the Republic, the months we call July and August were known as Quintilis and Sextilis respectively. Each month had three key days. The first day of each month, on which that month was "proclaimed" ("calare") by the High Priest, was the *calends* of the month. It is from this we get out term "calendar." The day in the middle of the month — the fifteenth day in March, May, July, and October, and the thirteenth day in the other months — was the *ides* which comes, perhaps, from an Etruscan word meaning "division." The ninth day before the ides, counting the ides itself as one day, was the *nones* ("nine"). Other dates were always spoken of as so many days before the next key day. Thus, July 16 would be "sixteen days before the calends of Sextilis." This was a ridiculously clumsy system, and in this book I shall use only the modern system of months and days.)

After the victory, the Gauls marched directly to Rome and, more fortunate than Porsenna, occupied it. This was the first outright foreign occupation of Rome in her history, and there was not to be another such event for eight hundred years more. Consequently, the later Roman historians made much of this unique disaster and filled the period with legends.

As many of the people as possible fled Rome at news of the Gallic advance, while those capable of fighting barricaded themselves upon the Capitoline Hill for a last stand. The senators, according to the story, took their seats on the porches of their mansions to confront the Gauls fearlessly. (It seems a foolish thing to do and probably never happened, but it makes a good story.)

The invading Gauls looted and burned the city but stared in amazement at the senators sitting motionless in their ivory seats. Finally, one naïve Gaul reached out to touch the beard of one of the senators to see if it was a man or a statue. The beard is the sign of manhood in many cultures, and for any stranger to touch it is considered an insult. When the Gallic fingers closed upon the senator's beard, the senator promptly raised his staff and struck the Gaul. The Gaul, after the first moment of amazement had passed, killed the senator and this was followed by a general massacre.

The Gauls then laid siege to the Capitol and a famous story is told in connection with that, too. One night the Gauls, having discovered a comparatively easy route up the hill, crept silently upward while the Roman defenders were asleep. They had almost achieved their goal when geese (kept in the temple because they played a role in religious observances) were disturbed by the faint sounds of the climbing men and began to hiss and run about.

One Roman, Marcus Manlius, who had been consul two years earlier, was roused. He seized his arms, attacked and threw over the first of the Gauls who was just reaching the summit, and called on others to wake and give aid. The Romans managed to beat the Gauls back and the city was saved from utter defeat. In honor of this feat, Manlius was given the surname of Capitolinus.

The Gauls, growing tired of the siege, which had now lasted seven months, and suffering themselves from hunger and disease, agreed to a compromise peace; that is, they offered to leave Rome if the Romans paid them a thousand pounds of gold. Scales were brought and the gold began to be weighed out. The Roman general supervising the weighing noted that one golden object, of which he happened to know the weight, was recorded at considerably less than the true figure by the scales. The Gauls were using false weights in order to get more than a thousand pounds.

The general objected and Brennus, the Gallic chieftain, is supposed to have answered coldly, "Woe to the vanquished," and to have thrown his own sword into the scale on top of the weights — meaning that the Romans would have to supply gold equivalent to the weight of his sword over and above the admittedly false weights.

The Roman historians could not bear to leave it at this and therefore insisted on adding that the indignant Romans took up arms and drove the Gauls back, and that the Gauls were then completely defeated by an army led by Camillus returning from his exile just in time to say, "With iron, not with gold, Rome buys her freedom."

In all probability, though, this last bit is just a flattering story made up by the later Roman historians. It seems much more likely that the Romans had been thoroughly defeated, laid under tribute, and had paid the tribute, too.

Nevertheless the city remained in being, and Camillus, even if he did not actually defeat the Gauls, still performed a great service. With the city in ruins, the Romans debated whether it might not be best to move to Veii and make a new start there, rather than to stay in a town which by recent events seemed to have been turned into a place of ill omen.

Against this, Camillus argued with all his might and prevailed. The Romans remained at Rome and Camillus was hailed as "the new Romulus" and a second founder of Rome.

The Gallic invasion had a number of consequences. In the first place, it apparently destroyed the Roman records, so that we have no reliable annals concerning the first three and a half centuries of Roman history. There are only the legendary tales, more or less distorted and some clearly invented in later times, which have been recounted so far in this book. It is only after 390 B.C. that the legends cease and a reasonably accurate history can begin.

Second, as after the time of Porsenna's invasion a century earlier, there followed a time of economic upset in Rome. The poor suffered horribly and debtors were once again being enslaved.

Manlius Capitolinus, the patrician savior of the Capitol, saw a soldier who had once bravely served with him, being led off to slavery for debt. Moved by pity, he promptly paid off what the soldier owed with his own money. He then began to sell his property announcing that no one would suffer so cruelly as long as he could himself make the necessary payment.

The patricians were displeased with this, for such kindness and generosity made them look the worse by contrast and, what's more, put unsettling notions in the mind of the poor. They announced that Manlius was attempting to gain popularity with the people in order to make himself king. Manlius was seized and tried, but it proved impossible for even the patricians to convict him in sight of the Capitol which he had saved.

The trial was moved out of sight of the Capitol. The patricians then got their conviction and poor Manlius was executed in 384 B.C.

But again there was long drawn-out plebeian agitation for relief and, in the long run, this could not be denied. Camillus, though a patrician, saw that the plebeians would have to be pacified. He used his enormous influence in this direction, and

as a result the Licinio-Sextian laws were passed in 367 B.C.
(They were named after Gaius Licinius and Lucius Sextius,
who were consuls that year.)

These laws eased matters for the debtor once more and limited the amount of land one man could hold. By preventing
individuals from piling estate upon estate they removed one of
the driving forces that led landowners to be merciless to small
farmers whose land they wanted to annex. Furthermore, the
consulship was opened to the plebeians and it grew customary,
after a while, to select at least one consul from a plebeian family. After this, the distinction between patrician and plebeian
faded completely.

Throughout Roman history, thereafter, it was felt that the
Senate ruled in partnership with the common people. The laws
and decrees of Rome were put forth in the name of S.P.Q.R.;
initials as well-known to the Roman historian as U.S.A. would
be to the American. "S.P.Q.R." stands for "Senatus Populusque
Romanus" ("the Senate and the People of Rome").

Finally, the Gallic invasion had resulted, in a sense, in a new
deal for central Italy. The Etruscans were through, and the
power-vacuum that resulted was ready to be filled by any city
that could display the proper initiative.

Rome had been a center of resistance to the Gauls and, while
she had suffered severely, she had put up a respectable fight.
The city's rapid recovery afterward had earned it considerable
prestige.

Under the capable leadership of Camillus, Rome quickly
won back all lost ground. She held on to Veii and defeated
the Volscians of southern Latium in 389 B.C. Even the Gauls
were defeated when they drifted south for another invasion in
367 B.C.

Camillus died in 365 B.C., but the Romans continued to grow
stronger. In 354 B.C., the Latin cities had been compelled to
join in a Latin League that was no longer an equal alliance but
was clearly dominated by Rome. At the same time, the south-

ern portion of Etruria, up to forty miles north of the city, acknowledged Roman domination.

Rome ruled over some 3,000 square miles of west central Italy only a generation after she had been apparently crushed by the Gauls. By 350 B.C. she had become one of the four great powers on the Italian peninsula, the other three being the Gauls in the north, the Samnites in the center, and the Greeks in the south.

# 3

# THE CONQUEST OF ITALY

## LATIUM AND BEYOND

Let us pause now to see how the condition of the world had changed in the four centuries since the founding of Rome.

In the east, the Assyrian Empire was long since dead, vanished and forgotten. In its place an even vaster, more powerful, and better ruled realm had arisen, the Persian Empire. By 350 B.C., though Persia had passed its peak, it still ruled over large sections of western Asia, from the Aegean Sea to India, and it controlled Egypt in addition.

The Greeks had passed through a period of great splendor during the first century of the Roman republic. While Rome was slowly freeing itself of Etruscan rule, the Greek city of Athens reached a height of culture that was unique in world history.

Unfortunately, the Greek cities had fought among themselves constantly, and by the time the Gauls had penetrated central Italy, Athens was defeated in war so badly by its chief rival, Sparta, that it never recovered completely. Shortly afterward, Sparta, too, was defeated by the Greek city of Thebes. By 350 B.C., the quarrels of the Greek cities had reduced all of them to an endless tug of war with everybody losing and nobody winning.

In Sicily, south of Italy, there was a flash of Greek greatness, for while Rome was recovering from the Gallic conquest, the city of Syracuse was controlled by a strong ruler, Dionysius (dih″oh-nish′us). Almost all of Sicily came under his rule, only the western tip remaining Carthaginian. In addition, his power reached out over much of the Greek portion of southern Italy. By 350 B.C., however, Dionysius had been dead for seventeen years, and under his weak successors Syracuse declined rapidly.

An unexpected greatness arose, however, in a small land north of Greece. This was Macedon (mas′ih-don), whose inhabitants spoke a Greek dialect but who were considered at best semibarbarian by the cultured Greeks to the south.

Until 359 B.C., Macedon had been merely a backwater of no importance in history, but in that year an extraordinary man came to power as Philip II. Almost at once he smashed barbarian tribes on the borders of Macedon. These had made continuous troubles for Philip's predecessors on the throne and had kept Macedon occupied and unable to play a proper part in world affairs. Now Philip's hands were freed.

Furthermore, he established an alliance with Epirus (ee-pigh′rus), a land to the west of Macedon and situated on the seacoast just across a narrow fifty-mile stretch of ocean from the heel of Italy. Philip married into the Epirot royal family and then placed his brother-in-law upon the throne of Epirus as Alexander I.

Philip built a large and efficient army, of which the core was

a well-trained *phalanx* (fay'lanks). This consisted of foot soldiers set in very closely spaced ranks and files. The rear files
had long spears that rested on the shoulders of those before so
that the phalanx resembled a bristling porcupine. The phalanx, drilled into performing its maneuvers with precision, as it
moved forward in step or shifted position right or left, could
simply smash through less-organized armies in its path as
though it were a battering ram. (Indeed, the word "phalanx"
comes from a Greek term meaning a log of wood used as a battering ram.)

Philip supported his phalanx well with cavalry and with an
efficiently organized system of supply. By 350 B.C. he was making his power felt in Greece, and the Greek cities were beginning to try (vainly) to stop him.

None of this affected the Romans. Everything, even the rise
of strong rulers in Sicily and in Macedon, was too far away to
concern them in 350 B.C. For Rome, only two powers represented dangers: the Gallic tribes to the north and the Samnite
tribes to the east and south. These Rome sought every opportunity to weaken and render harmless.

Rome's first chance came through a kind of civil war among
the Samnites. The Samnite tribes in Campania were embroiled
with those of Samnium itself; and the Campanians appealed
for assistance to Rome. (Throughout the next few centuries,
Rome was always ready to listen to pleas for assistance, always
came through with what she promised, and always kept the
spoils for herself. Those who used the very dangerous weapon
of Roman assistance never seemed to learn just how fatal such
help was. The Campanian Samnites, being the first, might be
excused.)

In 343 B.C. the Romans formed an alliance with the city of
Capua and declared war upon the Samnites. There followed
the First Samnite War, which might be considered Rome's first
step to world dominion. It wasn't a particularly remarkable

war, but over the next two years of not very intense fighting the Samnites were expelled from Campania and Roman influence over the area was established. In 341 B.C. peace was agreed to on both sides without a clearcut victory for either.

Probably Rome felt it was prudent to make peace with the Samnites, without having won any really smashing victory, in order to prepare herself for trouble brewing closer to home. While Roman armies were fighting in Campania, the Latin allies were supposed to be holding off the Samnites of Samnium itself. The Latins, however, were by no means eager to do this. Many of them felt Rome to be an oppressive overlord, and certainly this seemed to be a golden time to revolt — with the Roman armies occupied elsewhere. In 340 B.C. the Latin War began.

Unfortunately for the Latins, their timing was wrong. By the time the revolt was actually mounted, Rome had caught wind of what was going on, had made her peace with the Samnites, and had sent her armies marching north again. In two pitched battles, the Romans completely routed the Latin allies. In one of them, the Roman consul Publius Decius Mus deliberately let himself be killed, thinking that by this sacrifice to the lower gods he could guarantee victory for his army. (Such a sacrifice might actually be useful, since the soldiers thinking the gods were now on their side might fight with redoubled fervor, while the enemy might be correspondingly disheartened.)

At her leisure, Rome now turned against those Latin towns still resisting and snuffed them out one by one. By 338 B.C., the stillness of death had spread over Latium.

For decades there had also been periodic skirmishing between the Romans and the Gauls. The Romans had won consistently, although they generally remained on the defensive against the well-remembered and still-feared enemy. Nevertheless, it was increasingly obvious to the Gauls that they were getting little profit out of fighting the Romans; and the Roman victories over the Samnites and the Latins seemed to promise less profit than ever for the future. In 334 B.C., the Gauls agreed to a general peace and retired to their fertile home in the Po Valley.

Both the Samnites and Gauls had been somewhat tamed and the Latin allies had been punished. Rome therefore settled down to reorganize her dominions which had now further grown to over some 4,500 square miles and contained a population of at least half a million.

She made no further attempt to pretend that she was merely the head of a league of allies. Latium was made Roman territory, and most of the cities had to abandon all forms of self-government and become mere colonies. They could no longer make any agreements among themselves and could deal with each other only through Rome. The laws that ruled them were established by Rome and it was to Rome only that they could look for judgment. However, they became eligible for Roman citizenship if they moved to Rome.

All this was not as bad as it sounds. By and large, Roman government was efficient. It may have been harsher than the sort of things we are used to, for the Romans did not have our idea of democracy; nevertheless, the Latin cities were ruled by Rome as well as they had ruled themselves. Furthermore, as part of a larger area, they were freed of the constant warfare among themselves. With peace came increased trade and prosperity.

Because of good government and good times, the Latin cities and the other Roman-dominated areas of Italy usually remained loyal to Rome, even when great disasters befell the city a century later and when rebellion might well have destroyed the Roman realm once and for all. (The moral is, as one can see, that conquests may seem glorious and may make exciting chapters in history books, but it is the dull, plodding, day-to-day task of decent government that finally achieves the lasting results.)

While the Romans were preoccupied with the Latin War, it might have seemed a good time for the Samnites to seize the opportunity to re-establish power over Campania. Roman luck held. For centuries the Romans never found it necessary to fight more than one major enemy at a time. Always when they fought one enemy, caution or trouble held back other enemies.

In this case, the Samnites were distracted by trouble elsewhere. For decades now, they and other Italian tribes had been pressing against the Greek cities of the south. At the time the Greek cities had been founded, three or four centuries before, the Italian natives had been completely disorganized and had caused no trouble. That time had passed and the Greek cities were forever calling in outside help, since they feared they could not themselves withstand Italian pressure.

In the past it had been to cities such as Syracuse and Sparta that the Greeks of southern Italy had appealed, but now other and possibly more dangerous helpers were near.

This came about through the rise of Macedon, which I mentioned earlier. Philip II of Macedon had extended his power, and in 338 B.C. he met the armies of the two most powerful Greek cities of the time, Athens and Thebes, and smashed them. The Greek cities fell under Macedonian domination and were to remain there for a century and a half.

All this the Samnites watched with concern, for while Philip was pushing southward, his brother-in-law, Alexander of Epirus, showed signs of wanting to duplicate these feats in the west. It was this danger that occupied the Samnites while the Romans crushed the Latin cities and made peace with Gaul.

To be sure, Philip was assassinated in 336 B.C., and his even

more extraordinary son, Alexander III (soon to be known as
"the Great"), turned eastward and led his invincible armies
thousands of miles away from Italy; but the smaller Alexander
of Epirus was still there staring across the sea at the Italian
heel.

In 332 B.C. the blow fell. Tarentum, the leading city of Magna
Graecia, called for outside help as she had done on several occasions before, and this time she appealed to Alexander of Epirus. Alexander responded eagerly, moved an army into southern
Italy, and won several victories over the Italian armies.

For a while, things looked black indeed for the Italians, since
Rome and Epirus concluded a treaty and the possibility arose
of the two powers catching the Italians, and Samnium particularly, in pincers. (The Romans frequently made treaties with
the nations beyond their neighbors, as a means of helping them
subdue their neighbors. Once that was done, the power that
had made the treaty became the new neighbor and the next
conquest, but, again, the non-Romans never seemed to learn
that lesson.)

Unfortunately for Alexander of Epirus, he was too successful
for the people of Tarentum. They wanted help but, apparently,
not that much help. Soon the Tarentines were beginning to fear
that a too-victorious Alexander would be more dangerous to
them than the Italian natives could be. They therefore withheld their support.

In 326 B.C. he was defeated at Pandosia, a coastal city on the
instep of the Italian boot, and was killed in the retreat. His successor was too involved with home politics to carry on plans for
western conquest, and the outside danger to Italy passed for
the moment.

This meant that the Samnites could now turn their attention
to Rome, and certainly they could feel little friendliness for a
power that had been more or less openly willing to aid Alexander of Epirus. In fact, in 328 B.C. while the Samnites were
busy fighting Alexander, the Romans had established a colony

at Fregallae (free-jel'ee), on their own territory, to be sure, but very close to the borders of Samnium. The Samnites felt that this was a step intended to strengthen Rome in a forthcoming war with Samnium — and they were quite right.

Both sides were just aching for a fight and were willing to use anything as an excuse. A local quarrel in Campania served the purpose, and the Second Samnite War began in 326 B.C.

Rome's wars had reached the stage now where they were affecting all Italy. Both Rome and Samnium searched for allies elsewhere on the peninsula.

East of Samnium were two regions: Lucania, just north of the Italian toe, and Apulia, just northwest of the Italian heel. The Italian tribes of these regions had fought against Alexander along with the Samnites, but as long as it was a question of Italy alone, they considered the neighboring Samnites to be more dangerous than the distant Romans. They therefore fought on the Roman side.

To the cities of Magna Graecia in the Italian toe and heel, the Lucanians and Apulians were the immediate enemy. Since these had sided with Rome, the Greek cities sided with Samnium.

For five years, fighting continued indecisive, but with the advantage resting rather on the side of the Romans. Then, in 321 B.C., came disaster for Rome. A Roman army in Campania received a false report (deliberately spread by the Samnites) that a city in Apulia, allied to Rome, was being hard pressed by a Samnite army. The Romans at once decided to march directly to the city's relief — which meant cutting straight across Samnium.

In doing so, they passed through a narrow valley just east of the Samnite town of Caudium, a valley which could be entered by but one path at one end, and left by but one path at the other. This valley was called the Caudine Forks (kaw'-dine).

The Samnites were waiting. The Roman army entered the

Forks without trouble, but when they reached the exit of the valley, they found the path blocked by rocks and felled trees. They about-faced at once and found the road by which they had entered to be filled by Samnite troops that had quietly filed in behind them. They were trapped, neatly and completely, and they had no hope of escape. It was the most humiliating event in Rome's history up to that point. It is one thing, after all, to be defeated after fighting bravely; it is another to be defeated as a result of sheer stupidity.

The Samnites might have slaughtered the Roman army to the last man, but this victory would have been at the price of casualties and it seemed to them they could accomplish the same purpose without fighting. They needed only to sit tight and let the Romans starve.

They were right. Eventually, the Roman army consumed its food and there seemed nothing left to do but ask for terms. The Samnites presented those terms. The generals who led the Roman army were to make peace in the name of Rome and were to agree that Rome was to give up all the territory she had taken from Samnium. Under those conditions the army would be released.

Of course, the Roman generals could not make peace; only the Roman senate could, and the Samnites knew that. However, the senate might be persuaded to ratify the treaty of peace signed by the generals if it were made worth their while. To make it worth their while, the Samnites kept 600 of the best Roman officers as hostages.

However, the Samnites had underestimated the determination of their enemy. When the generals and their beaten army returned to Rome, the senate met to consider what to do. One of the generals suggested that he and his colleague be surrendered to the Samnites for having deceived them by making a false agreement, and that the hostages be abandoned. Almost all the senators had relatives among the hostages, but they agreed. The generals were delivered to the Samnites and the treaty was not ratified.

The Samnites objected that if the Romans would not ratify the treaty then it was not the generals they ought to return but the entire beaten army that ought to be put back into the Caudine Forks. This, of course, the Romans would not do, and the Samnites killed the hostages but realized they had lost a great chance for a real victory by accepting the Roman word and letting an enemy army live. They were not to have another chance.

The Romans continued the war under the strong leadership of Lucius Papirius Cursor, who was five times consul (the first time in 333 B.C. and the last in 313 B.C.) and twice dictator. He was a harsh disciplinarian and not liked by his troops, but he won victories.

The Romans fought politically as well as militarily. They established colonies on the borders of Samnium — filling them with retired soldiers and Latin allies — so that they could be sure of the countryside, whereas the Samnites, if they tried to march toward Rome, would find themselves in a quagmire of hostility. The Romans continued to cultivate alliances with the tribes in the rear of the Samnites.

ROADS AND LEGIONS

At this time, another Appius Claudius, a descendant of the Sabine patrician (see page 29) and of the tyrannical decemvir (see page 32), was rising to power in Rome. He eventually came to be known as Appius Claudius Caecus (see′kus), or "the blind," since in later life he lost his eyesight.

In 312 B.C. he was elected *censor*, an office that had first been established in 443 B.C. after the Twelve Tables had been drawn up. There were two censors, elected for a period of a year and a half, and only the consuls ranked higher. To begin with, the office was open to patricians only, but in 351 B.C. plebeians were allowed to qualify, and after 339 B.C. one of the censors *had* to be a plebeian.

Originally, the functions of the censor had included the supervision of taxation. (The word "censor" comes from a Latin term meaning "to tax.") In order to make taxation efficient and just, the people had to be counted and the value of their property estimated. Thus was instituted a *census* every five years, and we still use that term today for a gathering of statistics concerning the population.

Then, too, the censor had the right to exclude citizens from public functions if they had been guilty of immoral actions. They could even degrade a person, eject him from the senate, or deprive him of some or all of the rights of citizenship if, by his actions, he proved himself unworthy. It is from this we get our modern notion of a censor as someone who supervises public morality.

Appius Claudius Caecus was responsible for a number of innovations. He was the first to bring about the extension of Roman citizenship to individuals who did not own land. This recognized the fact that a middle class was growing up in Rome; merchants and artisans — businessmen, in other words — whose prosperity arose from sources other than agriculture and whose existence had to be accepted. Claudius also studied grammar, wrote poetry, and was the first Roman to write out his speeches. He is considered the father of Latin prose, and, with him, one sees that Rome was becoming more than a collection of farmers and soldiers. Culture was beginning to penetrate the city; and some Romans began to think as well as to act.

Appius Claudius' most important action, however, came in

312 B.C., when he supervised the building of a good road from Rome southeastward through Latium and Campania to Capua, a distance of 132 miles. It may have been covered with gravel at first, but by 295 B.C. it was paved throughout with blocks of stone. (In later years it was extended across Samnium and Apulia, down to the Italian heel itself.)

This was the first paved road that Rome built, but in later centuries, when she ruled a vast section of the ancient world, her roads were to spread everywhere and serve as the routes along which armies could be shuttled from one part of the realm to another as the occasion rose.

All the roads started from Rome, of course, and we still use the phrase "All roads lead to Rome" to mean that something inevitable will happen no matter what attempt is made to avoid it. The roads were built to last and were one of the glorious accomplishments of the Romans, for at no previous period in world history was so large an area brought into such close and efficient communication.

The Roman roads (slowly deteriorating with the centuries) served Europe's population for a thousand years and more after the end of the Roman period of history. Nothing better was produced, really, until the mid-nineteenth century, when a network of railroads began to cover the land.

The road built by Appius Claudius was not only the first but is also the best known of the Roman roads. To the Romans it was Via Appia, after the censor, and to us it is the Appian Way.

Its immediate purpose was to serve the Roman army as an efficient means of getting to Campania and back so that it might the better fight the Samnites. For this, the road worked well.

In addition, Roman skill in the art of war was improving in the furnace of the hard battles with the stiffly-resisting Samnites.

In the days before the Gallic invasion, the Romans fought much as other armies did. They collected the battleworthy men into a single mass that was not so large as to be unwieldy. This mass, containing from 3,000 to 6,000 men was called a *legion* (from a Latin word meaning "to collect").

The legion was armed with long spears and lunged at the enemy in unison, hoping that the weight of the charge would disrupt the enemy line. Which side won the battle depended on which side could catch the enemy by surprise, or off-balance, or outnumbered. All things equal, it might depend on which side charged with fiercer bravado, or which side could hold up for just long enough to allow reinforcements to come smashing in.

Throughout the ancient world, this attack-in-mass was used. It was brought to its highest pitch of perfection in the Macedonian phalanx — which was unbeatable, as long as it worked perfectly.

In the fourth century B.C., however, the Romans changed the legion into a world-conquering machine. According to tradition, the change started with Camillus. During the long siege of Veii, he kept the army in being over long periods, instead of merely for short campaigns during those times that his soldiers could be spared from their farming chores. To keep men in battle for long periods meant that the soldiers had to be paid, and Camillus was the first to institute such payment. It also meant that there was time for soldiers to be trained in maneuvers more complicated than that of merely charging at a given signal.

The legion came to consist of a complex body of men, including 3,000 heavily-armed men as the core, 1,000 lightly-armed men for more rapid maneuvering, and 300 horsemen (or cavalry) for still more rapid maneuvering. The legion was drawn up in three lines, all carrying short, heavy swords. The first two lines carried two short, heavy, throwing spears as well, while the third line carried the more usual long spears.

The first two lines were divided up into small groups called *maniples* (from a Latin word meaning "handful") made up of 120 men each. The maniples were placed with spaces between and the two lines were so arranged that the maniples were in checkerboard position.

The first line could advance on the enemy, throw their spears, charge in with their swords. Having wreaked considerable havoc, they could fall back, and the second line, fresh and unwearied, could do the same, while the third line remained as a reserve that awaited developments, such as the arrival of enemy reinforcements.

If it should happen that a sudden attack by the enemy, or some other misfortune, should drive the first line back, the maniples of the first line could retreat into the spaces between the maniples of the second line. Retreat would thus convert the legion into a solid phalanx which could (and on many occasions did) stand fast and immovable.

The legion was perfect for hilly and uneven county. A solid phalanx could always be upset if it could not march as a perfect unit. The Macedonian phalanx, for instance, had to have level ground to be really effective. The legion, on the other hand, could spread out. The maniples could make their way about obstructions and then come together again, if necessary. The phalanx was a fist that was deadly but that could never be opened. The legion was a hand in which the fingers could be spread out, nimbly and sensitively, but which could close into a fist at any time.

The developing art of legionary warfare was placing the Romans at more and more of an advantage over the Samnites. This was shown all the more so when in 312 B.C. the Etruscan cities, mere shadows of their early greatness, took action. A long period of peace, enforced by treaty, had come to an end, and it seemed to them that, with Rome occupied in the south, it was time for Etruria to strike for liberty.

But the Romans, nothing daunted, sent legions north and south, and fought a two-front war vigorously. The Roman general, Quintus Fabius Maximus Rullianus, made his mark here. Earlier in the war against the Samnites, Fabius had (against orders) attacked and beaten a Samnite army during the absence of the dictator, Papirius Cursor. Papirius, on returning, was fully determined to punish and perhaps execute Fabius, for to that rigid man, victory was no excuse for disobedience. To the soldiers, however, it was, and Papirius, facing a virtual rebellion, had to let Fabius go.

Then Fabius repaid Rome by leading an army far into northern Etruria and defeating the Etruscans wherever he met them. They were forced to drop out of the fight in 308 B.C.

Meanwhile, Papirius Cursor steadily pushed the Samnites completely out of Campania and in 305 B.C. invaded Samnium itself. The Samnites saw no way out but to make peace, if only to gain a breathing space so that they might later renew the fight. In 304 B.C. peace was signed and the Second Samnite War was ended. The Samnites gave up all Campania, but preserved their essential strength in Samnium.

SAMNIUM AND BEYOND

Rome was by no means blind to the fact that the Samnites were not yet crushed. During the years of peace, she strengthened herself in every direction. She annexed territory east of Latium and north of Samnium, reaching the Adriatic Sea for the first time. In this way she interposed a solid band of Roman territory between the Samnites on the southeast and the Etruscans and Gauls on the northwest. She founded cities in the Appenine mountains (that run down the length of the Italian peninsula like a backbone) to serve as centers of strength in offense and resistance in defence.

The Gauls, naturally, were apprehensive about Rome's growing power. The city that they had taken and pillaged a century before had somehow risen out of its ruins and grown mighty. It was now in control of 15,000 square miles of central Italy. It stretched from sea to sea and no other Italian power could make headway against it.

Too late (Rome's foes were always too late), the Gauls decided to join the enemies of Rome on the peninsula and crush the upstart power.

Lucania furnished the occasion for a new war, for Lucanian envoys came to Rome complaining that the Samnites were picking on them again, in defiance of treaty agreements. That was all Rome needed. Quickly she invaded Samnium and the Third Samnite War began in 298 B.C.

The Samnites, however, decided not to meet the Romans alone this time. A Samnite army forced its way northward and joined the Etruscans and Gauls. United, they faced Rome.

For the Romans, it was a frightening combination. They had not forgotten the Gauls, and the name was still calculated to make Roman hearts uneasy.

Fabius Maximus, who had ravaged Etruria in the previous war was sent northward again. In 295 B.C., the opposing armies met at Sentinum, about 110 miles north of Rome and only 30 miles south of the Gallic border. The Romans had met the Gauls considerably more than halfway.

In the battle that followed, the Samnites and Gauls held firm against the Roman onslaught for a long period of time, but the Etruscans melted away when the Romans sent a detachment to raid Etruria. Fabius's fellow-consul was Publius Decius Mus, son and namesake of the consul who had devoted himself to death for the sake of victory during the Latin War. The son decided to do the same now and, after appropriate religious rites, dashed into the front line to seek death — and found it.

Finally, the Romans had their way. The Samnite remnant retreated hastily and the Gauls were virtually wiped out. The Roman victory was complete, for the enemy losses had been three times the Roman.

The terror of the Gallic name was ended. The Gauls took no

more part in the fight; they had had enough; and the nightmare of 390 B.C. was lifted forever from the Roman mind. The Etruscans made a separate peace in 294 B.C. and the Samnites were left fighting alone.

Papirius Cursor invaded Samnium. In the southeastern section of that region, fully 160 miles southeast of Rome, the Roman army (fighting ever farther from home) met and defeated the Samnites at Aquilonia in 293 B.C. For three more years, the Samnites fought on despairingly and then, in 290 B.C., gave in again.

Even now, Rome felt in no position to demand too great a sacrifice of the stubborn foe that had now been fighting her, with short interruptions, for half a century. Samnium was forced to enter into alliance with Rome, but it was an alliance of near-equals. Samnium did not have to give up her self-government, but she could no longer fight independently; Samnites could march to war only under Roman generals.

With Samnium quiet, Rome consolidated her hold in Etruria and among the Gallic tribes east of Sentinum. By 281 B.C. all of Italy was under her control from the southern border of Cisalpine Gaul right down to the Greek cities of the south. She controlled about half of the peninsula.

And yet, as always, with a conquest completed, danger arose beyond the conquest.

The Greek cities of the south stared in amazement and fright at the new colossus that towered over them. A hundred years before, Rome was an unknown city, crushed by Gallic barbarians (an event just barely mentioned in the works of a single Greek philosopher of the time). Then, for a century afterward, it remained merely another one of the native Italian tribes which the cultivated Greeks shrugged off as mere barbarian nuisances. Now the Roman armies were everywhere — and everywhere victorious.

Some Greek cities made the best of it by joining the Romans since they could not beat them. Neapolis (the present-day

Naples), far northwest of the main Greek power, joined Rome in alliance.

Tarentum, the leading city of Magna Graecia, was not minded, however, to knuckle under to the barbarians. She looked abroad for help, as she had been doing for quite a while now. It was Tarentum that had brought in Alexander of Epirus against the Italians a half-century earlier (see page 50).

While Rome was deeply engaged with Samnium, the Tarentines thought they had their man in Sicily. A capable general, Agathocles (uh-gath'oh-kleez), had made himself master of Syracuse, Sicily's largest city, in 316 B.C. From Syracuse, he extended his rule over almost all of Sicily, and for a moment he looked like the champion of the Greek cause everywhere in the west.

However, the Carthaginians, who had been fighting the Greeks in Sicily for two centuries, bestirred themselves and sent a large army against Agathocles. They defeated him badly in 310 B.C. and penned him up in Syracuse itself.

Agathocles then had a most daring notion; one that was to have important consequences a century later. He decided to carry the fight to Carthage itself. He slipped out of Syracuse with a small army and made for the African coast, evading the Carthaginian fleet.

The Carthaginians were caught by complete surprise. For centuries they had had no important land enemies in Africa, and they had been sure no enemy could approach by sea while the Carthaginian navy ruled the waves. Their city and its approaches were undefended, therefore, and Agathocles could raid and ravage at will. The Carthaginians were forced to sign a peace treaty with him in 307 B.C., and he was left more strongly master of Sicily than ever.

The Tarentines called Agathocles into Italy now, and for several years he maintained himself there. The Romans, busily engaged in mopping up the Samnites and in consolidating their gains, paid little attention to him.

Under a man of Agathocles' type, the united Greeks of the west might have become strong enough to withstand the Romans. However, Agathocles could not make the Tarentines remain firmly with him any more than the previous helpers of Tarentum had been able to. The Tarentines wanted help, but they didn't want to be troubled in their own easy and prosperous way of life while they were being helped, nor did they want their helpers to be too dangerously successful.

Agathocles was approaching the age of seventy and gave up the fight. He left Italy, dying soon after in 289 B.C.

Tarentum, therefore, found herself alone once more and facing a Roman giant that was stronger than ever. Nor was there any chance that Rome would leave the Greek cities in peace. There were always local quarrels and crises that gave her opportunities for interference.

In 282 B.C., for instance, Thurii (thyoor'ee-igh), a Greek town on the Italian toe, called for Roman help against the inroads of the Italian tribes of Lucania, which were still maintaining a precarious independence. The Romans responded promptly and occupied Thurii.

Tarentum, dismayed at the appearance of a Roman force in the heart of Magna Graecia, was desperate enough to take action on her own. When Roman ships appeared off the shore, the Tarentines sank the ships and killed the admiral. (The ships were small ones, for Rome had not yet developed a real navy.) Elated by this unimpressive success, the Tarentines then sent an army to Thurii and drove out the small Roman garrison.

Rome, not quite ready to fight in southern Italy, and still settling affairs farther north, decided to turn the other cheek for the moment. She sent envoys to Tarentum to arrange a cease-fire and to request the return of Thurii. The Tarentines laughed at the Roman manner of speaking Greek, and as the Roman ambassadors were leaving the government center, some hoodlum in the crowd deliberately urinated upon the toga of one of them. The crowd laughed uproariously.

The indignant envoy proclaimed ominously that the stain would be washed out in blood, returned to Rome, and displayed the soiled toga to the senate. The senate, in a fury, declared war on Tarentum in 281 B.C.

But now Tarentum was truly frightened. A joke was a joke, but the dour Romans seemed to lack a sense of humor. The Tarentines cast their eyes abroad for help, and fortunately an even greater general than Agathocles was at hand, and eager to take up the Tarentine quarrel.

**Southern Italy**

# 4

# THE CONQUEST OF SICILY

## PYRRHUS

While the Romans were engaged in their fifty-year struggle with Samnium, the son of Philip of Macedon carried through the most astonishing military feat of ancient times — perhaps of all times. With his small and superbly trained army, including the Macedonian phalanx, Alexander the Great crossed into Asia Minor and marched the length and breadth of the Persian Empire, winning every battle against every foe. He carried Greek arms and Greek culture to the deserts of Central Asia, to the northwestern border of India, to Egypt. The entire vast Persian Empire fell under his control.

In 323 B.C., however, Alexander died in Babylon, at the age of 33. He left only a half-wit brother and a baby son to succeed him. They were soon done away with, and his generals fell to quarreling over the Empire.

They fought each other ceaselessly and by 301 B.C., after a gigantic battle in Asia Minor, it seemed obvious that no one of them was ever going to win everything. Alexander's empire was permanently in pieces.

The main Asiatic portion — including Syria, Babylonia, and the broad regions to the east — fell under the rule of Alexander's general, Seleucus (see-lyoo′kus), who made himself king. His descendants were to rule for centuries over what is usually called the Seleucid Empire (see-lyoo′sid).

Egypt was under the control of another of Alexander's generals, Ptolemy (tol′uh-mee). His descendants, all named Ptolemy, ruled as kings over Egypt, and therefore that land in that period of its history is known as Ptolemaic Egypt (tol″uh-may′ik).

Asia Minor was broken up into a series of small kingdoms, which there will be occasion to discuss later on. Taken all together, these Macedonian-ruled portions of the Persian Empire make up the Hellenistic kingdoms, and by 281 B.C., when Rome and Tarentum were squaring off for battle, all were firmly established. All of them, however, were too far distant to lend a hand to Tarentum and, besides, were far too preoccupied with bickering among themselves.

Closer at hand was Macedon itself, but it was greatly weakened by the fact that so many of its best men had travelled abroad to become the rulers and soldiers of vast realms to the east and south. It was further weakened by the fact that the old Macedonian royal family had petered out and that competing generals fought for rule. In 281 B.C., indeed, Macedon was suffering from a state of absolute anarchy and could help no one.

Contributing to that anarchy was the kingdom of Epirus on the western border of Macedon. The king of Epirus, since 295 B.C., was Pyrrhus (pir′us), the younger son of a cousin of the Alexander of Epirus who had once invaded Italy (see page 50).

As it happened, Pyrrhus was, of all the Hellenistic rulers of the time, the best general by far. Furthermore, he was the closest of all of them to Tarentum. And then, too, he was essentially a romantic, never happier than when he was engaged in some military adventure. (In fact, his great failing was that he never stopped to secure a victory as the Romans always did, but was always off on a new adventure before the old one had been battened down.)

Pyrrhus had helped along Macedonian misery by invading Macedon in 286 B.C., and he actually held it for seven months before he was forced out. Now, for five years, he had been rusting away in peace and was ready for anything as long as it meant fighting.

To him, therefore, the Tarentines turned, for he was made to order. He was only fifty miles away; he was a great general; and he was dying to fight. What more could the Tarentines ask?

Pyrrhus answered the call, of course, and in 280 B.C. he arrived. He wasn't there just to help Tarentum, to be sure. He had plans of his own. He was going to make himself the head of a Greek army that was to defeat Rome and Carthage and establish as great an empire in the west as his distant cousin, Alexander the Great, had established in the east. With him, Pyrrhus brought 25,000 veteran troops, trained in the phalanx technique, which the Romans were now going to face for the first time. It was no longer Italian tribes, fighting bravely but without science, that the Romans were to face. This time they would be opposing a trained general, master of all the arts of war.

Nor was it only men that Pyrrhus brought. When Alexander had reached India in his victorious march, he found the Indian armies fighting with huge, tusked beasts — elephants. They were used as we use tanks nowadays; to terrify the opposing army and to crush them by sheer weight. Alexander was genius enough to defeat the elephants, but his generals saw no reason why they should not make use of them. For a generation, elephants had fought on one side or the other (sometimes on both) of every great battle in which the Macedonians had been engaged.

Pyrrhus brought twenty elephants into Italy, and got to work at once. His first task was to handle the Tarentines. If they wanted help, they were going to have to pitch in. He closed the theaters and the clubs, and started drilling the citizens. The Tarentines cried out in horror and Pyrrhus sent the loudest criers to Epirus. That quieted the rest.

Then, that same year, he marched out to meet the Romans at Heraclea (her″uh-kle′uh), halfway between Tarentum and Thurii. He chose a spot of ground level enough for his phalanxes and drew up his cavalry and his elephants. The Romans stared with terror at the huge beasts. They had never imagined such creatures could exist and they called them "Lucanian oxen."

The Romans tried to attack, but Pyrrhus' phalanx held immovable, and when he sent the elephants forward, the Romans had to retreat — but in good order. The first battle between phalanx and legion had given victory to the phalanx, but Pyrrhus was not fooled. He rode gloomily over the battlefield, noting that the Roman dead had their wounds in front. They had not turned to run, even from the elephants.

They might be non-Greek barbarians, Pyrrhus thought, but they fought like Macedonians.

The victory at Heraclea emboldened some of Rome's scarcely conquered enemies to dare to rise once more. The Samnites in particular witnessed the Roman defeat with joy and joined Pyrrhus at once.

Pyrrhus, not too eager to continue fighting the Romans, felt that it might be just as well to arrange a peace with Rome on a live-and-let-live basis. He therefore sent Cineas (sin′ee-as), a Greek noted for his oratorical ability, to Rome as his representative, in order to persuade the Romans to make peace.

Cineas faced the senate, and his skillful speech almost moved the senators to agree to peace. According to the story, however, it was at this moment that the old censor, Appius Claudius Caecus, came on the scene. The hero of the Second Samnite War, and builder of the Appian Way, was now old and blind. He was too feeble to walk, so that he had to be carried into the senate chamber.

His words were not feeble, however. In his quavering voice, he set up a simple requirement. No peace with Pyrrhus, he said, as long as a single one of his soldiers remains on the soil of Italy. The senate promptly took up that cry and Cineas departed, his mission a failure.

Pyrrhus had to fight. He marched northwestward into Campania, taking city after city, advancing to within twenty-four miles of Rome itself, but he could not shake the loyalty of the Latin cities, and was forced to return to Tarentum for the winter.

During that winter, the Romans sent envoys to Pyrrhus to negotiate for the ransom and return of Roman prisoners. The chief envoy was Gaius Fabricius, who had been consul two years previously.

Pyrrhus received Fabricius with elaborate honors and tried to persuade him to argue the Roman senate into making peace. Fabricius refused. When Pyrrhus offered him increasingly large bribes, Fabricius, although a poor man, refused them all. To test Fabricius further (according to the Roman story) Pyrrhus had an elephant secretly brought behind him and made to trumpet. Fabricius never moved a muscle.

Struck with admiration, Pyrrhus, who was a generous and chivalrous ruler, ordered the prisoners released without ransom.

Fabricius had a chance to return this generosity during the next summer's campaign. When Pyrrhus' physician came secretly to the Roman camp and offered, for a bribe, to poison the Epirote king, the indignant Fabricius had the would-be assassin bound and returned to Pyrrhus.

Since attempts at peace continued to fail, Pyrrhus marched

northward again in 279 B.C. He managed to maneuver the Romans into a second battle on level ground at Ausculum (aws'kyoo-lum), about 100 miles northwest of Tarentum. Again, the Romans charged the phalanx without being able to move it. Again, Pyrrhus brought up his elephants and again the Romans had to retire. In this battle, one of the Roman consuls was Publius Decius Mus, grandson and namesake of the consul who had gone to his death to defeat the Latins, and son and namesake of the consul who had gone to his death to defeat the Gauls. The new Decius, it is said, now did the same, but this time the sacrifice didn't work. Pyrrhus won anyway.

The legion and phalanx had met a second time, and for a second time the phalanx had won. It was also the last time.

Nor was this second victory a very satisfying one. Pyrrhus' losses had been heavy, particularly among the troops he had brought with him, and this was serious, for he could not trust the Greek troops of Magna Graecia. Still less could he rely on the loyalty of his Italian allies.

Therefore, when one of his companions tried to congratulate Pyrrhus on his victory, Pyrrhus snapped back, "Another such victory and I shall return without a man to Epirus." It is from this that the phrase "Pyrrhic victory" comes, meaning a victory so costly that it has the effect of a defeat.

Pyrrhus was so weakened by his Pyrrhic victory that he felt in no position to pursue the retreating Romans. Let them go! Nor could he count on reinforcements from home, for while Pyrrhus was fighting in Italy, bands of Gauls had suddenly descended upon Macedon, Epirus and upper Greece, and paralyzed the whole region. (Pyrrhus might have been better engaged fighting at home to save his own land.)

Pyrrhus sought an honorable way out and found it in the fact that Rome now made an alliance with Carthage. That African city had been fighting Greeks for centuries, and as the Romans were now fighting them, too, why not an alliance?

But that gave the king of Epirus a logical way to stop fighting the Romans, so terrible even in defeat. He could cross over into Sicily and fight Carthage, the ally of the Romans. In 278 B.C. he left for Sicily.

There, he faced two enemies. First there were the Carthaginians and secondly there were the Mamertines ("sons of Mars"), who were actually Italian troops imported into Sicily by Agathocles to act as his personal bodyguard. Such mercenary soldiers (that is, soldiers who serve for pay rather than out of loyalty to a particular homeland) can be very useful, for they will fight as long as they are paid and are very loyal to the one who pays them. Furthermore, since war is their profession, they will usually fight bravely, if only to increase their rate of pay for the next battle by showing themselves to be valuable.

However, if payment fails, they are liable to seize what they need or want from the helpless population about them; and they usually have no hesitation in plundering the population they are hired to defend. The Mamertines, after Agathocles' time, therefore became a bitter burden to the Greek population.

Pyrrhus struck successfully at both groups, penning them up in different angles of the three-angle island; the Mamertines in the northern angle and the Carthaginians in the western one. However, the Sicilian Greeks grew restive under Pyrrhus' insistence on warlike discipline and, since the Romans were making progress in Italy in his absence, the Tarentines were screaming for him at the top of their lungs.

He sailed back to Italy in 276 B.C. and once again marched northwestward into the heart of Italy. In 275 B.C., he was ready for a third battle, this time at Beneventum, about forty miles west of Ausculum.

But the Romans, having faced the elephants and the phalanx twice, had worked out a defense against them. They attacked in a hilly region without allowing Pyrrhus to draw up his phalanx on flat ground. Furthermore, before charging, they had archers shoot arrows dipped in burning wax at the elephants. The elephants, stung by fire, turned tail and ripped through Pyrrhus' own lines. The phalanx, trying to form on the uneven ground, was shaken to pieces and was helpless. The Roman legions attacked, and Pyrrhus' third battle was an utter defeat.

He fell back on Tarentum, washed his hands bitterly of any further attempt to fight the Romans, and left for Epirus and further wars in Greece. He died three years later in the streets of a Greek city when a woman dropped a roof tile on his head. To the end of his life, he continued winning battles and losing wars.

Meanwhile, in 272 B.C., the Romans took Tarentum, and destroyed all her capacity for making war but left it its self-government. The last Greek city in Magna Graecia to remain free was Rhegium (ree'jee-um) at the extreme end of the Italian toe. The Romans took it in 270 B.C.

It was next the turn of the Samnites. Rome was grimly determined to punish them for the help they gave to Pyrrhus. In a single campaign (sometimes called the Fourth Samnite War), what was left of Samnite freedom was destroyed in 269 B.C. Etruria also was mopped up, and in 265 B.C. the last free city in Etruria was taken.

CARTHAGE

Rome now controlled all of Italy south of the border of Cisalpine Gaul. This border lay on the small Rubicon River (roo'bih-kon). In later centuries, even when the tide of Roman conquest had flowed far beyond that mark, the Rubicon River was still considered the boundary of Italy.

Not all of Roman Italy was ruled in the same way. In fact, Rome had a variety of methods of control and used them all.

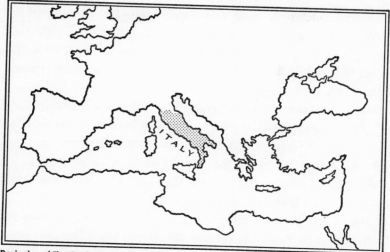

Beginning of First Punic War — 264 B.C.

Some areas were completely Roman and their inhabitants had full rights of citizenship (and could even vote if they came to Rome to do so). In some cities, Roman colonists took over — men of military experience with their families. They remained as garrisons in possibly hostile territory. Other places were in alliance with Rome, with a greater or lesser degree of self-government. Still other areas, where Rome had experienced considerable enmity, were held under tight control with little, or no, self-government. Different cities or areas could change their status, according to their behavior, being promoted to greater rights as a reward for loyalty, or demoted as a punishment for disloyalty.

In all cases, though, Rome held the strings and so arranged matters as to prevent different cities from making common cause. By placing different cities under different systems of government, she made it more unlikely that the two would find grounds for common action. All through her history, Rome maintained her ascendancy partly by dividing the governed areas from each other and partly by binding the interest of each, as far as possible, to Rome, either through fear or through hope. The policy of "Divide and rule!" became so famous that it has been a familiar phrase to succeeding generations down to our own time.

Rome now ruled over 50,000 square miles, with a population of about 4,000,000. A century after she had been crushed by the Gauls, she had raised herself to a world power, on a par with Carthage and with the various Hellenistic kingdoms.

As a world power, and the one that had risen latest and most rapidly, Rome was bound to arouse the envy and apprehension of the older powers. In particular, it was now the turn of Carthage to be alarmed, for she and Rome were the two great powers of the western Mediterranean and Carthage felt (quite rightly, as it turned out) that there was room for only one.

I left Carthage at the time of its founding, with the mythical tale of Dido and Aeneas (see page 8). At first, Carthage was only one of a series of colonial towns in the western Mediterranean founded by the Phoenicians, though the most successful one. Shortly after 600 B.C., however, Nebuchadrezzar of Babylon conquered Phoenicia and destroyed its power. That placed the Phoenician colonies on their own and they clustered about Carthage, whose navy now became the strongest in the west.

Carthage found her chief enemy in the Greek colonists who by that time had been expanding westward for two and a half centuries, flooding into Italy and Sicily. To combat these Greeks, Carthage was willing to ally herself with the native powers on the Italian mainland. At first, this meant the Etruscans, and in the Battle of Alalia (see page 21), about 550 B.C., Greek expansion was brought to a permanent halt.

Under her first strong military leader, Mago (may'goh), Carthage extended her influence over the large island of Sardinia, west of Italy, and over the smaller Balearic islands (bal"ee-ar'ik) 200 miles west of Sardinia. On the easternmost of these islands, he is supposed to have founded a town that in ancient times was called Portus Magonis ("Port of Mago") and that even today is known as Port Mahon.

Carthage established trading posts here and there along the coasts of the western Mediterranean and explored beyond the Mediterranean, too. There are dim stories of expeditions into the Atlantic that reached the British isles, of others that explored the western coast of Africa and may even have circumnavigated that continent.

Carthage's chief and enduring conflict in the centuries of her greatness was with the Greeks in Sicily. The Greeks had settled the eastern two-thirds of the island, but the Carthaginians had the western third, including Panormus (puh-nawr'mus), the modern Palermo, on the northern shore, and Lilybaeum (lil"uh-bee'um) at the western tip.

The fortunes of war in Sicily swayed back and forth without ever coming to a halt at complete victory for one side or the other. When the Carthaginians had capable generals, they would master all the island except for Syracuse. That city they could never capture. When the Greeks came under forceful leadership, as under Dionysius, Agathocles, or Pyrrhus, they would master all the island except for Lilybaeum. That city they could never capture.

Pyrrhus failed at Lilybaeum, too, and when he left Sicily, he said, in clear-eyed prophecy, "What a battlefield I leave for the Romans and Carthaginians."

Until then, Carthage and Rome had been friendly for two and a half centuries, for they had had a common enemy in the Greeks. As early as 509 B.C. when Rome was still under the Tarquins, Carthage had signed a trade treaty with her. In 348 B.C., this treaty was renewed, and even as late as 277 B.C., Carthage and Rome formed an alliance against Pyrrhus.

But now Pyrrhus was gone and the Greek cities of Italy were

taken. There remained, however, for Carthage, the old battle-ground of Sicily. Syracuse was still strong, and, after Pyrrhus' departure, her General Hiero (high'uh-roh) was the most prominent Greek in the west. He had fought well under Pyrrhus and he was a man of courage and ability.

Hiero's first feat of arms was against the Mamertines, whom Pyrrhus had left penned up in Messana (meh-say'nuh) in the northeastern corner of the island (see page 71). They were emerging now and spreading havoc. Hiero marched against them, defeated them in 270 B.C., and restricted them to Messana again. The grateful Syracusans made him king, as Hiero II.

Once he had made his rule secure, Hiero decided to return to Messana in 265 B.C. and, in alliance with Carthage, wipe out the Mamertine stronghold altogether. This he might well have done, but the Mamertines, reflecting that they were Italian soldiers after all, sent out an appeal for help to the Italian world-power of Rome.

Rome always answered such appeals, and an army under Appius Claudius Caudex (a son of the old censor) crossed into Sicily and, in 263 B.C., easily defeated Hiero's forces.

Hiero did not wait for a second defeat. He saw well where the future lay, retreated to Syracuse at once and signed a separate peace with Rome. Till the end of his long reign (he ruled for fifty-five years, dying in 215 B.C. at a time when he was over ninety years of age), he remained a loyal Roman ally. Syracuse was left at peace and in full enjoyment of her self-government. It was the most peaceful and prosperous half-century Syracuse had ever known, and in the twilight of Greek power elsewhere Syracuse had her Golden Age.

The war continued between Rome and Carthage, however. To Rome, the Carthaginians were "Poeni" (their version of "Phoenicia," the land from which the Carthaginians had originally come). This first war with Carthage is therefore called the First Punic War.

# THE ROMANS AT SEA

Perhaps the Romans looked for a quick and easy war. The Greeks, after all, had on several occasions been able to defeat the Carthaginians. Only fifteen years before, Pyrrhus had defeated them handily, and Rome had in turn defeated Pyrrhus.

It may have looked all the more as though the Romans were justified in being optimistic after they won a great victory over Carthage at Agrigentum (ag″rih-jen′tum) on Sicily's southern shore in 262 B.C. However, the Carthaginians all through their history seemed to fight best with their backs to the wall. They forced the Romans to struggle desperately at every step, and their far west bulwark at Lilybaeum seemed impregnable.

They had never lost Lilybaeum to any Greek, and the Romans did not think they would do better. Nor could they sit down to besiege Lilybaeum and starve it out as long as the Carthaginian navy could freely bring food and supplies into the port.

The Romans therefore made a daring decision. They would fight and defeat the Carthaginians at sea.

It seemed like a mad resolve, for Carthage had a long history of excellence at sea. She had the largest navy in the western Mediterranean and a centuries-long tradition of sea trade and sea warfare. As for the Romans, all their many victories had been on land. They had ships, of course, but small ones; none that could possibly dare approach Carthaginian ships of war. The Romans didn't even know how to build large ships; How, then, could they hope to battle at sea?

Fortunately for Rome, a Carthaginian quinquereme (a ship with five banks of oars, instead of the three banks in the much smaller Roman triremes) happened to be wrecked at sea and cast up on the coast of the Italian toe. Romans studied the wreckage and learned how to build a quinquereme. They undoubtedly had help in this from their Greek subjects (for the Greeks, too, had a long naval tradition).

The Romans proceeded to build a number of quinqueremes, and while they were a-building, they trained the crews on land.

This was not as hard as it might sound, since the Romans had no intention of trying to outmaneuver the skilled Carthaginian sea captains, for there they would certainly fail. Instead, they fitted their ships with grappling hooks. It was their intention to make straight for the enemy, fix themselves to the Carthaginian ships firmly and permanently by means of the hooks, and then send their own men swarming onto the Carthaginian vessels. The Romans intended to set up the equivalent of a land battle to be fought on the decks of ships.

In 260 B.C. the Romans were ready. A small detachment of their fleet was captured by the Carthaginians, and this may have led to a certain Carthaginian overconfidence. At any rate, the main body of the Roman fleet, freshly hacked out of the Italian forests, set sail under Gaius Duilius Nepos (dyoo-il'ee-us nee'pos). It was he who had designed the grappling hooks. They were beams with spikes affixed underneath. They were raised high as the Roman ship approached and were released to come down heavily when within reach of the enemy ship. The spike would be driven deep into the enemy deck and the two ships would remain together thereafter.

The Roman ships encountered the Carthaginian fleet off Mylae (migh'lee), a seaport just fifteen miles west of Messana. The ships joined, the beams dropped, the spikes held, the Roman soldiers dashed upon the surprised Carthaginians and it was no contest. Fourteen Carthaginian ships were sunk, and thirty-one were taken. The queen of the seas had been defeated by a rank newcomer, first time out. Duilius Nepos received the first naval triumph in Roman history.

Nevertheless, the Carthaginian will to resist held. Their strongholds in western Sicily remained firm, and the Carthaginians had ships enough and skill enough to keep them supplied.

The Romans, therefore, decided to go a step farther and take a leaf out of the book of Agathocles; they would attack Carthage on her home grounds as he had done (see page 61). In 256 B.C., a huge fleet of 330 quinqueremes was outfitted and placed under the command of Marcus Atilius Regulus, who was then consul.

The fleet rounded the eastern side of Italy, its heel, and sailed along its southern coast. About halfway along that coast, off a site called Ecnomus (ek'noh-mus), they met a still larger Carthaginian fleet. A second naval battle was fought, the largest ever fought up to that time, and again the Romans were victorious. With Carthaginian sea power temporarily shattered, the way was clear and the Romans made straight for the Carthaginian coast.

The situation was exactly as it had been in Agathocles's time. The Carthaginians had not learned their lesson; that their homeland was not immune from war. It was still unarmed and undefended, and Regulus had no difficulties in defeating the hastily assembled Carthaginian armies and in seizing control of the area. He finally appeared under the walls of Carthage herself, and when Carthage, frightened to distraction, was ready to make peace, Regulus set such extreme terms that the Carthaginian government decided to try battle instead. They might as well go down fighting.

In Carthage at the time was a Spartan named Xanthippus (zan-tip'us). Sparta was long past its great days of military prowess, but the old tradition still lived in the hearts of many individual Spartans. Xanthippus spoke out boldly and told the Carthaginians they were being defeated not by the Romans but by the incompetence of their own generals.

So well did he talk and so confident did he sound that the

distracted Carthaginians gave him the command. He scraped together an army and to it added 4,000 cavalry and a force of 100 elephants. In 255 B.C., he led them out against the Romans who had been weakened some time before when a large fraction of the army had been called off to the fighting in Sicily. Regulus might well have retreated, but he decided that Roman pride demanded he stand and fight. He fought, was defeated, and taken prisoner. The first Roman invasion of Africa thus ended in complete failure.

The Roman senate, at news of this, sent its fleet with reinforcements to Africa. This fleet defeated Carthaginian ships that tried to block its passage, but then ran into a greater enemy. Had the Romans been more experienced, they would have recognized the signs of a coming storm and have known that even Roman ships must seek harbor before a storm. The storm came, the Roman fleet was destroyed, and thousands of Roman soldiers drowned.

The Carthaginians, further heartened at this, sent reinforcements, including elephants, into Sicily. The Romans, however, reacting as though possessed by fiends, had a new fleet built in three months. This fleet sailed to Sicily where it helped take Panormus. It then cruised along the African coast without doing anything serious, and when it moved back to Rome, it too was caught by a storm and was destroyed in turn.

The war continued uselessly in Sicily, and in 250 B.C. the Carthaginians thought they might as well agree to a compromise peace. They sent an embassy to Rome to suggest it, and Regulus, the captured Roman general, accompanied the embassy in order (so he promised) to back the plea for peace. Regulus gave his word of honor to return to Carthage if the embassy failed.

However, when the embassy arrived at Rome, Regulus, to the surprise and horror of the Carthaginians, rose before the senate to say that prisoners like himself, who had surrendered instead of dying in battle, were not worth saving and that war should be continued to the end. He then returned to Carthage where he was put to death by torture by the angry Carthaginians. (This story may be untrue. All we know of the Carthaginians is what we are told by Greek and Roman writers, the inveterate enemies of Carthage. They loved to tell atrocity stories, and no Carthaginian writings in self-defense or in counterattack survive.)

In 249 B.C., the Romans built another fleet and sent it against Lilybaeum, which still, after fifteen years of war, remained firmly in Carthaginian hands. This fleet was under the command of Publius Claudius Pulcher ("Claudius the handsome"), a younger son of the old censor and the brother of the Appius Claudius who had first led a Roman army into Sicily.

Instead of maintaining the siege at Lilybaeum, Claudius Pulcher decided to attack the Carthaginian fleet at Drepanum (drep'uh-num) twenty miles to the north. As was usual in those days, the priests on board waited for favorable omens from the chickens. The chickens, however, would not feed — which was a very bad omen. Claudius Pulcher was one Roman who had no use for such superstitious rubbish. He seized the chickens, tossed them into the sea, and said, "Well, if they won't eat, let them drink."

However, if the admiral wasn't superstitious, the sailors were. The heart went out of them at this sacrilege.

What was still more serious was that Claudius Pulcher did not keep his movements secret and lost the advantage of surprise. The Carthaginians were ready for him and defeated him, destroying his fleet. The Roman leader was promptly recalled, tried for high treason (to the chickens, I suppose), and was heavily fined. He committed suicide shortly after.

Now finally, the Carthaginians found the man they had needed all along. He was Hamilcar Barca (huh-mil'kahr bahr'-kuh), who was made leader of the Sicilian armies in 248 B.C. while still quite young. Had someone like him been in command all along, the Carthaginians might have won. As it was, he found himself trying to support a cause that was essentially lost.

Nevertheless, he performed wonders. For two years, he raided the Italian coast, and then, pouncing on Panormus, he seized it by surprise and continued slashing raids in Sicily. The Romans could neither catch nor stop him. And still Lilybaeum held out firmly against the Romans.

In those years, however, it was the salvation of the Romans that they simply never gave up. In 242 B.C. they built still another fleet, and with it defeated the Carthaginian fleet off the western coast of Sicily. That ended all possibility of reinforcements and supplies for the daring Hamilcar.

Reluctantly, Hamilcar decided there was no choice but to make peace on any terms. The Carthaginian realm had become so disrupted by the long war that it faced absolute disaster. In 241 B.C. Hamilcar arranged peace, and after twenty-three years, the First Punic War was over.

It was a clear Carthaginian defeat. They were driven out of Sicily, which became completely Roman except for the easternmost section ruled by Hiero II of Syracuse, Rome's loyal ally. Furthermore, Carthage had to pay a heavy indemnity. Even so, Carthage got off lightly. If Rome had not herself been exhausted by her efforts, the war would undoubtedly have been forced further.

## THE FIRST PROVINCES

Sicily was the first territory outside the bounds of Italy proper to fall into Roman hands. Its greater distance and its separation by sea made it seem different to the Roman government. The lands of Italy were coming to be looked upon as an "Italian confederacy," an increasingly unified homeland; but Sicily was a strange land, containing Greeks, Carthaginians, and native tribes that had been subjugated for centuries and had little in common with the Italians.

Rome therefore looked upon Sicily as conquered property that could form no integral part of the complex governmental system imposed on Italy. A magistrate was sent out to Sicily and his range of duties ("provincia") included the complete government of the land. His edicts were its law, and it was his job to collect tribute from the territory and make its ownership and administration profitable to Rome.

The term "provincia" came to be applied to the territory itself and Sicily was the first *province* of Rome, organized as such in 241 B.C. Naturally, when a magistrate was sent out to rule a province, he usually took care that not all the money he collected was sent to Rome. Some stuck to his own hands. It was taken for granted that a Roman government official who was assigned to a province would enrich himself. It followed that the provinces tended to be badly ruled (not always of course, for even in the worst of times, there are honest officials now and then).

Sicily did not long remain Rome's only province.

The long war that had brought Carthage to the brink of ruin had left her commerce paralyzed and her business affairs in chaos. She had fought her wars with mercenary troops for the most part, and she now lacked the money to pay them. The mercenaries promptly revolted and attempted to take their fees (and more) by looting the city.

Hamilcar, the only Carthaginian who could bear up with indomitable spirit under the disasters that were overwhelming Carthage, took the leadership of what loyal troops he could find and after a desperate three-year fight destroyed the mercenaries in 237 B.C.

Rome watched, without directly interfering, perfectly willing to let Carthage tear herself apart. In 239 B.C., mercenaries on the island of Sardinia, which was still Carthaginian, offered to give up the land to Rome, since otherwise they were in considerable danger of being destroyed by Hamilcar. Rome promptly agreed and sent an occupying force in 238 B.C.

Carthage, quite rightly, protested that this was a breach of the treaty of peace. Rome contemptuously declared war and offered to withdraw the declaration only if Carthage gave up not only Sardinia but also Corsica (the island just north of Sardinia). Carthage, helpless, had to agree, and Sardinia and Corsica became Roman territory.

It took several years for the Romans to crush all resistance among the native tribes of the islands, but by 231 B.C., Sardinia and Corsica were sufficiently pacified to be organized as a second province.

Such was the state of affairs, now, that Rome could look abroad and find that all was in a state of profound peace. For the first time since the reign of Numa Pompilius, five hundred years before, the temple of Janus was closed.

But Rome's successes had brought with them new responsibilities. Now that she was a strong naval power, she had to be concerned with the matter of piracy on the high seas.

Such piracy, at the time of the First Punic War, centered about the eastern coast of the Adriatic Sea, a region known as Illyria. Under the mighty Macedonian kings, Philip II and Alexander the Great, the Illyrians were under firm control. During the disorders that followed the death of Alexander, the Illyrian tribes regained independence and freedom of action — which meant piracy.

The coast (now that of Yugoslavia) is rough, with many islands, and the natives could make a profitable business out of freebooting. Their light ships could run out to strike quickly and could then lose themselves among the islands if they were pursued by war vessels. The Greeks, south of Illyria, suffered immensely from these piratical raids.

Macedon, east of Illyria, might have seemed the natural power to turn to. By 272 B.C., after the death of the war-making and troublesome Pyrrhus, it had come under the firm rule of

Antigonus II (an-tig'oh-nus), grandson of one of the generals of Alexander the Great. His descendants, the "Antigonids," continued that rule for a century.

Unfortunately, Macedon was continuously involved in the eternal political quarrels of Greece and in wars with Ptolemaic Egypt and apparently had neither time nor inclination to waste on Illyrian piracy. The Greeks therefore turned to the new power of Rome as a natural alternative. She had just proven her strength at sea and her vigor in general — and she was just across the Adriatic from Illyria.

Rome, willing as always, sent ambassadors to warn the Illyrian queen of the consequences of Roman displeasure. The queen promptly had them killed. Rome next sent two hundred ships, which settled the affair in 229 B.C. A second campaign in 219 B.C., against the Queen's successor, put a final end to Illyrian piracy.

As a consequence of the Illyrian War, Rome took over the Greek island of Corcyra (kawr-sigh'ruh), which had been an Illyrian possession for half a century. It lay just off the southern tip of the Illyrian coast and fifty miles southeast of the Italian heel.

The Greeks were overjoyed at the end of the Illyrian pirates and treated the Romans with every mark of respect. They allowed the Romans to participate in some of their religious festivals, a sign that they considered the Romans to be civilized people on a par with the Greeks themselves.

Even while the Illyrians were being crushed, a greater danger had to be handled in the north. The Gauls, reinforced with contingents from their kinsmen beyond the Alps, suddenly launched a new invasion southward in 225 B.C. They raided into Etruria, reaching Clusium, the old city of Lars Porsenna. There they stopped, apparently lost courage, and retreated.

The Romans followed under the leadership of their consul, Gaius Flaminius. Flaminius was unusual among the Roman leaders in that he had what today would be called democratic notions. When he was tribune in 232 B.C., he managed to force through a measure distributing land to plebeians despite the opposition of the aristocrats of the senate; and, in particular, against the determined opposition of his own father. Flaminius encouraged the establishment of games for the plebeians, and he tried to discourage the entry of senators into commerce (where they could use their political power to enrich themselves). It is not surprising then that he was popular with the Roman people and unpopular with the senators.

Flaminius was not, unfortunately, a very good general. He usually attacked without first thinking through the situation. He was defeated in his first battle with the Gauls and beat them only after he had been strongly reinforced. After a second victory in 222 B.C., however, the Romans were left in complete control of Cisalpine Gaul.

Flaminius strove to make that victory secure by extending a road leading northward from Rome. He began that task in 220 B.C. when he was censor, and by the time he was through the Flaminian Way was driven across the Appenines to the shores of the Adriatic at the borders of Cisalpine Gaul. In case of any Gallic uprising, Roman troops could be on the scene in double-quick time.

With Roman colonies established in Cisalpine Gaul, Roman power was extended to the Alps. Rome was now in control of about 120,000 square miles of territory. She ruled over all the region that makes up the modern Republic of Italy (which includes Sicily and Sardinia) and over Corsica and Corcyra in addition.

# 5

# HANNIBAL

## FROM SPAIN TO ITALY

Anyone watching Rome's century and a half of steady victories over the Samnites, the Gauls, the Greeks and the Carthaginians; her expansion from a small patch in the center of Italy to lord of all the peninsula and of all the seas about it, would never have guessed that she was at the brink of disaster. Yet she was — for she had an implacable enemy, a single man, the Carthaginian general, Hamilcar Barca.

Hamilcar was completely aware that he had outfought the Romans wherever he had met them in Sicily and Italy. If his nation was defeated, it was only because he had been born too late and had grown old enough to fight only after the war was lost. He himself had not been defeated and he resented the Roman victory hotly.

Nor could he tell himself philosophically that war was war,

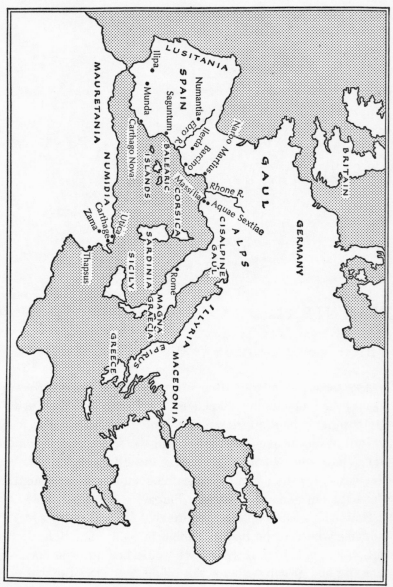

The West

that Rome would be satisfied with her conquests, and that Carthage should forget the past and begin anew in peace. He might have brought himself to think so if the loss of Sicily were all that was involved. The Romans had taken that island after a fair fight of many years and had paid enough in blood for it. Rome's extortion of Sardinia and Corsica, however, at a time when Carthage was helpless, must have struck Hamilcar as the act of a ruthless bully.

After that, Hamilcar decided, there was no use expecting friendly treatment from Rome. Carthage might expect to be slowly crushed by an implacable and pitiless foe. Carthage had to be prepared to fight the Roman enemy again, and to make that possible, Carthage must be strengthened. What she had lost in Sicily, she must make up elsewhere.

In 236 B.C. Hamilcar, therefore, persuaded the Carthaginian government to place him in charge of an expedition which he led to Spain. Carthage already had outposts on the Spanish coast, and it was Hamilcar's aim to broaden those outposts and extend Carthaginian influence into the interior.

There, over the next few years, while Rome concerned herself with Illyria, Hamilcar built a new empire for Carthage. Traditionally, he founded the city of Barcino (bahr′sih-noh), named for himself and now known as Barcelona. He died in 228 B.C., fighting against native Spanish tribes.

His son-in-law Hasdrubal (has′droo-bal) succeeded to his power and extended the Carthaginian rule over Spain still further by peaceful means. He founded a town which was called Carthago Nova in Latin, meaning "New Carthage," and this has come down to us as Cartagena.

By the time the Romans had cleared the decks of the Illyrians and the Cisalpine Gauls, they found, to their unpleasant surprise, a Carthage that was stronger than ever before. They had not minded the initial Carthaginian thrust into Spain. Rome had felt at first that it would be good strategy to keep Carthaginian energies occupied in a direction so remote from Rome. She had not, however, counted on quite so much Carthaginian success. She therefore took steps to limit it.

Rome forced Hasdrubal to agree that the Carthaginian power was to be confined south of the Ebro River. In addition to that, the independence of the Greek town of Saguntum (suh-gun'tum), about eighty miles south of the Ebro, was to be guaranteed.

In 221 B.C. Hasdrubal was assassinated, but if the Romans thought that this would end the danger from Spain, they were quite wrong. Hamilcar Barca had left a son, a young man called Hannibal, who was now twenty-six years of age and quite old enough to take over.

Hannibal, born in 247 B.C., was only a boy when his father took him to Spain after making him swear an oath to be at eternal enmity with Rome. The lad was trained by his capable father in the art of war, and, as it turned out, Hamilcar Barca shared with Philip II of Macedon (see page 45) the fate of being a remarkable father destined to be vastly overshadowed by a still more remarkable son.

With Hasdrubal dead, Hannibal assumed command of the Carthaginian forces in Spain and almost at once began to lay his deep plans into motion.

For two years he tested his army. He used it skillfully in order to conquer areas of Spain that had not yet become Carthaginian. The army itself, feeling the touch of a master, grew ever more confident.

Saguntum, in turn, grew ever more nervous. She had every reason to suspect that Hannibal intended war and she knew that she was the first object in his way. She sent for help to Rome. Rome at once sent ambassadors to the camp of young Hannibal to warn him that he would bring disaster on himself if he didn't settle down, but the Carthaginian general paid no attention.

In 219 B.C., Hannibal deliberately infuriated Rome by laying siege to Saguntum and taking it after eight months. The

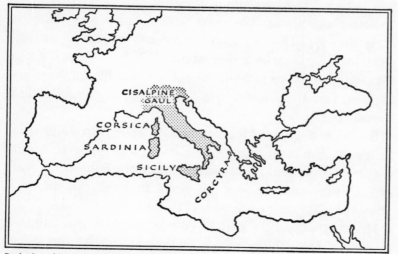

Beginning of Second Punic War — 219 B.C.

Romans sent another embassy to protest but Hannibal treated it with calculated scorn; warning them coldly that they had better leave his camp or he would not be responsible for their safety.

In this way, Hannibal accomplished two things. He forced Rome to declare war, for the insult was too great for her to accept. Second, he forced Carthage to back him up despite the fact that the merchant princes who ruled Carthage feared war and hated the brilliant and too-independent family of Hamilcar Barca. Rome's angry demands were so extreme that Carthage had to accept war rather than surrender. Thus began the Second Punic War.

In 218 B.C., Hannibal, with an army of 92,000 men (including a number of elephants) crossed the Ebro River, the northern limit of Carthaginian rule in Spain, and advanced northward. He had to fight the native tribes as he marched, but he was in no hurry. He didn't want the Romans to guess his plans.

They didn't. Rome assumed she would fight the Carthaginians overseas, in Africa and in Spain, and therefore sent troops to both those places. The army sent to Spain was under the leadership of the Roman consul, Publius Cornelius Scipio (sip'-ee-oh). It had been his father who had wiped out the last Carthaginian resistance in Sardinia and Corsica fifteen years earlier, and now the son was sent to engage the son of Hamilcar Barca.

But when Scipio and his men had left Italy by sea and sailed for Spain, Hannibal made his dash. He was going to reverse matters. Greeks and Romans had carried the fight to the walls of Carthage; well, he was not going to await the enemy in Spain, he was going to carry war to the walls of Rome.

He went around the eastern edge of the Pyrenees and then made his way rapidly across southern Gaul. At the Rhone River, hostile Gallic tribes tried to block him, but he brought some ships up for a feint, crossed farther up the river while the tribes were concentrating on the ships, and fell upon them from the rear. He defeated them completely and then moved straight for the Alps.

Certainly the Romans expected no danger from the north, for the Alps were a protective rampart which few men would care to tackle. Hannibal did, however. He managed to get his army across the Alps, including even a few of his elephants, in one of the great military feats of history.

When Scipio landed in Spain, he must have felt a prize fool, for he found his enemy gone. He pursued in all haste, but by the time he reached the Rhone, Hannibal had already crossed it. Scipio did not try to cross the Alps after the amazing Carthaginian but traveled back to Italy by sea, hoping to confront him in Cisalpine Gaul at the other side of the Alps, if, indeed, Hannibal did not find himself utterly lost in the craggy, snow-swept passes of these rough mountains.

Hannibal made it all right. He had lost a large number of men in fighting his way through hostile tribes. He had lost most of his elephants in the dreadful crawl over the Alps in the autumn season of the year. He arrived in Italy with less than a third of the men with whom he had left Spain five months before. But it was the best third, hardened by adversity into a superb military force and fighting under a man they loved; one who was soon to be recognized as one of the greatest generals of all time.

## THE ROMAN DISASTERS

In 218 B.C., the bewildered and humiliated Scipio, finding an enemy army of 26,000 men boldly stationed in Cisalpine Gaul, marched north, livid with fury.

The armies met first at the Ticinus River (tih-sigh'nus), a stream that enters the Po River from the north. There the opposing cavalries had a brief skirmish and the Romans were defeated. Scipio himself was badly wounded and, according to the story, would have been killed had not his nineteen-year-old son (and namesake) rushed to his rescue. We shall hear more of Scipio's son later.

Scipio and his army managed to retreat across the Po and fell back eastward to the Trebia River (tree'bee-uh), a stream that enters the Po River from the south. There he waited for the army of his fellow consul, Tiberius Sempronius Longus, while facing Hannibal warily. The stream divided them; the Romans on the east, the Carthaginians on the west.

Hannibal wanted battle; he was terribly afraid the Romans might retreat and keep their army in being; whereas if they fought he was confident of destroying them. Therefore, when Sempronius' army arrived, Hannibal didn't move a finger to prevent them from uniting their forces. United, they might feel strong enough to fight.

Scipio had had enough of Hannibal for a while and favored

a retreat despite the strengthened army. Sempronius, however, who had not had to face Hannibal, was all for fighting and would not consider for a moment any craven suggestions about retreating.

It was Hannibal's intention to make the Romans cross the river if he could. He did this by sending a detachment of cavalry to the Roman side. The Romans attacked them and, after brief resistance, the Carthaginians fled. The Romans pursued hotly; and the Roman infantry, suddenly scenting victory, plunged into the river after them.

It was winter now and the water was icy. The Romans emerged on the other side, soaked and freezing, and as the fleeing cavalry scuttled to one side, the Romans found it was not merely the cavalry they were pursuing but the entire Carthaginian army which waited for them at the ready — and nice and dry besides.

The Roman legions fought bravely, hacking through Hannibal's lines, but the Carthaginian cavalry, reinforced, wheeled about and, with the help of the elephants, swept in on the wings and routed the Roman horsemen. Then, Hannibal's younger brother, Mago, whom Hannibal had concealed with two thousand men, charged up at the crucial moment and attacked the Romans from the rear.

By sheer fighting, part of the Roman army extricated itself, but only after the most severe losses. The Romans kept garrisons in two fortified cities on the Po River, Placentia and Cremona, but otherwise had to abandon all of Cisalpine Gaul, which they had conquered only four years before. The Gauls were delighted to see this turn of events and promptly joined forces with Hannibal. Whatever losses he had suffered making his way into Italy were more than made up for.

Scipio, who had been unable to stop Hannibal, was now sent back to Spain to see what he could do there in Hannibal's rear, while other generals prepared to face the terrible Carthaginian.

If the Romans had been angry before, they were beside

themselves now. Hannibal was marching southward and he simply had to be stopped. A new army under Flaminius, the conqueror of Cisalpine Gaul, was sent to stop and destroy him.

Flaminius did not have far to go to meet Hannibal. The Carthaginian had marched his way across northern Etruria in utter contempt of Roman power and then, in the spring of 217 B.C., marched eastward passing by Lake Trasimenus (tras"ih-mee'-nus). In the course of this march, Hannibal lost the sight of one eye, but with his remaining eye he could still see better, as it proved, than many Roman generals with two.

Flaminius was in furious pursuit but, unfortunately for Rome, he was still a rather poor general. He was so anxious to meet and destroy the Carthaginian, that he took no time for caution, no time to send scouts forward to reconnoiter. Perhaps Hannibal had learned enough about Flaminius to feel he could count on that.

At Lake Trasimenus, Hannibal noted a narrow road skirting the lake and lined on the other side by hills. He placed his entire army behind the hills and waited. The Roman army came snaking along the narrow road in the morning and a light mist helped keep them in ignorance of the waiting enemy. When the Romans were spread out completely into a long, narrow line along the road, the Carthaginians came down all along that line and simply slaughtered them. The Romans scarcely even had a chance to defend themselves and lost ten men to one. The army was wiped out and Flaminius with them.

To Roman horror, the second army sent against Hannibal, although greater than the first, had suffered an even greater defeat.

The Romans were furious no longer; they were terrified. Never since the Gallic sack of Rome almost two centuries earlier had they felt in such danger. Hannibal seemed a magician, against whom no enemy could stand.

The Romans appointed a dictator, Quintus Fabius Maximus, the grandson and namesake of the general who had defeated the Gauls nearly eighty years before (see page 96).

Fabius made no move to advance toward Hannibal. He viewed his task to be that of keeping his army intact and patiently waiting his chance.

Hannibal might then have marched straight for Rome but he knew better. He might defeat incautious Roman generals in the field, but his army was still small and far from home. He did not think he could carry out an actual siege against Rome herself; not without help. This help he expected to get from the Italian allies of Rome.

It was that hope which led him first east and then south. By skirting wide around Rome he marched through the territory of tribes, particularly those of Samnium, whom he wanted to rouse against Rome. To encourage them to do so, he released all Italian prisoners without ransom. Then (he hoped) with all of Italy behind him, and with the city of Rome friendless and alone, he could attack and crush it.

In this respect, however, Hannibal's strategy fell short. The Roman military machine might falter, but the Roman realm had been built on political understanding, even more than on armed might. The Italian cities appreciated the prosperity and efficient government which Roman dominion had brought. They might long for independence, but if they sided with Hannibal they knew they would get not independence but Carthaginian domination, and surely that would be much worse than Roman rule.

Moreover, Fabius, the Roman dictator, took just the action that least suited Hannibal. Instead of risking an open battle, he merely marched and countermarched along Hannibal's flanks, cutting off groups of Carthaginians, nibbling here and nipping there. But he always avoided an outright fight, no matter how Hannibal tempted him. Fabius gained the added name of Cunctator (kunk-tay'ter) or "delayer" because of this policy. (To this day, a "Fabian policy" is one of delay and patience, and the avoidance of an outright forceful struggle.)

Fabius, by his tactics, was slowly rubbing out Hannibal's army, but as the months passed, the Romans grew less and less satisfied with this way of doing things. It seemed ignoble and beneath Roman dignity. After the Romans had had time to recover from the shock of two successive defeats, it seemed to them that Hannibal wasn't so frightening after all. All that was needed, many of them thought, was firmness and resolute attack. Fabius Cunctator, it seemed, was just a coward, unworthy of the name of Roman.

One of the most fire-eating of the critics of the Fabian policy, Gaius Terentius Varro, was elected consul in 216 B.C. (537 A.U.C.); and, along with him, a more cautious man, Lucius Aemilius Paulus.

Fabius was called home and the two consuls were committed to the policy of finding Hannibal and fighting him. They found him at Cannae, near the Adriatic Sea and nearly 200 miles southeast of Rome. (Hannibal had travelled almost the length of Italy in the year and a half since he crossed the Alps.)

The consuls divided the command, leading the army on alternate days. When it was Varro's turn to command, he could hardly wait to fight. He had a larger army than either Sempronius or Flaminius had had and he outnumbered Hannibal nearly two to one — 86,000 against 50,000. Surely it was impossible for Romans to lose a battle in which they had such an advantage.

Hannibal, despite his disadvantage in numbers, seemed willing to humor Varro, and give him the battle he wanted. The Carthaginian infantry was pushed forward in a semicircle and, when the Romans attacked, it was slowly driven back. The Carthaginian line straightened as it fell back, and then began to bend backward.

Through it all, though, the ends of the Carthaginian lines did not move. The forward-moving Romans did not seem to care about the ends of the line. The Carthaginian center seemed to be caving in; surely, one more push and the Carthaginian line would break and the battle would be over.

But in their eagerness to push forward, they were pushing into the interior of what had become a U-shape. They were being forced so closely together they could scarcely find room to wield their swords so that their very superiority in numbers was working to their disadvantage. At Hannibal's signal, the ends of the Carthaginian line closed in, and the Carthaginian cavalry, which had pushed the Roman cavalry out of the way and circled wide, fell upon the Roman rear.

The Roman army was in a sack and Hannibal merely tightened the neck and let the Roman soldiers die. They were killed by the tens of thousands and the consul, Paulus, died with them. Hardly any escaped. (Varro was one of those who did, but he killed himself rather than go back and face Rome.) It was the greatest defeat Rome was to suffer in the age of its greatness.

The Romans had thus sent out a third army, stronger than the first two, and had suffered a third defeat, worse than the first two. Indeed, Cannae has always been considered the classic "battle of annihilation," and there perhaps has never been a better example of a weak army so completely wiping out a stronger one through the sheer genius of its commanding general.

To be sure, there have been other generals who have defeated huge armies with small forces. Alexander the Great defeated huge Persian armies and Robert Clive defeated huge Indian armies, each with relatively tiny forces. However, the huge armies were poorly led and poorly organized, while the small armies of Alexander and Clive were better armed and better led. Hannibal, however, was fighting the best army in the world, for the Romans were simply unbeatable for centuries before Hannibal and became unbeatable again for centuries after him. There are many, then, who consider Hannibal to have been the greatest general who ever lived.

# THE TURN OF THE TIDE

The Battle of Cannae placed Rome at the very brink of disaster. The watching world, seeing the Romans suffer three gigantic defeats in three years, felt certain that they were witnessing the fall of the Roman upstart.

Some of the Italian allies, feeling that Rome was through, decided they might as well join Hannibal and get in on the winning side before it was too late. Capua was the most important of the cities that opened its gates to the Carthaginian. Abroad, allies of Rome deserted — Syracuse being the most notable of these.

In Sicily, Hiero II of Syracuse had died at just about the time of Cannae. His grandson, Hieronymus (high"er-on'ih-mus), succeeded to the throne and decided to switch sides. If the Romans were forced to make peace, they would certainly have to give Sicily to Carthage and the Carthaginians would show no mercy to a Syracuse that had held out for Rome. He did the only safe thing he felt there was to do and joined Carthage now to secure good treatment later.

As a further shock to Rome, Macedon formed an alliance with Hannibal. Wherever Rome looked, she seemed to see walls of hostility closing in on her.

Facing a hostile world, Rome set an example of resolution such as the world has rarely seen before or since. She would hear of no peace; would listen to no counsels of despair; she even forbade any public signs of grief for the thousands lost at Cannae. Grimly, despite her three defeats and her hundred thousand dead, she began to build a new army and to plan strong action, even in this hour of disaster, against every enemy.

Never, in any of her victories, before or later, was Rome as admirable as she was now in the day of her disaster.

She recognized that Hannibal, though unbeatable in the field, must eventually wither away if she could only keep reinforcements from reaching him. For that reason, she made no further attempt to fight the Carthaginian in Italy, but she redoubled every effort to fight him outside Italy.

In Spain, the Roman armies fought under two Scipios, the general who had lost at the Ticinus River (see page 93) and his brother. The fighting was not very successful but it was useful, for Hannibal's brother, Hasdrubal, who commanded in Spain, was kept too busy to send Carthaginian reinforcements to Italy.

In 212 B.C., both Scipios died in battle, but the son and namesake of the general, the young man who had saved his father's life at the Ticinus, took over. He proved a dashing general indeed, and for several additional years he held Hasdrubal in check.

Meanwhile the Roman fleet in the Adriatic saw to it that no reinforcements for Hannibal arrived from Macedon. (Indeed, it was one of the great shortcomings of Hannibal's strategy that he didn't understand the importance of destroying the Roman control of the Mediterranean. It was odd for a Carthaginian to be so splendid on land and so unfeeling for the sea.) Rome even sent an army into Macedon to make sure that the Macedonians would be kept busy at home.

Then there was Syracuse. Immediately after Cannae, the Romans elected Marcus Claudius Marcellus as consul. He had been one of those most active in defeating the Cisalpine Gauls, a few years before Hannibal had entered Italy. He had then made himself extremely popular with the Romans by managing to drive off Hannibal's forces when they attempted to capture the city of Nola (near Naples) shortly after Cannae. It was not much of a check for Hannibal, but any victory over the Carthaginian, however slight, was cause for rejoicing among the Romans.

Marcellus now moved into Sicily, defeated an invading Carthaginian army, and laid siege to Syracuse.

Things did not go too well. Many of the Syracusan soldiers had once served in Roman legions and, if captured, they knew they would be whipped, then executed as traitors, so they fought desperately. Then, too, a scientist named Archimedes (ahr''kih-mee'deez) was a citizen of the city. He was over seventy at the time, but he happened to be the greatest scientist and engineer the ancient world ever produced.

Archimedes got to work building machines of various sorts: catapults to hurl missiles, stones, or burning liquids at the Roman ships. He was supposed to have devised cranes that would lift ships and overturn them, even lenses to set them afire by concentrated sunlight. Undoubtedly, the story of one man against an army, of Greek brains against Roman brawn, was exaggerated in later generations, especially by Greek historians. Nevertheless, Marcellus had to stand off from Syracuse and keep the city under distant siege for two years. While it proceeded, the Carthaginians took a number of Sicilian cities.

Finally, partly through treachery, partly through the carelessness which left a section of the wall unguarded during a night festival, Roman troops were able to enter the city in 212 B.C.

The usual sack began, with the victorious troops looting, burning, and killing. Marcellus had given strict orders that Archimedes was to be taken alive, for he was gallant enough to respect a worthy foe. Archimedes, however, oblivious to the sack about him, was drawing figures in the sand and attempting to work out a geometric problem (or so the story goes). A

Roman soldier ordered him to come along, and the Greek scientist said, imperiously, "Don't disturb my circles!" Whereupon, the soldier killed him.

Marcellus, distressed at this, gave Archimedes an honorable burial and saw to it that his family was kept from harm. He then went on to clear Sicily of the Carthaginians.

But what of Italy itself and of Hannibal?

The Romans had finally learned their lesson. They wanted no more battles in Italy with the Carthaginian. The policy of Fabius was adopted for thirteen years and Hannibal was hounded everywhere he went; snapped at, snarled at, lunged at; but whenever Hannibal turned to fight, the Romans retreated quickly.

It was not dashing and noble, but it worked, and little by little, Hannibal was worn out. Many say that Hannibal lost his chance when, after Cannae, he didn't immediately march on Rome and assault her. However, Hannibal was there on the spot, and certainly he was one of the most capable, daring, and fearless generals who ever lived. If he felt it was not yet time to assault Rome, he was probably right.

Rome, after all, was still strong, and not enough of Italy had yet broken away from her. Hannibal's original troops might have worked miracles, but most of the old campaigners were dead and Hannibal had to depend on mercenaries and on Roman deserters for future battles.* After two years of tremendous deeds, he may well have felt they deserved a rest, so he wintered after Cannae in Capua.

There is a story that the ease and luxury of Capua unmanned Hannibal's hardened veterans and spoiled them. This, however, is probably romantic nonsense. His army was good enough to remain undefeated for thirteen years, and if they won no

---

* It is an amazing tribute to the force of Hannibal's personality that, during the thirteen years after Cannae, his army, composed as it was of rag-tag troops that had no feeling of patriotism for a Carthage that meant nothing to them, and felt only a personal loyalty to a great commander, never once revolted.

great victories it was only because the Romans prudently refused to give them a chance to do so.

In 212 B.C., Hannibal marched southward to Tarentum and,
with the help of the Tarentines themselves, took the city and
penned the Roman garrison in the city's citadel. The Romans
seized the opportunity to lay siege to Capua, against which
their anger was particularly hot because of her quick surrender
to Hannibal after Cannae. Hannibal had to choose between
completing the job at Tarentum or marching back to relieve
Capua.

He dashed back toward Capua and the Romans faded away
at his approach. When he returned to Tarentum, the Romans
returned to Capua. It was very frustrating for Hannibal, and in
211 B.C. he decided to gamble on a supreme demonstration; he
would go through the motions of making a lunge at Rome herself. He did so and reached the very edge of the city. Tradition
says he threw a spear into it. However, the Romans didn't
flinch but made ready for a siege and did not even recall their
troops from Capua.

Furthermore, word reached Hannibal that the land upon
which his army was encamped had been put up for sale and
had been bought by a Roman at its full price. Confidence in
the fact that the land would remain Roman for all Hannibal
could do thus seemed to be supreme.

Hannibal was forced to retreat and that was a great moral
victory for Rome. Rome's firmness impressed all who had been
waiting for the city to collapse under Hannibal's hammer
blows. A succession of Roman victories in different theaters of
the war emphasized this.

In 211 B.C., shortly after Hannibal's fruitless lunge at Rome,
the Romans retook Capua and revenged themselves fearfully
on the Capuan leaders and population. In 210 B.C. they took
Agrigentum in Sicily and wiped out Carthaginian power there.
In 209 B.C., young Scipio took New Carthage in Spain, while
old Fabius retook Tarentum.

Only one thing now stood between Rome and complete victory and that was Hannibal himself. He was still in Italy, still undefeated, still dangerous. For all their victories, the Romans dared not attack him even now.

Yet if Hannibal was to do anything but die slowly, he had to have reinforcements. He could not get them from Carthage; he never did. The Carthaginian leaders were strongly suspicious of Hannibal, fearing (as governments often do, and sometimes with justice) that a general who was too successful might be as dangerous as a victorious enemy. Carthage therefore held back and tried to win the war by fighting elsewhere than in Italy and leaving Hannibal with nothing but his genius.

Hannibal had to look to Spain where his brother Hasdrubal was in charge. In 208 B.C. Hasdrubal, in response to Hannibal's increasing desperation, decided to repeat his brother's feat of ten years before. He dodged the Romans, marched across Spain and Gaul, clambered over the Alps and descended upon Italy with a new army. He was none too soon, for Hannibal, despite heroic endeavors, was losing ground steadily. About the only event in 208 B.C. that was favorable to the Carthaginian was the death of Marcellus in a petty skirmish.

It was now up to Hannibal, in the south of Italy, to join forces with his brother in the north. And it was up to the Romans to stop him from doing so.

One Roman army remained in the north to dog the footsteps of Hasdrubal, while another hung about Hannibal. The Roman armies dared not combine and attack Hannibal under any circumstances; nor did they quite dare to combine and attack Hasdrubal, lest Hannibal, unwatched, join his brother before the battle could be completed.

Then came the great turning point of the war. Hasdrubal sent messages to Hannibal setting a marching plan and a meeting place. Through a series of accidents, the messengers were taken and the messages fell into the hands of the Romans. The general watching Hannibal knew exactly where Hasdrubal intended to march, and Hannibal did not! Under the circumstances, the Roman general, Gaius Claudius Nero (an able man who had served under Marcellus) felt justified in disobeying orders. Abandoning the watch on Hannibal, he hastened northward.

The combined Roman army met Hasdrubal's forces on the banks of the Metaurus River, about 120 miles northeast of Rome, near the Adriatic. Hasdrubal tried to retreat but couldn't find a ford across the river, and wasted time looking for one. When he did find one, it was too late. The Romans were upon him and it was fight or be slaughtered.

The Carthaginians fought heroically, but Hannibal was not there, and the Romans won a complete victory. Hasdrubal died with his army, and the news of this reached Hannibal in a horrible manner. The Romans found the body of the dead Hasdrubal, cut off his head, carried it southward to Hannibal's army, and threw it into the camp.

Hannibal, gazing with sorrow at the dead features of his loyal brother, knew that the war was lost. He was to get no reinforcements and the Romans would keep on going and going and going, until even he himself would have to give up.

But he had no intention of doing so without a defeat in the open field. He retired to Bruttium (brut'ee-um), the Italian toe, and stood at bay for four more years. Still the Romans dared not attack him directly.

## VICTORY IN AFRICA

New men were arising in Rome, however. The chief of these was young Publius Cornelius Scipio, who had succeeded his father and namesake as leader of the Roman forces in Spain in 210 B.C.

Scipio, who had been at the disaster of Cannae and had been one of the few who survived (luckily for Rome), followed an enlightened policy of conciliation in Spain, managing to win over the native tribes to the Roman cause. He was unable to stop Hasdrubal from taking his ill-fated army to Italy, but it made what was left of the Carthaginian forces in Spain that much easier to fight.

In 206 B.C., the Carthaginians sent reinforcements into Spain and a great army gathered to crush Scipio. The opposing armies met at Ilipa (il'ih-puh) in southwestern Spain, about sixty miles north of where Seville stands today. Here it was the Romans who were outnumbered and the Romans who had the masterly general. For several days the armies faced each other without fighting, watching each other narrowly, waiting, it would seem, for some favorable moment when one or the other could spring savagely. The entire procedure seemed to become automatic, like a repetitious dance, each army being led out from camp to field in late morning.

Then one day, instead of marching out in late morning, with the legions in the center and the Spanish allies at the wings, Scipio attacked at dawn with the allies in the center and the legions at the wings.

The surprised Carthaginians were caught without breakfast. Their best troops faced the Spaniards who simply held them fast with a minimum of fighting. The Romans at the wings swept round the weak contingents they faced, and surrounded and destroyed the Carthaginian army.

Two great results followed the battle of Ilipa. First, Carthage had to evacuate Spain, losing the empire Hamilcar Barca had begun to build twenty years earlier. Second, the Romans discovered they had a general at last, one who was good enough to fight Hannibal with at least a reasonable chance of winning.

It was time now for the Carthaginian allies to begin breaking away. One of these was Massinissa (mas"ih-nis'uh), king of Numidia (nyoo-mid'ee-uh), a realm to the west of Carthage, occupying the territory of modern Algeria. Scipio came to a secret agreement with Massinissa, who from this point on was a loyal Roman ally.

Scipio returned to Italy in 205 B.C. and found himself the darling of the city. He was still only thirty-two, too young to qualify for the consulship, but he was elected consul anyway.

Hannibal was still in Bruttium, still dangerous, always dangerous. However, Scipio felt there was no need to fight Hannibal. Why not do as Agathocles and Regulus had done in their times? Why not carry the fight to Africa once more and attack Carthage herself?

This was opposed by the older generals, particularly by Fabius, partly because they felt it to be dangerous (after all, neither Agathocles nor Regulus had succeeded in actually defeating Carthage) and partly because they were jealous of the young man.

But Scipio was far too popular to be denied. When the senate refused to assign him an army, volunteers flocked to him by the thousands, and in 204 B.C. he sailed for Africa. There Massinissa joined him openly, and the Numidian cavalry that had been a mainstay of Hannibal's army in Italy was now turned into the terror of Carthage.

Scipio's victories quickly brought Carthage to the edge of despair. In anguish, the Carthaginians sent for Hannibal and then decided they could not wait for him to arrive. They agreed to a truce with Scipio, and accepted peace terms. Before the peace terms could be formally ratified, however, the faithful Hannibal had arrived with his army and Carthage broke the truce.

Now it was Scipio versus Hannibal, and the final battle of the greatest war of ancient times was fought at Zama (zay'-muh), a town about 100 miles southwest of Carthage, on October 19, 202 B.C. (551 A.U.C.).

Hannibal had retained all his old ability, but Scipio was almost as good a general and he had the better army. Most of Hannibal's men were Italian and Carthaginian mercenaries who could not be relied on to the end.

Hannibal had eighty elephants, more than he had had in any previous battle, but they were worse than useless to him. He began the battle with an elephant charge, but the Romans sounded the trumpets which promptly frightened some of the elephants back into Hannibal's cavalry, throwing them into confusion. Massinissa's horsemen charged at once and completed the removal of the Carthaginian cavalry. The remaining elephants passed through lanes between the Roman maniples; lanes that had been purposely left for them, and lanes the elephants deliberately took rather than face the spears of the legionnaries. (Elephants are quite bright.)

It was then the turn of the Romans to advance, and Scipio guided that advance with precision, throwing in successive lines of troops at just the proper intervals to be most effective. The Carthaginian front-liners fled, and only the last line, composed of Hannibal's tried and true veterans of the Italian campaign, remained. These fought as always, and the battle was truly Homeric, but Scipio deliberately held back, delaying in order to give Massinissa's horsemen a chance to return and attack from the rear (as Carthaginian horsemen had once served the Romans at Trebia and Cannae). This worked and Hannibal's fine army was cut to ribbons. In his entire career, Hannibal had lost only one pitched battle, but it was the battle of Zama he lost — and that outbalanced all his victories.

There was nothing left. Carthage had to surrender unconditionally. The Second Punic War was over and it was Rome, despite Hannibal and despite Cannae, that had gained the complete victory.

By the treaty of peace, signed in 201 B.C., Carthaginian power was broken forever. She was not wiped out completely, as some vengeful Romans would have liked, because Scipio held out

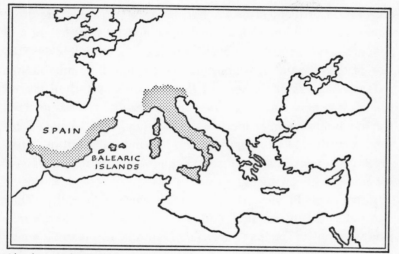

After the Second Punic War — 201 B.C.

against a too cruel peace, but it was bad enough.

Carthage's territory was limited to her African dominion (the northern part of what is now Tunisia) and, in particular, she had to give up Spain. She also had to give up her fleet and her elephants. She had to agree to pay a large indemnity over a period of fifty years, and to make no war, even in Africa, without Rome's consent.

Furthermore, Massinissa, as a reward for his help, was set up as monarch over an enlarged Numidia that was made independent of Carthage and allied to Rome. It was quite plain, moreover, that Massinissa had a free hand to annoy Carthage and take advantage of her in any way he chose, for Carthage could not defend herself without Roman permission, and Rome always sided with Massinissa. For fifty years after Zama, the long-lived Massinissa was to make life hell for Carthage. What had been the queen city of Africa was made to suffer in full for Rome's humiliation by the great Hannibal.

As for Hannibal, he forced the peace down the throat of a

reluctant Carthage after he had escaped with his life from
Zama. Hannibal knew that Carthage could no longer fight and
that any foolish resistance would result in the complete destruction of the city and death or enslavement for all its inhabitants.

Hannibal was made head of the government and all his old
ability was now turned to the ways of peace. He reorganized
Carthaginian finance, increased efficiency, and managed affairs so well that the city soon felt the pulse of restored prosperity. It was even able to pay off the indemnity forced upon it
by Rome with surprising speed.

Romans could view this only with extreme hostility. They
had not forgiven Hannibal and never would. In 196 B.C., a mission was sent to Carthage accusing Hannibal of planning a new
war and demanding that he be given up. Hannibal managed to
escape to the Hellenistic kingdoms in the east, however, and
remained in exile for the rest of his life. He never forgot his
hatred of Rome, but was nevermore able to strike against her.

Scipio returned to Rome as her greatest hero, her deliverer
from Hannibal. He was given the added name Africanus, and
it is as Scipio Africanus that he is best known today. However,
the senate could not forgive Scipio his youth and brilliance,
while Scipio's pride and his high opinion of his own ability offended many others. He was never able to play a great role in
Roman government thereafter.

Rome herself gained considerable territory. The province of
Sicily now included the whole island, for the dominions of
Syracuse were made part of it.

Then, too, Rome had fallen heir to Carthaginian dominions
in Spain. In 197 B.C. these were organized as two provinces,
Hispania Citerior ("Inner Spain") to the east, and Hispania
Ulterior ("Outer Spain") to the west. These two provinces,
however, included only the southern portion of the Spanish
peninsula. The northern portion remained under the control of
native tribes and was not to be completely subdued by the
Romans for nearly two more centuries.

The existence of Spain as Rome's first distant provinces forced certain important changes in Roman politics. Governors had to be sent out for periods of longer than a year, so that provincial leaders came to feel more and more independent of the home government. Then, too, it was impractical to try to send armies into and out of the provinces quickly enough to keep the farms at home ploughed and harvested. Instead, a standing army had to be established there; professional soldiers who spent all their time soldiering and no time farming. Thus, armies came to be loyal to their commanders rather than to distant Rome. For over a hundred years, however, the power and influence of Roman tradition kept the military in line. After that, there was to be gathering disaster.

Italy itself saw many changes, too. The regions that had helped Hannibal lost privileges. Cisalpine Gaul was settled thickly with Latin colonists and the Gallic population was slowly absorbed into the Roman way of life. Latin colonists filled the far south, too, and the Greek cities were so weakened that never again were they of any political importance. Etruria continued to decline and was more and more absorbed into Romanism, too.

Rome was ready, now, for the final push to universal power. All that remained in her way were the Hellenistic monarchies.

# 6

# THE CONQUEST OF THE EAST

## SETTLEMENT WITH PHILIP

In 200 B.C. Rome could take a clear look eastward in order to consider the state of the Hellenistic kingdoms. The nearest and most immediately dangerous of these was Macedon. There, a strong king, Philip V, had come to the throne in 221 B.C. and was strengthening the Macedonian grip over Greece.

Greece at this time was only a shadow of what it had once been. The chief Greek power lay in two associations of cities. One, in northern Greece, was the Aetolian League; the other, in southern Greece, was the Achaean League. They feuded with each other and with Macedon. Had they combined firmly, they might have held off Macedon, which had its own continuing troubles with surrounding barbarians and with other Hellenistic kingdoms, but the Greeks never managed to unite against a common enemy.

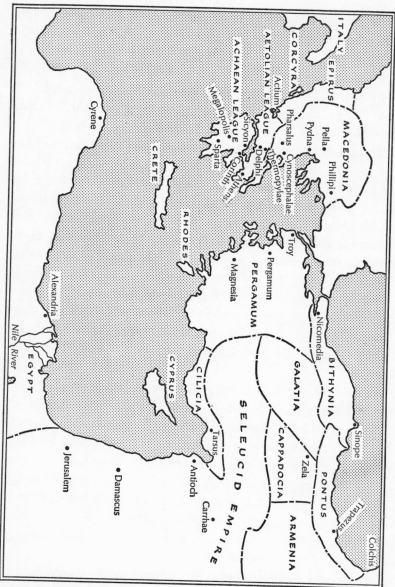

The Hellenistic East

Indeed, the Achaean League carried on constant warfare with Sparta, which was regaining some of her ancient vigor and which disputed the mastery of southern Greece with the League. So deadly was this rivalry, in fact, that the Achaean League actually called in the common enemy, Macedon, for help against Sparta. Macedon crushed Sparta in battle the year before Philip came to the throne, and now the Achaean League was little more than a Macedonian puppet.

Philip went to war against the still anti-Macedonian Aetolian League and quickly won victories over it. This war was broken off in 217 B.C., however, with a hastily patched-up peace, because Philip wanted his hands free for action against Rome, which had just lost the first couple of battles against Hannibal. After Cannae, Philip joined Hannibal in alliance but could send no reinforcements as long as the Roman fleet controlled the seas.

Rome was not satisfied with passive defense only. She formed an alliance with the Aetolians and Spartans, both of whom were anxious to repay Macedon for past humiliations, and sent a small force across the Adriatic. This was the First Macedonian War.

It was not much of a war, but it served to keep Philip off-balance while the tide of the war against Carthage turned. By 206 B.C., the Greek allies had had enough and were able to come to terms with Philip, who was anxious to get them off his back. Rome decided on a compromise peace in 205 B.C.

But that was by no means the end of the story for Rome. Philip had helped Hannibal; in fact, he sent a small detachment to fight with Hannibal at Zama after the end of the First Macedonian War. For this, he had to be punished severely; Rome was determined on that.

Rome had another reason for enmity with Macedon, too. Since Rome had beaten Pyrrhus and absorbed the Greek cities of Magna Graecia, she had been exposed to the beauties and allure of Greek culture. Noble Roman families were having their children educated by Greeks. The children, once they had learned Greek, read Greek literature and Greek history and fell in love with it.

Romans learned the Greek myths and adapted their own religion to those myths. They began to try to connect themselves to the Greek world by way of Aeneas and the Trojan War (see page 8). A Latin literature, in imitation of the Greek, came to be born.

The first Roman playwright of importance was Titus Maccius Plautus (ploh'tus) who was born about 254 B.C. His chief work was done in the decades before and after the Battle of Zama. He wrote lusty, slapstick comedies, about 130 of them, of which only twenty survive. He used plots he found, readymade, in Greek comedies.

A younger contemporary, Quintus Ennius, born in 239 B.C., had fought in Sardinia during the Second Punic War and had come to Rome in 204 B.C. He wrote tragedies and epic poems, also using Greek originals as inspiration. He was lionized by a number of Roman aristocrats, including Scipio Africanus.

With all this growing popularity of Greek culture, it was natural that many of the Roman aristocrats found added cause to hate Philip because he oppressed the Greeks. For some, war against Philip seemed almost a holy crusade on behalf of the Greek cause.

There remained the question, though, as to whether any Roman attempt to settle accounts with Philip might not bring the entire Hellenistic world down upon Rome. As Roman eyes surveyed the situation, this seemed doubtful.

Ptolemaic Egypt had been powerful under the first three Ptolemies, but the third had died in 221 B.C. Ptolemy IV had been a weak monarch, and when he died in 203 B.C., just before the battle of Zama, an eight-year-old boy, Ptolemy V, had come to the throne. There was no question of Egypt interfering against Rome. She would have all she could do to protect her own existence. Besides, Egypt had been an ally of Rome since

shortly after the defeat of Pyrrhus, when the wise Ptolemy II
had decided that Rome was a friend worth having, and Egypt
had been loyal to that alliance since.

Asia Minor was occupied by a number of small Hellenistic
kingdoms. The westernmost of these — just across the Aegean
from Greece — was Pergamum (pur′guh-mum). Pergamum's
great enemies were the larger Hellenistic kingdoms that neigh-
bored it, including Macedon. The king of Pergamum, Attalus I,
therefore allied himself with Rome, which he viewed as a natural protector.

The one Greek area that still maintained its independence
and prosperity, now that Syracuse was gone, was Rhodes, an
island in the southwestern Aegean Sea. It allied itself with
Rome for the same reasons Pergamum did. Athens, too, formed
an alliance with Rome.

That left the Seleucid Empire, which just then was reaching
the peak of its strength, and was the only Hellenistic kingdom
friendly to Macedon. Antiochus III (an-tigh′oh-kus) had come
to the Seleucid throne in 223 B.C. and had achieved a number
of successes. For one thing, his predecessors had lost the vast
regions of central Asia that had once been part of the Persian
Empire and that Alexander the Great had conquered. Now
Antiochus, after some difficult wars, had reconquered the area.
By 204 B.C. the Seleucid Empire stretched from the Mediterranean to India and Afghanistan.

It was a realm of impressive size. Antiochus came to be called
"Antiochus the Great" by his courtiers and, what's more, he
believed his own propaganda and considered himself another
Alexander. However, the eastern regions were held only very
precariously and Antiochus' real strength lay in Syria and Babylonia.

Once young Ptolemy V came to the Egyptian throne, it
seemed to Antiochus that the perfect chance had come to settle
a century-long war that had been proceeding, on and off, between the Seleucids and the Ptolemies. In 203 B.C., Antiochus

III formed an alliance with Philip V against Egypt, and began war with that country.

Pergamum and Rhodes, fearful that Antiochus might win and become altogether too powerful for the remaining Hellenistic kingdoms, appealed to Rome. Rome was aware of the danger, and aware also of her long-standing alliance with Egypt. The Romans also noted that after Hannibal had fled from Carthage, he had made his way to Seleucid dominions, and Antiochus was now harboring this great enemy of Rome. For all these reasons, Rome marked the matter down for future settling.

For now, however, the affair with Philip V took priority. At least Antiochus was not likely to interfere with the Romans in Macedon while he was busy in Egypt.

In 200 B.C., then, the Romans, after an appeal from Rhodes, sent an embassy to Philip V, ordering him to desist from activities considered harmful to Rhodes and to Pergamum. When Philip refused, the Second Macedonian War began.

Affairs proved disappointing to Rome, to begin with. She had expected all Greece to rise and join in the fight against Philip but this did not happen. What's more, Philip proved to have considerable ability as a general. For two years, therefore, matters continued at a frustrating stalemate.

The Romans then placed Titus Quinctius Flamininus (flam″ih-nigh′nus) in charge. He had served under Marcellus, the conqueror of Syracuse, and he was one of those Romans who admired Greek culture.

Flamininus took over with firmness and in 197 B.C. forced a battle at Cynoscephalae (sin″uh-sef′uh-lee) in Thessaly, a region in northeastern Greece. It was the first time the Macedonian phalanx had met the Roman legion since Pyrrhus's time nearly a century before. The armies were equal in number, but the Romans had on their side some excellent Greek cavalry and also a force of elephants.

Philip's army consisted of two phalanxes which did very well

for a time. However, the ground was moderately uneven so that
the phalanxes were thrown into some confusion. Furthermore,
the flexibility of the legion proved crucial. The Roman left
wing was being beaten by the phalanx facing it, when a Roman officer on the right wing (which was doing better) managed to detach a portion of his troops and attack the successful
phalanx from the rear. The phalanx found it difficult to maneuver rapidly enough to meet the new threat and was crushed.

The legion had proved its superiority, and Philip V was
forced to make peace, especially since other Macedonian ar-
ies were defeated by the Greeks in Greece and by the Pergamenes in Asia Minor.

As in the case of Carthage, Macedon was confined now to its
home territories. It had to give up its fleet, disband most of its
army and pay a large tribute. Philip was allowed to remain as
king, but he had learned his lesson. He was to make no other
move against Rome for the rest of his life.

Flamininus then went on to take care of what must have
been, for himself, the best part of the victory. In 196 B.C., the
year after Cynoscephalae, he attended a celebration of the
Isthmian Games (a religious and athletic festival held at the
great Greek city of Corinth every two years). There, with great
fanfare, he declared all the Greek cities free and independent
after a century and a half of Macedonian domination.

The Greeks applauded wildly, but for too many of them
freedom only meant the ability to indulge in their feuds more
freely. Sparta was under a ruler named Nabis (nay′bis) who
had reformed the city drastically and under whom it was gaining strength rapidly. The Achaean League called upon Rome
to take up Macedon's old role and defeat Sparta.

Reluctantly, Flamininus led his Romans against Sparta.
Sparta resisted with surprising vigor and Flamininus apparently did not have the heart to destroy the city. He forced a
compromise peace on all the Greeks and in 194 B.C. returned
to Rome with his army, leaving Nabis in power. The Greeks

warred again after he left, however. In 192 B.C. Nabis was assassinated and Sparta lost her last battle. She was never to
fight again.

## SETTLEMENT
## WITH ANTIOCHUS

And what of Antiochus? While Rome marched against Macedon, Antiochus invaded Egypt. Antiochus won an important
victory in 200 B.C. and seized Asiatic territories that Egypt had
held for nearly a century. His armies advanced in Asia Minor,
too.

In 197 B.C. Attalus of Pergamum died. His son, Eumenes II
(yoo'mih-neez) confirmed the alliance with Rome and begged
Flamininus, who was just closing in on Philip, to order Antiochus out of Asia Minor. Flamininus sent messengers to deliver
that order, but Antiochus felt no need to obey since he was winning everywhere. He finally signed peace with Egypt in 192
B.C. and held all the ground he had conquered.

Yet when Antiochus stopped to draw breath he found his
ally, Macedon, crushed and the Romans dominating Greece.
It seemed quite obvious to him that Rome would not remain at
peace with him while he held territories conquered from Roman allies, and the question was whether he ought not to strike
first.

Two considerations persuaded him. First, the Aetolian
League had already tired of the new situation since Philip's defeat. Since Rome had fought against Sparta, the Achaean
League was pro-Roman; and since the Achaean League was
pro-Roman, the Aetolian League had to be anti-Roman. The
Aetolian League therefore appealed to Antiochus to free them
of the Roman yoke.

Secondly, Hannibal arrived at Antiochus' court from the pro-

vincial city of Tyre in 195 B.C. His one great obsession was the
defeat of Rome, and he urged Antiochus to the battle, offering
to lead another army into Italy if the Asian king would give
him one, and promising to defeat the Romans if only Antiochus
would invade Greece in order to provide a distraction.

Antiochus' vanity urged him to pose as the deliverer of the
Greeks and the avenger of the Macedonians, but he did not
follow Hannibal's advice. He did not give the Carthaginian an
army but decided to put his main effort into Greece, relying
on Aetolian promises that the Greeks would rise to join him.

In 192 B.C., Antiochus took the plunge, swept up what was
left of Asia Minor, crossed the Aegean Sea, and led an army
into Greece, beginning the Syrian War.

Of course, the Greeks did not rise to join him. Furthermore,
despite the desperate warnings of Hannibal, Antiochus gave
himself up to feasting and celebration.

In 191 B.C. came the moment of truth. A Roman army met
the forces of Antiochus at Thermopylae (ther-mop'ih-lee) on
the Aegean coast just forty miles south of Cynoscephalae. The
Romans won an easy victory, and Antiochus, terrified, hastened
back to Asia.

The Romans were not satisfied, however. Antiochus could
not be allowed to retain the territory of Rome's faithful ally,
Pergamum. A Roman fleet, aided by ships of Pergamum and
Rhodes, defeated Antiochus' navy, and the legions piled ashore
in Asia for the first time in their history. At their head was Lucius Cornelius Scipio, brother of Scipio Africanus. (The Roman
senate had been reluctant to place Lucius in charge, but Africanus offered to go as second in command and that made everything all right.)

Battle was joined in 190 B.C. at Magnesia, about forty miles inland from the Aegean. Scipio Africanus was sick in bed during
the battle, but the Romans won anyway without very much
trouble, so that Lucius Scipio received the added name of
"Asiaticus."

Antiochus was through. In the peace treaty that followed, Antiochus had to agree to get out of Asia Minor. Pergamum and Rhodes were strengthened at Seleucid expense, and the Greek cities on the Aegean coast of Asia were liberated. Antiochus was also saddled with a large indemnity of what would today be worth about thirty million dollars.

One other point. Antiochus had to agree to give up Hannibal to the Romans. He felt it would be dishonorable to do this, however, and arranged, therefore, to allow Hannibal to escape. The great Carthaginian fled to Bithynia (bih-thin'ee-uh), a Hellenistic kingdom northwest of Pergamum. There he remained as a valued adviser to the Bithynian king, Prusias II (proo'shee-as). When Bithynia had a small war with Pergamum, Hannibal led the Bithynian fleet to victory in a naval battle. That attracted the attention of the Romans, however. Pergamum was their ally and Hannibal their deadly enemy.

Flamininus himself was sent to Bithynia in 183 B.C. to demand Hannibal's surrender. The Bithynian king was forced to agree, but when Hannibal saw the soldiers arriving to surround his house, he quickly deprived Rome of her final victory by taking the poison he always carried on his person. Thus died Hannibal, thirty-three years after his victory at Cannae and nineteen years after his defeat at Zama.

Scipio's life after the Battle of Magnesia also entered the shadows. When he returned from Asia, he found that his political enemies in Rome were beginning an investigation of his handling of the indemnities paid over by Antiochus and were accusing him and his brother of keeping some of the money for their own use.

Lucius Scipio was ready to produce the account books, but Africanus, either because he was too proud to submit to investigation or because he was guilty, seized the books and tore them up. His enemies insisted this meant the brothers were guilty. Lucius was heavily fined and Scipio was prosecuted in 185 B.C. for having taken bribes from Antiochus. He might have been condemned, but he reminded the court that the day was the anniversary of the Battle of Zama. At once, an acquittal was forced by the cheering crowd. In 183 B.C. Scipio died, the same year in which Hannibal did.

## SHADOW OVER GREECE

At the time of the deaths of Hannibal and Scipio, Rome could no longer be challenged, either east or west. Everywhere along the Mediterranean coast, the land was either Roman, allied with her, or terrified of her. Nevertheless, she had so far made no actual annexations in the east. She had labored only to weaken any strong power and to make sure that all weak powers depended only on her.

Yet she was not entirely at ease. Macedon remained cause for apprehension. Philip V had supported Rome in her war against Antiochus and was careful to do nothing to offend her in the years after Cynoscephalae. However, he worked with might and main to strengthen Macedon internally and to make it strong in the north. Also, he skillfully fed discontent among the Greeks who were by now as annoyed at Roman domination as they had ever been at Macedonian domination, for actually the "freedom" they had been granted consisted only of a change of masters.

Philip was planning for the future, slowly and carefully, and had one son executed out of suspicion that he was too genuinely pro-Roman. In 179 B.C., Philip died with his plans not yet matured. He was succeeded by a son, Perseus (pur'syoos), who continued strengthening Macedon and trying to build up an all-Greek union. Eumenes II of Pergamum took fright finally and began sending missions to Rome, begging the senate to take action before it was too late. Rome recognized the danger at last and in 172 B.C. began the Third Macedonian War.

Perseus was promptly abandoned by the Greeks and Bithynians on whom he thought he could count, but he faced up to the situation just the same and led into the field the largest Macedonian army since the days of Alexander the Great a century and a half before.

The Romans did not do very well at first. The Macedonians fought with their old-time vigor and for several years held off the best the Romans could send against them.

Finally, the senate placed a new general in charge. This was Lucius Aemilius Paulus, son of the consul who had died at Cannae. Paulus had served ably in Spain against the native tribes and now, as a man of about sixty, he took over the Macedonian war with energy.

In 168 B.C., he forced Perseus to battle at Pydna (pid'nuh) on the Aegean shore of Macedon. Once again, and for the last time, the phalanx faced the legion. As long as the battle remained on level ground, the phalanx was unbeatable; it moved forward with its long spears, like a dreadful porcupine and swallowed up the legion. However, as the ground became uneven, cracks began to appear in the phalanx. Paulus ordered his men into the cracks as fast as they appeared, so that the phalanx was broken up and annihilated. The phalanx never fought another battle.

This time Rome decided to have done with Macedon altogether. Perseus was taken prisoner to Rome, and died in captivity there, while Paulus received a triumph and the added name of "Macedonicus." The Macedonian monarchy was abolished 155 years after the death of Alexander the Great. In place of the monarchy, four small republics were established.

Rome still did not annex any territory in the east, but she was strongly annoyed at the tendency of the Greek people to sympathize with Perseus, and lashed out in punishment. Roman armies ravaged Epirus, partly for its present actions, and partly in memory of Pyrrhus, a century and a quarter earlier.

Rhodes was another victim. She had supported Rome loyally in the wars against Philip V and Antiochus III, but had seemed hesitant in the case of Perseus. As a result, Rome established a trade depot on the island of Delos, about 160 miles northwest of Rhodes, and diverted her own trade there. Rhodes, which depended on trade for its prosperity, began to decline, and its great days were over, although it continued as a more or less free city for two more centuries.

Another victim was the Achaean League. It had been thoroughly pro-Roman since the defeat of Philip V, and it had offered help in the war against Perseus, although an important segment of its leadership had wished to remain neutral. Rome refused the help, feeling, perhaps, that the Greeks were not to be trusted. After the war, it was decided to punish the League for lukewarmness. A thousand of its leading men were carried off as hostages to Rome.

Among the men so carried off was Polybius (poh-lib'ee-us), who had led the cavalry force sent by the Achaean League to aid the Romans against Perseus. Since Polybius was known to be one of those who had favored neutrality, the Romans had not been impressed. Fortunately for himself, Polybius was a cultured man who gained the friendship of the conquering Roman general, Paulus Macedonicus, and served as tutor to his sons.

Paulus' younger son (who had fought with his father at Pydna) was adopted by the son of Scipio Africanus, and became known as Publius Cornelius Scipio Aemilianus. He is much more commonly known as "Scipio the Younger," while his eminent grandfather by adoption is sometimes called "Scipio the Elder."

Scipio the Younger was one of the leading examples of the Greek-admiring ("phil-Hellene") Romans. He introduced into Rome the custom of shaving the face, a custom picked up from Greece, where Alexander the Great had started it. He also cultivated men of learning, both Greek and Roman.

In Scipio's circle, for instance, was Gaius Lucilius (lyoo-sil'-ee-us) who was the first Roman to write satires; that is, literary compositions intended to hold up vice and folly to ridicule.

Another member of the circle was Publius Terentius Afer, usually known among English-speaking people as Terence. By birth, he was a Carthaginian and had been brought to Rome as slave to a senator. The kindly senator, recognizing the young slave's ability, had had him educated and then freed him. The young freedman bore his old master's family name.

Terence became famous for writing plays which, like those of the older Plautus, were drawn from Greek themes and were sometimes little more than translations from the Greek. His plays were notable for their elegance of language and Terence helped convert Latin from a language of soldiers and farmers to one of cultivated men. His plays were less vigorous and comic than those of Plautus, however.

The tendency in Rome to begin to admire everything Greek was not universal. There were Romans of the old school who distrusted and despised what seemed to them to be dangerous foreign notions. The most important of these men was Marcus Porcius Cato. He was born in 234 B.C. and had fought under Fabius against Hannibal. He served at the Battle of Zama and there acquired a hatred of Scipio whom he accused of extravagance. He later fought well in Spain and in the war against Antiochus.

Cato was a model of old-fashioned Roman virtue; completely honest and completely bound to duty, but cold, cruel, sour, miserly, and narrow-minded. He was heartless to his slaves and lacked any tender feelings for his wife and children. In 184 B.C. he was elected censor and he cracked down ruthlessly on all signs of what he considered immorality. He fined Lucius Scipio Asiaticus, for instance, for kissing his own wife in the presence of their children (though there his dislike of the Scipios may have influenced him). He is often called "Cato the Censor" in memory of his censorious efficiency in that office.

Cato showed no favor in any direction and conducted everything he could get his hands into with rigid economy and efficiency. Later Romans (who didn't have to deal with him) greatly admired him, though they didn't follow his example.

Cato was one of the first important prose writers in Latin. He wrote a history of Rome and a treatise on agriculture. He is supposed to have been taught Greek by the poet Ennius (see page 115). Nevertheless, he remained strongly suspicious of everything Greek.

Since Polybius and the other Greek hostages in Rome had Scipio the Younger for their friend, they naturally had the Scipio-hating Cato for their particular enemy. For years, Polybius tried to use his influence with Scipio and others of the phil-Hellenic group to allow the Achaean hostages to return to their homes, but Cato was always there to block any such action. Nor did Scipio fight very hard against Cato, for he rather admired the stern old man and was himself a rock-ribbed conservative in many respects, for all that he had a liking for Greek ways.

A break finally came when Scipio the Younger had a chance to win military glory. Though Rome had established herself in Carthaginian Spain, the native tribes in the north had been fighting stubbornly for half a century against the Roman advance. Scipio the Younger went to Spain in 151 B.C. and, by skillful diplomacy and intelligent handling, pacified the tribes and brought back peace. When he returned to Rome, his reputation had increased to the point where Cato grudgingly agreed to let the Greeks go.

He did this, however, in the most churlish possible way. When the senate was debating whether or not to release the Greeks, Cato rose and said, "Have we really nothing to do but to sit here all day, debating whether a parcel of old Greeks are to have their coffins made here or in Greece?" So the Greeks were released after seventeen years of exile.

Polybius paid back his debt to the Scipios many times over,

for he wrote a history of Rome during her period of rise to world mastery. Portions of the history still survive, and the story of Rome during her most heroic period can be best heard by us through the words of this Greek so tardily released by Rome.

The cruel treatment of the Greek hostages, imprisoned for so little reason, and the general tightening of the Roman grip, inflamed the anti-Roman feelings of Greece. They waited their chance.

## THE END OF CARTHAGE

Ever since the battle of Zama, Carthage had struggled to live, concentrating on her own internal affairs and trying, above all things, not to rouse the Romans against her. However, the Romans needed very little excuse. They would never forgive Carthage for Hannibal's humiliating victories.

Massinissa, with Roman connivance, did everything he could to irritate and annoy the Carthaginians. He insulted them, raided their territory, and when Carthage complained to Rome, she gave no help.

The Roman who was most furiously anti-Carthaginian was, of course, Cato. In 157 B.C., he was part of a Roman mission that traveled to Africa to settle one more dispute between Massinissa and Carthage. Cato was horrified to find that Carthage was prosperous and her people well off. This seemed insupportable to him and he began a campaign to end it.

From that moment on, he ended every speech, on whatever subject, with the final phrase, "Praeterea censeo Carthaginem esse delendam" ("I am also of the opinion that Carthage ought to be destroyed").

Actually, it was more than mere prejudice on his part. Carthage, recovering her trade, was competing with Italy in supplying wine and oil, and the Italian landowners (of whom Cato was one) suffered. But, of course, private profit is often hidden under a careful coating of great patriotism.

In 149 B.C., Cato finally got his chance. The actions of Massinissa had finally goaded Carthage into actually taking up arms against her tireless foe. There was a battle, which Massinissa won, and the Carthaginians at once realized that Rome would now consider that Carthage had made war without permission and had therefore broken the treaty of peace.

Carthage sent men to explain, and ordered her generals executed. The Romans, however, had their excuse. Even though Carthage had lost the battle and was completely helpless and was, moreover, willing to do almost anything to have peace, Rome declared war.

The Roman army landed and the Carthaginians made ready to agree to whatever demands were made, even giving up all their weapons. What the Romans demanded, however, was that Carthage be abandoned; that the Carthaginians build a new city not less than ten miles from the sea.

This, the horrified Carthaginians would not do. If their city was to be destroyed, they would be destroyed with it. With the courage and strength of despair, the Carthaginians locked themselves in their city, manufactured arms out of almost nothing, fought and fought and fought without thought of surrender. For two years, the astonished Romans found that every attempt to beat down the maddened enemy failed.

During this period, Carthage's two enemies, Cato and Massinissa, both died, the former at eighty-five years of age, the latter at ninety. Neither of these cruel old men was able to live to see Carthage destroyed. Both spent their last days watching Roman arms humiliated again by a Carthaginian adversary.

By her great final stand, Carthage won the pity and admiration of all later generations, and the Roman war against her can only be thought of as a cowardly and ignoble act.

Finally, in 147 B.C. Scipio the Younger was sent to Carthage.

End of Third Punic War — 146 B.C.

He put new energy into the campaign and perhaps the magic of the name, even though it was only an adopted one, helped. In 146 B.C. (607 A.U.C.), Carthage was finally taken and burned to the ground. Those of its inhabitants who did not choose to die in the flames were slaughtered or enslaved, and Scipio the Younger gained the added name of "Africanus Minor" ("Africanus the Younger").

Carthage was levelled to the ground and her territory was annexed to the Roman dominion as the Province of Africa. The Romans of the time intended that no city was ever to stand on that site again. A hundred years later, however, a new Carthage was founded — but a Roman one. The old Carthaginians of Phoenician descent were gone forever.

Polybius had not stayed in Greece long, but had hastened to Africa to be with his friend Scipio, and to witness the great event that would serve to conclude his history. He reports that Scipio watched Carthage burn with thoughtful eyes and quoted to himself from Homer's poems. Polybius asked him what he was thinking, and Scipio replied that history had its ups and downs and he could not help thinking that perhaps someday Rome herself would be sacked as Carthage was being sacked now.

Scipio was, of course, right. Some five and a half centuries later, Rome was indeed sacked, and the invaders were to come from — Carthage!

While the Romans struggled with Carthage in the final battle, new disorders broke out in the east. Greece and Macedon were in virtual anarchy. The Romans did not rule the area themselves, but neither did they allow any strong native governments. This meant the whole realm was a prey to endless politics on land and piracy on the sea. The four republics into which Macedon had been formed squabbled among themselves constantly.

It seemed to many Greeks that the time for striking a blow for freedom had come. A Macedonian adventurer named Andriscus (an-dris′kus) claimed to be the son of Perseus and declared himself king of Macedon in 148 B.C. He gained allies in Greece, and made an alliance also with the poor, dying city of Carthage.

The Romans promptly sent an army under Quintus Caecilius Metellus, who easily defeated Andriscus in what is called the Fourth Macedonian War. That was the end of any lingering independence Macedon might have had. It was transformed into a Roman province in 146 B.C., and thus Rome finally began to annex eastern territory outright.

But matters had gone too far in Greece. The Achaean League found itself so eager to defy Rome that they could not pull back. Metellus's envoys were insulted and Metellus was forced to march southward. He was an admirer of Greek culture and he hoped to handle Greece as gently as possible, but in 146 B.C. he was replaced by Lucius Mummius, a man of little learning. Mummius had gained some military experience in Spain and cared nothing for the Greeks; he was intent only on earning a triumph.

The chief city of the Achaean League was Corinth. At the approach of Mummius, Corinth surrendered and offered no resistance, so that the Achaean War was over before it had really begun. But that was not what Mummius wanted. He treated Corinth as though she had been taken by storm, looting and killing. The inhabitants were sold as slaves and priceless works of art were carted away to Rome.

Mummius, who had no understanding of art, proceeded to make himself ridiculous for all time by the directions he gave the captains of the ships on which great paintings were loaded. "Don't let them be damaged," he said, "or you will have to replace them." The Achaean League was dissolved and the last miserable sparks of Greek freedom were extinguished.

In the far west, too, Roman arms were engaged. The native tribes of western Spain ("Lusitania," making up the territory of modern Portugal) rose against the cruelty of Roman governors, under the leadership of a Lusitanian shepherd, Viriathus (vir"ee-ay'thus). For ten years, from 149 to 139 B.C., Viriathus conducted a successful guerrilla war against the Romans. At one time he trapped a Roman army in a mountain pass and forced a temporary peace. In 139 B.C., however, Roman money purchased the treachery of some of Viriathus's friends, and the Lusitanian was assassinated.

Even so, the Lusitanians held out. Once more Scipio the Younger was called upon. In 133 B.C. he finally (after a long siege) captured the city of Numantia in northeastern Spain. It had been the center of resistance and northern Spain became Roman. Indeed, what independence existed among the natives of Spain was now to be found only in the extreme northwest.

In that same year, Rome gained her first foothold in Asia itself. The king of Pergamum, Rome's loyal and longtime ally, was Attalus III. He had come to the throne in 138 B.C., had no direct heirs and expected none. If he died without doing something about it, his land would simply be squabbled over by other kingdoms in Asia Minor and the Romans would interfere to the harm of all. He felt it wise to greet the inevitable with a smile. He made a will leaving his kingdom to Rome.

When he died in 133 B.C., Rome accepted the gift and reorganized the land as the Province of Asia. She had to overcome a rebellion on the part of some Pergamenes who didn't want to become Roman, but that caused her little difficulty and by 129 B.C. the land was quiet.

In 133 B.C., then, the Romans could look upon a Mediterranean world which was almost entirely theirs. A century earlier, they had controlled Italy only. Now almost all of Spain was theirs, as well as north Central Africa, Macedon, Greece and Pergamum, and the islands of the western and central Mediterranean. Elsewhere along the shores of the sea were kingdoms which were nominally independent, but were either Roman allies or, at the very least, cowed and submissive.

Ptolemaic Egypt continued under the rule of feeble kings who were careful to court the favor of Rome, and who were little more than Roman puppets.

The Seleucid Empire alone retained some strength for a while. Antiochus III died in 187 B.C., but under his sons the realm recovered from the damage done it by Rome. In 175 B.C. Antiochus IV came to the throne. He had been sent as hostage to Rome after the Battle of Magnesia and had been educated there. Nevertheless, once king, he imagined he could still fight the Egyptians in the old-fashioned way. He tried to do so and won some victories, but the Romans stepped in and made him back off.

Antiochus IV, sullen in defeat, looked for easier battles elsewhere. Judea was under his control, so he attempted to declare Judaism illegal and to force the Jews to accept Greek culture. The Jews revolted and under the family of the Maccabees established an independent kingdom.

After the death of Antiochus IV in 163 B.C., the Seleucid Empire began its final decline. Native tribes in the east, which had been subdued first by Alexander the Great and then by Antiochus III now established their independence once and for all, and by 129 B.C. had even taken Babylonia. After that the mighty Seleucid Empire was restricted to Syria alone and spent all its energies on civil wars between different members of the Seleucid family, each of whom wanted to succeed to the worthless throne. They, too, could offer no further resistance to Rome.

# 7

# INTERNAL TROUBLES

## WEALTH AND SLAVERY

In a very obvious way, Rome profited from her conquest of the Mediterranean world, particularly through her victories over the opulent East, where long centuries of civilization had accumulated wealth. The tribute drawn from Carthage, Macedon, and Syria, the spoils wrung from the provinces, the profits brought in from trade conducted on Roman terms, meant that a flood of wealth poured into the city.

In 167 B.C., in fact, after the battle of Pydna and the final defeat of Macedon, so much wealth came to be at the disposal of the Roman authorities that Roman citizens were freed of all direct taxation. They were supported by the people they had conquered.

But Rome had not made herself the greatest power in the world without also paying for it. A hundred years of fighting had completely changed Roman society.

Before the Punic wars, the small farmer was the backbone of Rome. He tilled his farm part of the year and fought in the army the rest of the time. Campaigns were brief and close to home.

A century of warfare, however, had killed off many of these stout hearts (there were fewer Roman citizens in 133 B.C. than in 250 B.C.) and had ruined others economically. Large sections of Italy had been devastated by Hannibal, or by the Romans themselves in punishment for joining the Carthaginian.

Furthermore, campaigns had grown longer and more distant from home. No longer could men be both soldiers and farmers. Soldiers had to be professionals, with arms their way of life.

As for the money that poured into Rome, while it benefited all Roman citizens to some extent, it benefited some a great deal more than it benefited others. Senators, administrators, officials, generals were enriched. Those to whose hands foreign wealth had managed to stick invested in land, buying up the farms of the small farmers whom war had ruined. Agriculture came to be conducted in large plantations rather than by small families, so that farming as well as fighting came to be professionalized.

Slaves flowed into Italy, too, from Africa, Greece, Asia and Spain, and this made the plight of the small farmer even worse. Slaves could be used to do the farm work in large gangs under overseers whose only task was to squeeze every ounce of work out of the unfortunates under their control. The owner could live in Rome, far from any sight of human suffering and therefore from any need to feel responsible for it. (Such "absentee ownership" always encourages bad treatment of tenants and slaves.) The small farmers who managed to hang on to their land despite the havoc of war could not compete with the slave gangs.

As a result, many men tended to flock from the Italian countryside into Rome, there to find what work they could. A large class of *proletariat* arose in the city. (This word comes from a Latin term meaning "to bring forth children," since to the ruling aristocracy, the poor seemed to have no use other than to produce youngsters to serve in the legions.)

A Roman citizen inside of Rome had certain power. However poor he might be, he could vote, which meant that those aristocrats who hoped for high office had to take him into account. Clever, unscrupulous politicians saw, more and more clearly, that these Roman votes were for sale. They courted popularity by bidding against each other, voting food allotments at lowered prices to Roman citizens — and eventually distributing grain without charge. They also established free games and shows of all sorts. In this way, the people were bribed to fight the political battles of one leader against another, often against their own interests.

This policy, which worked to the enrichment of politicians and the ruin of Rome, is usually termed "panem et circenses." This is most often translated as "bread and circuses," but "circus" did not mean to the Romans what it means to us. The word is Latin for "ring," and it refers to the area (usually oval, actually) within which were held contests and shows for the amusement of the people. Chariot races, gladiatorial combats, fights with animals, enlivened the proceedings and made them the Roman version of our own vaudeville (a rough and bloody version, to be sure). It would be better to translate "panem et circenses," then, as "food and shows."

While the rich got richer and the poor got poorer, while the free farmer perished and the slaves multiplied, Rome did not advance politically. Down to the Carthaginian wars there had been a steady move toward broadening the base of government and making it more democratic. This came to a halt after Hannibal's invasion.

For one thing, during the dreadful danger of the Second Punic War, everyone recognized the need for a strong government. It seemed no time for political experiments. The senate supplied that strong government; indeed, it never ruled better in Rome's history than in the times of stress of the Second Punic War and afterward.

But no ruling group finds it easy to give up power voluntarily. The landowning aristocracy that made up the senate had no intention of changing a situation that found them so neatly in the saddle even after the real crisis had passed.

As a result, a great and tragic paradox came to pass, for Italy was cheated of repose.

Once Hannibal had been driven out of the peninsula, Rome had no need to fear that any foreign army would, in the foreseeable future, ever put her in danger on her home grounds. Indeed, for over five centuries Italy was not to feel the tread of a foreign army.

Yet Italy was not to experience peace. The narrow policy of the senate and its determination not to allow power to pass from its hands led to a new and more dreadful kind of war. There followed the war of slave against free, of poor against rich, of Rome against her allies, of Rome against Rome.

The first indication that a new era of social revolution was coming appeared in the form of the most dreadful of all wars — an insurrection of slaves.

Slaves were imported in particularly large numbers into Sicily, which had become little more than a huge grain plantation intended to supply cheap wheat for the Roman proletariat. The Sicilian slaves were treated more brutally than animals would have been, for they were less valuable and more easily replaced.

However, these slaves had, not too long ago, been free men themselves. Many of them had been respectable citizens whose only crime had been that of living in a conquered country; or soldiers whose only crime had been that of being defeated. With life worse than death, they needed only a leader to rise in mad desperation.

In 135 B.C., a Syrian slave named Eunus pretended that he was of the Seleucid royal family and took to calling himself

Antiochus. Probably no one took him seriously, but the pretense was good enough for the purpose, and the slaves rebelled.

In such a rebellion, the slaves, maddened by suffering and knowing well that no mercy would be shown them, looted and killed with complete abandon. The slave masters (who generally write the history books) detail the slave atrocities very carefully. The truth is, though, that once the slaves are crushed, as they almost always are, they are punished by even worse atrocities.

This First Servile War (from the Latin "servus" meaning "slave") was no exception. The slaves turned Sicily into a bloody horror for several years. They were strongest at Enna, in the very center of the island, and at Tauromenium (taw''roh-mee'nee-um), the modern Taormina, on the northeastern coast.

It took the Romans three years to put down the rebellion and they had to suffer a number of humiliating defeats at first. It was not until 132 B.C. that Sicily was quieted and the slaves drowned in their own blood.

Rome had had a good scare, though. Faced with such horrors and with the growing evidence of the economic decay of Italy, at least some of her leaders began to think that it was time for drastic reform.

## THE GRACCHI

Among those who saw the need for reform were two brothers, Tiberius Sempronius Gracchus (grak'us) and Gaius Sempronius Gracchus. Together they are usually referred to as the Gracchi (grak'igh). Their mother was a daughter of Scipio

Africanus and her name was Cornelia. (It was customary for women of noble families to bear the feminine version of the family tribal name. Publius Cornelius Scipio was of the Cornelian family and so his daughter was Cornelia.)

Cornelia's husband, who had served as consul twice and had fought with distinction in Spain, died in 151 B.C. at which time Tiberius was twelve and Gaius two years old. Cornelia devoted herself to the bringing up of her children (refusing all chances at a second marriage — which was most unusual for the time) and saw to it that they had the best Greek education.

She was inordinately proud of them. When another Roman matron on a visit, having displayed her jewelry, asked to see Cornelia's jewels, Cornelia called her sons to her. With one on each side, she said, "These are my jewels."

The Gracchi had a sister, Sempronia, who eventually married Scipio the Younger.

Tiberius, the elder of the Gracchi, fought well in the Roman armies. He was at Carthage, where he served under Scipio the Younger and where he is supposed to have been the first Roman to make his way over the walls. He also served with Scipio in Spain.

Tiberius was far more than a soldier, however, for his Greek education seems to have given him a more-than-Roman vision of the world. He was appalled at the social evils that were overwhelming Rome, and the slave war in Sicily seemed to be the last straw. Rome had to be reformed and made over.

In 134 B.C., at the age of twenty-nine, he stood for the office of tribune and was elected. He took office at the end of the year and at once began to press hard for land reform. He wanted to cut down on the huge estates, divide them into farms of moderate size and distribute them among the poor. This was all the more reasonable since there existed a law (over two hundred years old) which limited the size of estates, anyway. Once the land was distributed, Tiberius proposed it be made inalienable;

that is, it could not be sold and collected by the buyers into large estates again.

Naturally, the large landowners were horrified at this and were bitter opponents of Tiberius. (If it had been modern times, they would have denounced him as a Communist.)

The landowners took action. There were, after all, two tribunes, and if one of them objected to any governmental action, that action could not be taken. The other tribune, Marcus Octavius, was a friend of Tiberius', but when he was offered enough money he found he wasn't as much a friend as all that. Consequently, when Tiberius was on the point of carrying his law, with the approval of the vast majority of the Roman voters, the other tribune ordered proceedings stopped.

Tiberius, alarmed and frustrated, did everything he could to win Octavius back, but failed. In desperation, he then arranged to have Octavius voted out of office. With him gone, the law was passed and a committee was voted into office to put it into effect.

The removal of Octavius had, however, been illegal (strictly speaking) and the senatorial enemies of Tiberius used that against him. He was a revolutionary, they said, who was upsetting the government. Furthermore, his laws had been passed only after he had taken illegal action and therefore those laws had no force.

Tiberius realized that he was losing friends as a result of this sort of argument. He therefore endeavored to win back popularity by means of a rather radical suggestion. Attalus III of Pergamum had just died and left his land to Rome. Tiberius at once proposed that the Pergamene treasury, instead of being made state money with the senate in charge, as was customary, be distributed among the common people who would then be helped in establishing themselves on their new farms.

This further enraged the senators, and it seemed quite plain that Tiberius was only safe from harm as long as he was tribune (whom it was strictly forbidden to harm). When his term of office was over, his life would not be worth a copper coin. Tiberius therefore set himself up for re-election. But this, too, was considered by many to be illegal, and he was accused of trying to make himself king — an accusation which always brought up horrid memories of Tarquin to the average Roman.

When the day of the vote came, disorders grew and became riots. Tiberius' foes were better organized and Tiberius and many of his followers were killed. The body of the elder Gracchus was denied honorable burial and thrown into the Tiber.

The leader of the gang that killed Tiberius Gracchus was a member of the Scipio family, a second cousin of Cornelia. Such was his unpopularity as a result of the murder that the senate sent him abroad to keep him out of harm's way. He remained in exile the rest of his life, never daring to return to Rome.

Scipio the Younger was in Spain, completing the conquest of Numantia at this time. When he heard of the death of his brother-in-law, he was quite unmoved. He was himself a conservative who disapproved of Tiberius' views and he stated publicly that Tiberius had deserved death.

In 132 B.C. Scipio returned to Rome, along with Gaius Gracchus who had served with him and whose absence from Rome probably kept him from being killed along with his brother.

The battle between the conservatives and the reformers continued, of course, after the death of Tiberius Gracchus. Scipio became the leader of the conservative group. He was in the process of making major speeches against the land-reform laws when, in 129 B.C., he died suddenly in his sleep. The conservatives insisted he had been murdered by the reformers, but there is no definite proof of this.

Meanwhile the reformers pressed for a law that would make it legal for a tribune to be re-elected, so that if another one of their party gained power he wouldn't receive Tiberius' treatment. While Scipio lived, this move was blocked, but afterward, it was passed.

Gradually, the younger Gracchus came to the fore. In 123

B.C. (against the pleadings of his mother, who had seen one of her beloved sons die by violence and feared the same fate for the other) he ran for tribune and was elected.

At once he revived his brother's land-reform law (still in existence but, thanks to the influence of Scipio, not enforced) and began to put it into action. He introduced price-control measures to keep the distribution of the food supply from serving to enrich shippers and large landowners while the people starved. (This eventually became the basis of free food distribution to the Roman proletariat.)

He also reformed the voting system in Rome to give more power to the proletariat; and he reformed the system of taxing the provinces and of judging the law in such a way as to weaken the power of the senate in these respects. Gaius also improved the roads and set many public works into action. This served to employ people as well as to make life better.

Then, too, he attempted to introduce a system of colonization by which some of the sites ruined by Rome — Capua, Tarentum, Carthage — would be revived with Roman colonists. This was intended to draw off the proletariat from Rome, making useful citizens of them. Unfortunately, the proletariat preferred "panem et circenses" at Rome, and the colonization plan was a failure, though it deserved to succeed.

Gaius Gracchus was extremely popular as a result of all this and was easily elected tribune for a second term. In his second year, Gaius had in mind an important reform which was to allow all Italian freemen to become Roman citizens. This would have been a great measure that would have made Rome more popular throughout her realm — in Italy certainly, and elsewhere, too, since it would have become apparent that all Roman subjects might eventually become Roman citizens. From the more immediately political standpoint, it would have produced a large supply of new voters bound by gratitude to the reform party.

However, Gaius here touched on the prejudice of even the

poorer classes among the Romans. Why let a horde of foreigners become Roman? Why spread the food allotment and freedom from taxes any farther?

The conservatives fed this selfish view and took full advantage of Gaius's declining popularity. They maneuvered him into a wild-goose chase in Africa in connection with his colonization scheme, and elections approached in his absence. He was not re-elected for a third term.

Thereafter, the senators tried to repeal the colonization law, as a preliminary to doing away with other reforms. Again, there were riots and disorders and again there was death for the reformers. In 121 B.C., Gaius Gracchus was killed, and over the next ten years most of the reforms of the Gracchi were done away with.

Poor Cornelia, with both her sons gone, retired to seclusion at a villa near Naples, where she might pass away the time, devoted to literature and lost to the world. When she died, the inscription on her tomb did not read that she was the daughter of the great Scipio who had defeated Hannibal, but simply, "Cornelia, mother of the Gracchi."

With the death of the Gracchi passed the best hope of reforming Rome and moving her in the direction of something like our modern democracy. The Senatorial conservatives clung desperately to power and, in doing so, prepared increasing disaster for themselves.

## MARIUS

Although Rome lost her chance to develop into a completely healthy society, she did not enter into any obvious decline at once. Indeed, she extended her power over wider and wider regions for two more centuries, but at a slower rate than before and, except in one or two cases, against trivial opposition.

The Celtic tribesmen of western Europe were among the foemen who could put up an excellent fight. The Spanish tribes had defended themselves for three-quarters of a century before succumbing, and between the Spanish provinces and Italy itself lay a stretch of some 300 miles inhabited by other Celtic tribes. That stretch, between the Pyrenees and the Alps and extending from the Mediterranean Sea to the Atlantic Ocean, was Gaul, an area of about 250,000 square miles.

Gallic tribes had occupied Rome in 390 B.C., and others had raided Macedon and Greece in 280 B.C., so the ancient world knew well how formidable they could be. Rome had little occasion to fear them now, however. The tribes that had settled in the Po Valley (Cisalpine Gaul) were absorbed and Romanized, and their land was virtually part of Italy, even though it was still considered a separate province. Nor did the Gauls beyond the Alps cause any direct trouble.

On the Mediterranean shore of Gaul, however, was the city of Massilia, which had been founded by Greek settlers about 600 B.C. when Rome was still an Etruscan village. Massilia had flourished as a far western outpost of the Greek world. Her great rival in trade was, of course, Carthage, and so Massilia established a firm alliance with Rome throughout the Punic Wars. Afterward, she represented Rome's outpost in Gallic territory.

In 125 B.C., Massilia complained to the Romans that the Gauls were infringing on her territory. The Romans responded at once. For one thing, they always did, and for a second it gave the Roman senate a chance to get the consul, Marcus Fulvius Flaccus (flak′us), out of the city. Flaccus was a strong supporter of the Gracchi and the reform movement, and so the sooner he left Rome and the longer he stayed away, the better the senate would like it.

Flaccus defeated the Gauls and returned in triumph, but his reward a few years later was death along with Gaius Gracchus.

The Romans moved into southern Gaul permanently and established themselves along the route which Hannibal had once taken in passing from Spain to Italy. Twenty miles north of Massilia, they founded a military outpost in 123 B.C. and named it Aquae Sextiae (the modern Aix) after Sextius Calvinis, who was then consul. In 118 B.C. they established the town of Narbo Martius (the modern Narbonne) on the Mediterranean shore, about 120 miles west of Massilia.

The Roman portion of Gaul was organized as a province in 121 B.C., and when Narbo Martius became its chief city, the province came to be called Gallia Narbonensis. Since it was a most pleasant land, suitable for visits by tourists and vacationers, it quickly became *the* province to the Romans. It is still known by that name, for the southeastern corner of the later nation of France, with Aix as its chief city, is known as Provence.

Rome might have gone on to conquer all Gaul at that time, but that had to be delayed for three-quarters of a century, for other matters occupied her. For one thing some very nasty complications in Africa had arisen, complications which showed how quickly and revoltingly decay was spreading in the unreformed Roman government.

After the death of Massinissa of Numidia at the start of the Third Punic War (see page 128), the most remarkable member of his family was his grandson, Jugurtha (joo-gur'thuh). His uncle, who had succeeded Massinissa to the throne, sent the young man to Spain, partly to obtain military training for him and partly to be rid of him. There Jugurtha served under Scipio the Younger. Scipio was greatly impressed with the young Numidian and sent him back to his country with much praise and recommendation that he be given high office. After his uncle's death, Jugurtha came to share the government with a pair of cousins.

Jugurtha, however, saw no point in sharing anything. In 117 B.C. he had one cousin killed and the other driven into exile, making himself king of Numidia. This was obviously illegal (and immoral, too, though Rome was less concerned about that), and since Numidia was a Roman protectorate, it was up to Rome to see that this sort of thing did not take place. However, Jugurtha found the proper method for dealing with the new kind of Romans. When senators came to Numidia to investigate the situation, he gave them presents and they went back and told the Roman government that Jugurtha was a fine man who had done nothing wrong.

The Romans kept making settlements, such as dividing Numidia and letting Jugurtha's cousin have the less desirable half. Jugurtha made war against his cousin, killed him too, and by 112 B.C. had the entire country.

Rome could not quite accept the disgrace of having her orders flouted in this way and the senate had to send an army to Numidia in 111 B.C., thus beginning the Jugurthine War. This did not disturb Jugurtha, who simply bribed the general and was at peace once more. At this, the honest party at Rome (what there was of it) arranged to have Jugurtha ordered to the city to give a personal accounting. Jugurtha promptly came to Rome, bribed a tribune, and had the proceedings stopped. While in Rome, he even arranged to have one of his Numidian enemies assassinated.

Then, when he embarked for his return to Numidia, he is reported to have said grimly, "The city's life is for sale, and it would die if it could only find a purchaser."

The war with Jugurtha was recommenced, iron spears against golden coins, and the gold won. The Roman army was forced out of Numidia.

Somehow an honest general had to be found, and Rome was beginning to find a shortage of them. (It is hard to find healthy men in a sick society.) Finally, the Romans came across Quintus Caecilius Metellus, nephew of the general who had won the Fourth Macedonian War (see page 130).

Metellus, who was rigidly and old-fashionedly honest, left

for Numidia in 109 B.C., and Jugurtha, who had at last met up with a general he could not bribe, began to take a beating. He had to abandon regular warfare and confine himself to guerrilla fighting and raiding. For two years he managed to frustrate Metellus (as Fabius had once frustrated Hannibal).

Fighting under Metellus at this time was Gaius Marius, a grim character of no great intellect, but a hard fighter and a good hater. He was the son of a poor farmer and he hated the aristocrats. In 119 B.C. he had served as tribune and had showed himself a violent partisan of the popular (*i.e.* "people's") party, as the reform group is usually called.

Like Jugurtha, Marius had fought with Scipio the Younger in Spain. In 115 B.C. he had been in command in Spain on his own and had subdued some distant tribes who had not yet accepted the sovereignty of Rome. Now he was serving in Numidia, where his hate had perfect exercise against Metellus, who came of an old patrician family and who was about as conservative as it was possible to be.

It occurred to Marius that he was doing well enough in Numidia to have a good chance of being elected to the consulship as a war hero. He returned to Rome and used as his campaign issue the claim that Metellus was dragging out the war needlessly for his own benefit. This was not true but it was good politics. Marius was elected in 107 B.C. and promptly selected himself to replace Metellus in command of the army. This was in flat disobedience to the senate's wishes, of course, and the senate refused to grant him an army.

Grimly, Marius ignored the senate, gathered volunteers as Scipio Africanus had done a century before, made violent speeches against the conservatives, and had his way. He deliberately chose men for his army from among the poorer classes, men who would feel more loyalty to their general than to a city and a senate from which they had gathered few benefits. With them, he went back to Numidia.

Marius had, as his chief military aide, Lucius Cornelius Sulla, another capable soldier but one who was far more intelligent and whose sympathies were with the conservatives. Between the two of them, they mopped up Numidia and captured Jugurtha in 105 B.C. Sulla arranged the capture by means of some smooth diplomacy and the use of Jugurtha's father-in-law, Bocchus (bok'us), king of Mauretania (the region which now comprises modern Morocco), who, in return for money, agreed to turn against Jugurtha.

Jugurtha surrendered himself to Sulla rather than to Marius, and the conservatives at once tried to encourage the belief that it was Sulla and not the wild-eyed Marius who had won the war. This gave rise to a certain enmity between the two military leaders that was to have important consequences later. In 104 B.C. Jugurtha was brought to Rome and died miserably in prison.

After his death, the eastern part of Numidia continued to be under native rulers, while the western part was added to the kingdom of Mauretania.

But now an echo of the barbarian past arose to frighten Rome. From out the northern reaches of Europe came new tribes of barbarians; rough, uncouth peoples who had never heard the Roman name.

The Romans called them Cimbri (sim'brigh), and their original home may have been in what is now called Denmark, though this is by no means certain. They had been migrating here and there in central Europe, and in 113 B.C. they crossed the Rhine River and entered Gaul, pouring southward in a wild, unruly hoard.

Twice the Cimbri defeated Roman armies sent to stop them, but both times the barbarians made no attempt to enter Italy itself. They were content merely to kill soldiers who got in their way and, for the rest, claimed merely to be looking for homes where they could settle down. In their search, they wandered into Spain.

Rome was in a panic. It was the days of the Gauls all over

again. Roman armies were being defeated by barbarians while in Numidia other Roman armies had behaved disgracefully in the squalid war with Jugurtha.

Once Marius had completed the defeat of Jugurtha, however, the Romans turned to him at once as the one man they could count on against the terrifying menace from the north. The senate, itself desperate and not knowing where to turn, did not interfere when the frightened populace demanded Marius. In 104 B.C., Marius was elected consul for the second time, while he was still in Africa, and then, in a completely unprecedented manner he continued to be elected consul as long as the danger lasted, in 103, 102, 101, and 100 B.C., five years in a row. This was quite illegal, but the Romans felt the city to be in danger and decided it was no time for legalistic quibbling.

(Counting his election in 107 B.C., Marius was consul six times by 100 B.C. When he was a young man, there is a story that it had been prophesied to him that he was to be consul seven times all told. However, the seventh consulate was a long time coming.)

Marius whipped an army into line with a display of old-time Roman virtue. Again, though, he made use of the lower classes and developed a military force personally loyal to him. This may have been a tendency that would have developed even without Marius. Generals were becoming more important and more independent in a variety of ways. For instance, they took to making use of a personal bodyguard. Since the general was usually at least a praetor, if not a consul, the bodyguard came to be called the *praetorian guard*. Safe behind their spears, generals eventually grew strong enough to defy the Roman law.

Fortunately, Marius had time to organize, for the Cimbri wasted time in Spain, suffering a few sobering defeats. In 103 B.C. they were reinforced by another tribe which may originally have lived on the Baltic coast east of Denmark. This second tribe, the Teutones (tyoo'toh-neez), may have spoken a language ancestral to modern German. If so, they were the first

Germanic people to appear on the horizon of the ancient world. (From the name of this tribe we derive the word "Teutonic" as a synonym for "Germanic.")

Together the Cimbri and Teutones were 300,000 strong, according to some estimates, and now they were definitely making their way toward Italy.

In 102 B.C., Marius led his army into Gaul, encountered the Teutones on the Rhone River, followed them southward coolly, letting them wear themselves out in piecemeal attacks while he remained strictly on the defensive. Then, at Aquae Sextiae, came the real battle. The wild attacks of the barbarians broke against the disciplined ranks of the Romans, and when the Teutones had tired, a detachment of hidden Romans fell upon their rear. Caught in a vise, the barbarians were slaughtered without mercy, almost to the last man.

Meanwhile, however, the Cimbri had crossed the Alps and were pouring down into Cisalpine Gaul. The Roman armies facing them retreated to the Po Valley, almost to the borders of Italy itself. Marius left Gaul and joined the army at the Po. Under his driving leadership, the Romans re-crossed the river and met the Cimbri at Vercellae (vur-sel'ee), halfway between the Po and the Alps. Here, in 101 B.C., the Cimbri were annihilated. Rome was delivered and Marius was at the peak of his fame.

(Nor had Rome's only danger lain in the north. Taking advantage of the terror and disorganization in Italy, the slaves of Sicily rose again in 103 B.C. in the Second Servile War. For two years, Sicily again experienced terror and counter-terror.)

## THE SOCIAL WAR

By 100 B.C., though, Rome could draw her breath again.

Jugurtha was dead; the Cimbri and Teutones had been slaughtered; the slaves were quiet; all seemed well. It was time to consider the matter of reform once more.

Marius was in his sixth consulate and at the peak of his popularity. He wanted to use that popularity to pay off his obligations to his soldiers. To reward them, he needed farms, and that meant breaking up the large estates and the founding of colonies in which veterans could be established. In short, he needed the platform put forward by Gaius Gracchus.

For this, he turned to the popular party* with whom, in any case, he was in sympathy. Marius, however, was no politician. Uneducated and illiterate, he could make no skillful speeches nor invent clever policy. He was a soldier, no more, and an easy puppet for other cleverer men.

Thus Marius fell into the hands of the tribune Lucius Appuleius Saturninus (sat"er-nigh'nus), who a few years earlier had been removed from a political post by the senate and who had become strongly anti-senatorial in consequence. Saturninus pushed through the laws that Marius wanted, cowing the senators by the free use of rioting and mob violence. He even forced the passage of a clause compelling senators to swear to comply with the various laws being passed, within five days of passage. Only Metellus, the general under whom Marius had served in Numidia, refused to swear. He went into voluntary exile instead.

Saturninus, like Gaius Gracchus, pushed for the extension of

* We might speak of the "reform party" or the "popular party" or the "demagogs" or even the "democrats," but none of these names are really accurate, particularly not the last. After the time of the Gracchi, what really existed in Rome were two sets of unscrupulous, conniving and corrupt politicians (with a few exceptions on both sides), both of which were after power and the wealth that came with power, and not caring how they got it. One set of politicians, the senatorial conservatives, was in power, the other set, the anti-senatorial popular party, was out of power, and that was almost the only difference between them. Both sets worked hard to ruin the Roman Republic and, in the end, they succeeded.

Roman citizenship. As in the case of Gaius Gracchus, Saturninus roused the hostility of the lower classes in this way. The senate seized upon this hostility, organized the city rabble for its own purposes and, as a consequence, drove the radical tribunes to open rebellion. Violence and rioting increased on both sides. The senate declared the city in a state of emergency and called on Marius, as consul, to protect the government by capturing and imprisoning the leaders of his own party.

Marius was unable to think his way out of the dilemma, and in the end, impelled by what seemed to him his duty as consul, he obeyed the senate. In a pitched battle in the Forum, Saturninus and his partisans were defeated and forced to surrender. Then after the surrender they were killed by mob violence.

Marius found his popularity completely gone. The death of Saturninus ruined his standing with the popular party without doing anything to reconcile him to the conservatives. For a while, Marius was forced to retire from politics.

But the problem of reform would not down. There had grown up in Rome during the period of conquest a class of men who had become rich by speculation or through commerce or by collecting taxes for the government. (Rome put up the right to collect taxes at auction, with the high bidder getting it. She then had her supply of money without the trouble of going through all the administrative detail of the actual taxing. The high bidder went about squeezing money out of the province he had bought. Anything he collected over his bid was his profit, and he made sure to squeeze the last coin out of the unhappy provincials. If necessary, he lent them money to pay their taxes — but at a high rate of interest. Then he could squeeze both taxes and interest out of them.)

The rich men were not the senators, for this method of enriching one's self was not open to the old patricians who were debarred by custom from engaging in commerce and tax-collecting. Their wealth was supposed to come from the land.

The newly-rich were called the *equites* (ek'wih-teez) from a word meaning "horseman," because in ancient times only the rich could afford a horse, while the poor had to fight on foot. We might call them the "business class."

The senate looked down upon the business class but were often in a kind of unofficial alliance with them. While the tax collectors were making their money, the provincial governor (of the senatorial class) could easily rake in a share of the loot if he looked the other way and didn't inquire too closely into the methods being used.

When Gaius Gracchus was fighting the senate, however, he tried to win over the business class to the cause of reform by arranging to have them assume the function of jurymen. Until then, this had been the right of those of the senatorial class only. However, as the senators grew more and more corrupt, it became impossible to punish any of them, no matter how disgraceful their behavior, because the senators serving as judge and jury would not convict one of their own. (It might next be the turn of any one of the jurymen after all.)

Unfortunately, the equites were no better, but proved as corrupt and as careful of their own as the senators. Consequently, in addition to the usual aims of the reformers — such as land-distribution, the establishment of colonies, the extension of the citizenship — the reform of the judiciary became a prime concern.

In 91 B.C. a new reforming tribune, Marcus Livius Drusus, tackled this problem. He was the son of a fellow-tribune of Gaius Gracchus, one who had opposed Gracchus' reforms. The son, however, was a different matter, an idealist and a true reformer. He suggested that to the 300 senators be added 300 equites and that together they take up the judicial function. The idea was that the senators would keep a sharp eye on the equites and the equites would be as sharp with respect to the senators. Between the two of them, the new ruling class would be forced to be honest. Probably this wouldn't have worked;

the two classes would have made an alliance that would have allowed joint corruption.

To fight against such joint corruption, Drusus also suggested the establishment of a special commission to try all judges accused of corruption.

Both the senate and the equites would have nothing to do with this, so Drusus turned to the people with the usual popular program of land reform and colonization. As usual, he also added the admission of the Italian allies to citizenship and, again as usual, that roused the prejudiced group.

The senators and equites were able to block all of Drusus's laws even after they had been passed, and Drusus himself was mysteriously assassinated. His murderer was never found.

For many Italians the murder of Drusus was the last straw. For two centuries they had been faithful allies of Rome in good times and bad. By and large they had even remained with Rome after the dark day of Cannae. Where was their reward?

Surely, it would not be too much to give them the citizenship. It would mean they could vote, but only if they would travel to Rome, since Roman custom insisted on the presence of the actual voters in Rome. The Italians could not be expected to flock into Rome from distances of hundreds of miles every time a vote came up, so it wasn't likely, as many Romans who fought the grant of citizenship maintained, that the Italians would control the government.

(Unfortunately, the Romans never made use of "representative government," in which far-off districts could elect individuals to take up residence in Rome and represent the interest of their constituents in the senate.)

Even aside from the vote, Roman citizenship was desirable. As Roman citizens, the Italians would have greater rights in the law-courts, would be freed of various taxes, and would share in the spoils flooding in from foreign conquests. Moreover they would seem more important and more appreciated in their own eyes.

Surely, citizenship was not too great a return for their loyalty, and yet over and over again during the space of half a century, they had been disappointed. Those Romans who backed citizenship for the Italians were driven out of office and usually killed by the senatorial die-hards and their henchmen. After each such senatorial victory, joyful Italians who had come to Rome in expectation of the grant of citizenship were driven harshly away.

Well, then, if Rome didn't want the Italians, the Italians didn't want Rome. In angry fury, various Italian districts declared themselves independent of Rome and formed a separate republic they called Italia. They established their capital in Corfinium about eighty miles east of Rome.

Naturally, this meant war, and what followed is usually called the Social War, from the Latin word for "allies." The Italian tribes who rose against Rome in 91 B.C. were, however, of the Samnite group for the most part, so that one might almost call what followed the Fifth Samnite War.

Rome had no thought of giving in, but she was caught by surprise. The Italians had been preparing for the day, and no sooner did they announce their defection than their armies were in the field and their cities were in a state of readiness for defense. As for Rome, she was unprepared. Even her walls had been allowed to fall into disrepair since the days of Hannibal, over a century earlier.

Rome's hastily gathered armies met initial defeats, particularly in the south against the Samnites, where the consul Lucius Julius Caesar found himself badly beaten. Caesar, in order to keep the Etruscans and Umbrians north of Rome in line, as far as possible, decreed in 90 B.C. that Roman citizenship be granted to those Italians who remained faithful.

The senate, very much against its will, was forced to ask Marius (who had now returned from a tour of the East) to lead the Roman troops, but they avoided giving him full power. Marius' heart was not entirely in his job, for, of course, he had favored giving citizenship to the Italians. Now he had to fight his own people, so to speak, on behalf of the hated senate as at the time when he had destroyed Saturninus. Marius therefore attempted to avoid fighting and, when forced into battle, tried to keep casualties to a minimum.

However, after Lucius Caesar died, Marius' old aide of Numidian days, Sulla, succeeded to the command of the Roman armies in the south. He did not have Marius' inhibitions but prosecuted the war vigorously. In 89 B.C., the Italian rebels were being driven back everywhere.

This warmed every senatorial heart. Their man, Sulla, had had to fight under Marius' command against Jugurtha and against the northern barbarians. Now, at last, Sulla was fighting independently and was doing far better than Marius. The senate had a military champion at last.

The rebellious Italians were further weakened by the Roman offer to grant citizenship to all Italians who applied for it within sixty days. Since citizenship was what they had originally been demanding, many Italians gave in. The Samnites held out to the end, but by 88 B.C. the Social War was over.

Gone was the last spark of native Italian freedom. The Samnites were virtually wiped out. Rome even saw to it that the native Italian language, Oscan (belonging to the same language family as Latin), was discouraged. Latin became the language of almost all Italy.

It might seem that Rome had caused herself a great deal of trouble thanks to the narrow-minded folly of her Senatorial conservatives. They had granted citizenship to the Italians anyway. Why had they not done so three years earlier and saved themselves a great deal of death and destruction?

The Roman change of heart came about, as it happens, not because they suddenly saw the light, or out of a feeling of affection for the allies and repentance for the wrongs done them. Actually, a new and completely unexpected danger had arisen in the East, which for a century had been so quiet and docile. To meet this new danger, Rome simply had to have peace and quiet at home, and citizenship for the Italian allies was the price she paid.

# 8

# SULLA AND POMPEY

### PONTUS

The new danger arose in Asia Minor, which until then had never given serious trouble to Rome. The western third had once comprised Rome's loyal ally, Pergamum, and now for forty years this had been Roman territory as the Province of Asia.

Northwest of this province was Bithynia which a century before had been the last refuge of Hannibal (see page 121). Now it was as complete a Roman puppet as Pergamum had ever been.

East and southeast of Bithynia were a series of other kingdoms, all of which had been set up after the death of Alexander the Great. On the eastern Black Sea coast, for instance, was Pontus, which took its name from the Greek name for the Black Sea.

Pontus had originally been part of the Persian Empire but had been held to it by rather loose ties. After Alexander the Great had conquered the Persian Empire and then died, Pontus shook loose from all attempts of the Macedonian generals to seize control. In 301 B.C., it established its complete independence under Mithradates I (mith''ruh-day'teez), a ruler of Persian descent.

South of Pontus were Galatia (guh-lay'shee-uh) and Cappadocia (kap''uh-doh'shee-uh) whose history parallels that of Pontus. Galatia received its name from the fact that Gallic tribes who had invaded Asia Minor two centuries before had settled there.

East of Pontus, stretching from the Black Sea to the Caspian Sea, south of the lofty range of the Caucasus mountains was Armenia.

Of these kingdoms, Pontus, under a line of vigorous kings (all called Mithradates) flourished most. She fought off the larger Hellenistic monarchies, finding her most dangerous enemy in the Seleucids. When Antiochus III was humbled by the Romans, Pontus had the opportunity for expansion and seized control of the Black Sea all the way westward to the boundary of Bithynia.

When Rome took over Pergamum, Mithradates V was king of Pontus. As did the other kings of Asia Minor, he formed an alliance with Rome and was careful never to do anything to offend that conquering city. Nevertheless, he did his best to increase the power of Pontus and to annex portions of Galatia and Cappadocia, working hard to get Rome to agree to such power increases. In 121 B.C., however, he was assassinated by his own courtiers and his eleven-year-old son succeeded to his throne as Mithradates VI (sometimes called "Mithradates the Great").

All sorts of stories about Mithradates VI are told. He avoided being killed or even dominated by his guardians and relatives through sheer ability and courage. He received a thorough education and was said to have learned twenty-two different languages. Perhaps the most famous story told about him is that he took small quantities of all kinds of poisons in order that his body might develop an immunity to them. In that way, he hoped to avoid assassination by poison. (This is possible only for a few poisons, by the way.)

Once Mithradates VI became old enough, he began a vigorous program of expansion, chiefly in the direction away from Roman dominions. He took control over the fabled land of Colchis (kol'kis), which Jason and his Argonauts had once visited in order to obtain the Golden Fleece, according to the Greek myths. His power extended over the northern shores of the Black Sea, too, where six centuries before, Greek cities had been established on what is now the Crimean peninsula. He tightened Pontic control over Galatia and Cappadocia and formed a tight alliance with Armenia.

All this he could do without Roman interference, for Rome's attention was firmly fixed upon Jugurtha in the south and on the barbarian hordes in the north. She had no time to be concerned with an oriental kinglet fighting his way through distant mountains and seashores.

Mithradates hated Rome which, during his youth, had casually annexed some territory he considered his own and which lorded it over the native kings of Asia Minor. He watched these conquering people being humiliated in Africa and panicking before northern barbarians. They won in the end, but then Italy itself burst apart in civil war.

Mithradates must have felt he had nothing to fear. In 90 B.C. he was beyond doubt the strongest power in Asia Minor (except for the Romans), and he moved westward, taking over the kingdom of Bithynia.

Despite the Social War, Rome reacted at once. Bithynia was her loyal ally and Rome had to stand by her. Firmly she ordered Mithradates out of Bithynia, and the Pontic monarch, surprised at Roman anger, left. However, Rome next en-

couraged Bithynia to invade Pontus in retaliation and
Mithradates exploded in rage. He took up arms against Rome
herself and thus began the First Mithradatic War in 88 B.C.

Mithradates had prepared well. His armies, led by experienced Greek generals, swept through Asia Minor like wild-
fire. He not only occupied the various native kingdoms, he even
took over the Province of Asia itself. Then, as though to burn
his bridges behind him, he ordered every Italian trader in Asia
Minor to be killed, and 80,000 of them are supposed to have
been murdered in a single day, though this number is probably
a gross exaggeration.

Mithradates next sent an army into Greece. The Greeks, astonished that anyone could resist the all-conquering Romans,
joined Mithradates in considerable numbers, and the entire
Roman dominion in the east seemed on the point of collapse.

The Romans were flabbergasted at this sudden irruption of
their greatest enemy since Hannibal. It was important that they
take action at once and yet they could not, even though two
men qualified for the honor of leading the Roman armies, for
each was supported by one of the two powerful parties in Rome
and neither would give way. The two were, of course, Sulla the
conservative, and Marius the radical. Both had been in the East
in recent years and both had dealt with Mithradates.

The senate knew which of the two it wanted and quickly appointed Sulla to lead an army against Mithradates. This
Marius could not endure. He approached the tribune, Publius
Sulpicius Rufus, who was on the senatorial side but who was
also overwhelmed by debt. Marius, it is strongly supposed,
promised to pay off those debts out of the profits of the war, and
Sulpicius Rufus veered to the popular side at once. He pushed
through a law which made the votes of the new Italian citizens
more important and brought numbers of them to Rome. They
voted Marius into command against Mithradates.

This was only natural on the part of the Italians. Marius had
favored them before the Social War and had fought them

gently during the war, while Sulla had been the chief agent of their defeat.

So now there were two generals appointed to lead Roman armies against Mithradates and neither could do so until the matter was settled. Sulla managed to escape from Rome and joined the army that had been assigned to him and that was waiting near Naples.

He did not, however, take it to Greece. He dared not as long as his enemy, Marius, was in control of Rome. Instead, he did an unprecedented thing. He marched his army toward Rome. For the first time in Roman history, a Roman general at the head of a Roman army marched against the city of Rome itself. (Even Coriolanus, who marched against his native city four centuries earlier did so at the head of an enemy army.) Thus began the First Civil War of Roman general against Roman general. Others were to distract Rome in the next half century.

Marius tried to defend Rome but the turbulent population could not stand against Sulla's army, led as it was by a determined and capable general. Marius and Sulpicius Rufus were forced to flee. The latter was caught twenty miles south of Rome and killed, but Marius made his way down the Italian coast, narrowly escaping death more than once, making always for Africa. Finally, he managed to find safety on a small island off the Carthaginian shore.

## SULLA IN CONTROL

Sulla was now undisputed proconsul (that is, someone who is not actually a consul but leads armies as though he were one) and felt it safe to leave Italy.

In 87 B.C., he landed in Greece and began a grim march eastward. He defeated the Greek armies, and in 86 B.C. he laid siege to Athens. It had been many long years since Athens had been able to fight gallant battles with strong enemies. For two centuries she had been nothing more than a kind of "university town" given over to schools of philosophy and dreams of past greatness.

Yet when Mithradates' armies appeared in Greece, Athens was tempted into one last fling. She opened her gates to him and indulged in the delights of being anti-Roman.

Now Sulla was at her gates and where were Mithradates' armies? Some were defeated and some were retreating. Sulla carried the city in 86 B.C. and allowed it to undergo a violent sack by his soldiers. It was a final blow to the ancient city. It never lifted its head again to take any independent action, however slight.

Sulla then moved northward, continuing to defeat enemy armies with considerable ease, and worked his way around the northern shores of the Aegean Sea and into Asia Minor. By 84 B.C. Mithradates saw that further resistance was useless and made peace. The peace was harsh enough. He had to give up all his conquests, surrender his navy, and pay a huge indemnity.

And at that, he got away lightly. Sulla found it necessary to have a quick peace, for he could not afford the necessary delay that would have been involved in the complete destruction of the Pontic king.

The trouble was back home in Rome. Naturally, once Sulla had left Italy, the popular party, which he had temporarily crushed, raised its head again.

A consul, Lucius Cornelius Cinna, elected just as Sulla was leaving for Greece, was of the popular party and tried, unsuccessfully, to stop the departing general. Once Sulla was gone, Cinna attempted to carry through some of the laws favored by the popular party. In this he was opposed by the other consul and was driven out of Rome.

Outside Rome, however, he called upon the Italians for support and brought back Marius from his island exile. Together, they marched against Rome and took her.

By now Marius was about seventy years old and, apparently, nearly mad with anger against his old senatorial enemies. He had saved Rome from Jugurtha and the barbarians fifteen years before and his reward had been his continual humiliation at the hands of the senate and their favorite, Sulla.

He indulged himself in an orgy of revenge and slaughtered his enemies wherever they could be found. This included as many senators as he could lay his hands on, and from this holocaust the senate never fully recovered. Its dignity had been destroyed, and thereafter no Roman general had any hesitation in following his own plans without regard for what the senate might say.

In 86 B.C. Marius and Cinna forced their own election as consuls, and Marius thus became consul for the seventh time as (according to the story) had been foretold him in his youth. He died, however, eighteen days after that election, leaving Cinna in sole control of the city.

All depended now on what action Sulla would take. The popular party sent a general with an army to Asia Minor to take over from Sulla, but it is hard to replace a victorious general. The new army deserted to Sulla's side and its general committed suicide.

Sulla left two legions in Asia Minor and took the rest of his army back to Italy. What followed was almost a renewal of the Social War. Cinna and the other reformers had most of their strength among the Italians, and these now once again faced a Roman army in 84 B.C. and the same general they had faced five years before.

The Italians had no more luck this time. Cinna died in a mutiny and the popular party was forced back and back. Finally, in 82 B.C. Sulla won a great victory over the Italians at the Colline Gate at Rome (the very gate which Hannibal had approached on his great raid a century and a half before). This put an end to all resistance and the First Civil War was over.

Sulla was completely victorious. He celebrated a magnificent triumph and gave himself the added name of Felix ("happy"). He revived the old office of dictator that Cincinnatus had once held (see page 36), and in 81 B.C. (672 A.U.C.) became dictator of Rome. It was not an emergency office for a sharply limited time, however, as it had been in Cincinnatus's time. He took the office for an indefinite period, and he might as well have been an absolute monarch, or a dictator in the modern sense.

It was now Sulla's turn to set up a series of executions of thousands of his political enemies. Many of the popular party, including some senators, perished now. This was not entirely a matter of mere cruelty or blood-lust. Many of those who were listed for execution ("proscribed") had committed no particular crime against Rome or against Sulla, but they did own property. Once executed for treason, their property belonged to the city of Rome. It could be put up for auction and Sulla or his friends could bid for it. Since no one dared bid against them, Sulla's people gained property for virtually nothing. To execute people was thus one way of rewarding and enriching one's self and one's friends.

One of those who might have been executed was a young aristocrat named Gaius Julius Caesar, a nephew of the unsuccessful Roman general of the Social War whom Sulla had replaced. Young Caesar was the nephew of Marius's wife and his own wife was the daughter of Cinna. Sulla ordered him to divorce his wife, but Caesar had the courage to refuse. Caesar's death might have followed, but he was saved as a result of the pleas of his aristocratic family. Sulla reluctantly let Caesar live but said sourly (and truthfully), "Watch out for him. In that young man is many a Marius."

Sulla occupied himself in restoring the power of the senate, and in reducing the power of all influences that were against the senate. He appointed new senators in place of those killed by Marius, and doubled the size of the senate from 300 to 600. He included equites among the senators (as Drusus had suggested doing ten years earlier) so as to tighten the bond between the landowners and the businessmen. He drastically weakened the offices of censors and tribunes and decreed that it would be treason for any general to take his army out of the province assigned him. He also revised and updated Rome's law code by freeing it from a too-narrow dependence on the old Twelve Tables (see page 32), allowing praetors to establish new precedents to meet new needs, but he carefully reserved all judicial functions to senators alone.

Sulla also savagely punished those areas of Italy that had been active on behalf of Marius. What remnants were left of the Samnite and Etruscan culture were completely wiped out. This, too, he turned to the advantage of the senate, for he settled his soldiers on vacated land, hoping that they might serve as a strong base on which the power of the senatorial party might rest in the future.

By 79 B.C., Sulla felt that his reforms were completed and that what he considered Rome's good old days were restored. He therefore resigned the dictatorship and turned all power back to the Senate. The next year he died at the age of sixty.

But Sulla's reforms meant nothing. His changes in the law code survived, but all else began to crumble at once. The senate could not be brought back to what it had once been, and it remained at the mercy of generals from that time on.

During his dictatorship, Sulla attempted to keep matters quiet in the east. Some of the minor generals on the spot tried to earn glory by skirmishing with Mithradates (sometimes called the Second Mithradatic War), but Sulla stopped that and enforced peace in 81 B.C. under the terms that ended the first war.

Mithradates, however, knew he could not relax. Disorders

at home might keep the Romans from exerting their full strength just now, but he could not rely on those disorders forever. The Romans would never forgive his slaughter of the Italians in Asia Minor in 88 B.C. any more than they had ever forgiven Carthage for the slaughter at Cannae. The proof of this was that the Roman senate was careful not to ratify peace with Mithradates, so that the peace which existed remained only as a personal arrangement with Sulla; and in 78 B.C. Sulla was dead.

Mithradates therefore felt it only natural to prepare for a renewal of the war and seek some favorable opportunity for striking. Such an opportunity came in 74 B.C. when Nicomedes III (nik″oh-mee′deez) of Bithynia died without heirs. Nicomedes III had always been a loyal henchman of Rome and had fought Mithradates constantly. Now, with death approaching, he took what he felt to be the logical action to keep Bithynia permanently out of the hands of his Pontic enemy. He willed Bithynia to Rome, and it became a Roman province.

Mithradates declared this will to be invalid and with a large army entered and occupied Bithynia. Thus began the Third Mithradatic War, and, once again, Mithradates began by carrying all before him.

Sulla, when he had departed from Asia Minor, had left his second-in-command in charge. This was Lucius Licinius Lucullus (lyoo-kul′us), a nephew of Metellus Numidicus, who had fought against Jugurtha.

Lucullus, an efficient but a stern and unlovable man, had left the minor skirmishing of the Second Mithradatic War to his lieutenants and had spent his time reorganizing and reforming the administration of Asia Minor. In the process, he also heavily fined the cities that had helped Mithradates, and some of the money disappeared into his own coffers.

Now, with Mithradates on the rampage again, Lucullus took firm action. He defeated Mithradates in a series of battles and drove him back to Pontus. In 73 B.C. he invaded Pontus itself and forced Mithradates to flee eastward to Armenia.

Armenia was then ruled by a strong monarch, Tigranes (tigh-gray'neez), who had come to the throne of Armenia in 95 B.C. and had strengthened it by conquest and reform just as Mithradates had done in Pontus. In fact, Tigranes married the daughter of Mithradates and the two kingdoms usually acted in alliance. Tigranes had helped Mithradates from the beginning although he had hitherto been careful not to take actual military action.

It was to the court of his son-in-law that Mithradates now fled. Tigranes, impressed by the Roman victories, might have given him up, but the Roman ambassadors who came in 70 B.C. to demand him were needlessly arrogant and the offended Armenian decided to fight.

Lucullus promptly invaded Armenia and defeated Tigranes' large but not too well-trained army, took the Armenian capital in 69 B.C., and sent both Tigranes and Mithradates flying. Lucullus took off in pursuit. Lucullus' harsh, stern character did not, however, recommend itself to his men. They found themselves moving ever eastward into craggy mountains under the lead of an unpopular general, and they mutinied. Lucullus was forced to retreat westward as a result, while both Tigranes and Mithradates managed to recover at least parts of their territory.

Lucullus was able to do nothing more with his rebellious troops, and in 66 B.C. he was called home. In Rome, he was just as unpopular as in Asia Minor and he did not try to enter politics. The popular party managed to delay his triumph, but he had it at last, along with the added name of "Ponticus."

He then retired to a pleasant villa and made use of the money he had extorted from the luckless inhabitants of Asia Minor to support himself in cultured luxury.

Lucullus became particularly renowned for the elaborate dinners he gave and the costly dishes he had prepared. He was supposed to be the first to bring a small red fruit to Rome from Cerasus (ser'uh-sus), a city in Pontus. The Romans called the fruit by the name of the city, which became "cerise" in French and "cherry" in English.

Lucullus fed many guests at his table and once, when a particularly elaborate dinner had been prepared, his servants asked for whom the dinner was intended since no invitations had been issued.

"Tonight," Lucullus explained, "Lucullus has Lucullus as guest," and he dined alone.

Ever since then the phrase "Lucullus dines with Lucullus" has been used as an expression representing extreme luxury, while a "Lucullan feast" is the ultimate in eating.

To be sure, Lucullus enjoyed the finer things in life, too. He patronized poets and artists, enjoyed their company, collected a magnificent library, and wrote (in Greek) a history of the Social War, in which he had fought under Sulla.

## NEW MEN

With the death of Marius and of Sulla, new men began to rise to prominence in Rome. The most successful of these, at first, was Gnaeus Pompeius (pom-pee'us), who is usually known in English as Pompey (pom'pee).

He was born in 106 B.C. and, as a young man, fought alongside his father against the Italian allies in the Social War. Although the family was a plebeian one, and although Pompey's father tried to maintain a cautious neutrality in the struggle between Marius and Sulla (until a bolt of lightning killed him in 87 B.C.), young Pompey's sympathies were on the side of the senatorial aristocrats.

While Marius and Cinna were in control of Rome, Pompey kept discreetly out of sight, and just managed to stay alive. Upon hearing that Sulla was returning from Asia Minor, he hastened quickly to his side, raising an army on his behalf. He fought alongside Sulla and did well enough to earn the dictator's gratitude.

Sulla sent him to Sicily to take care of the pro-Marius forces there, and this Pompey did so well that when he returned in 81 B.C. Sulla let him have a triumph even though he did not qualify on two counts: he was not a government official and he was under age. Sulla also indulgently bestowed upon him the additional name of "Magnus" ("the Great"), which was rather overdoing it.

Pompey's military career continued fortunate even after the death of Sulla. In 77 B.C., he defeated a Roman general, Marcus Aemilius Lepidus (lep'ih-dus) who had turned against Sulla's policies. Lepidus had to flee to Spain, which was then the center of the pro-Marius faction.

Spain was at that time under the control of the general Quintus Sertorius. He had retreated westward when Sulla had taken over Rome. He fought in Spain and in northwestern Africa and, eventually, was asked by certain rebellious Spanish tribes to lead them against the Roman government.

This Sertorius did, setting up what amounted to an independent Spain in 80 B.C. He was an efficient general and an enlightened one, treating the native Spaniards well, attempting to civilize them on the Roman model, establishing a native senate and setting up school for the native youngsters. What's more, he defeated the regular Roman forces sent against him.

It seemed natural to Pompey to pursue the defeated Lepidus, and in 77 B.C. he persuaded the senate to send him to Spain that he might take care of both rebels. Actually, he didn't. Lepidus died soon after reaching Spain, but Sertorius was more than a match for the new young general. Pompey, defeated and embarrassed, had to appeal to Rome for reinforcements. This might have been sufficient indication that Pompey was not really a general of the first rank, but his luck held. In 72 B.C., Sertorius was assassinated (with Roman money undoubtedly paying off the assassin), and the movement he had supported in Spain quickly collapsed. The undeserving Pompey got all the credit for it.

While Pompey was in Spain, Italy faced a new kind of disaster.

The Roman interest in gladiatorial shows had become evil and disgusting. Originally, the shows had been exercises in which armed opponents displayed their ability to attack and defend themselves efficiently. There was value to this, because it helped keep soldiers in shape and the practice served to save their life in actual battle.

However, as foreign slaves poured into Italy, it became customary to draw the gladiators from among them. The Romans didn't much care what happened to slaves, and it seemed amusing to them to have such gladiators fight each other to the death, or to have them face wild animals. They would be bet upon wildly, as we, today, bet upon prizefighters.

Some particularly good gladiators might last a long time and even win their freedom in the end, but for most it was a short, hard life and a bloody death.

One gladiator was a man from Thrace (the region north of the Aegean Sea and east of Macedon) named Spartacus. He had been captured by the Romans (perhaps after he had deserted from the Roman army) and, because of his size and strength, was sent to a gladiator's school. In 73 B.C., he persuaded a number of fellow-gladiators to break out of the school and to use their arms against the Roman masters instead of against each other.

Seventy gladiators broke out, and soon they were joined by slaves eager to strike a blow for their own freedom. Thus began the Gladiatorial War or the Third Servile War. In the first two wars of this type, it had been Sicily that had suffered. Now it was Italy that faced the horrors of a slave war and, what's more, this time the slaves were under a skillful commander.

For two years Spartacus defeated every Roman army sent out against him. At the height of his power he had 90,000 men under his command and controlled almost all of southern Italy. In 72 B.C. he fought his way northward to the Alps intending to leave Italy and gain permanent freedom in the barbarian regions to the north. His men, however, misled by their initial victories, preferred to remain in Italy in reach of the rich loot, and Spartacus had to turn south again.

At last the Romans found the man to save them in the praetor Marcus Licinius Crassus. Crassus, born about 115 B.C., was the son of a well-known conservative family. His father and brother were among those who died at the hands of Marius and Cinna, and he had saved his own life only by leaving Italy in a hurry. When Sulla returned, Crassus, like Pompey, joined him at once and, again like Pompey, he became one of Sulla's favorites.

Crassus was one of those who did well as a result of Sulla's proscriptions. He gathered up all the estates he could from among those that were confiscated and did not hesitate (according to the stories) to arrange for the execution of innocent people whose estates he felt he would like to have. He gained a horrible reputation as a monster of greed, but he became the richest man Rome had ever seen and was called Crassus Dives (dy′veez) or "Crassus the Rich."

Many stories are told of Crassus's unscrupulous chase after gold. Rome had numerous rickety wooden apartment houses in which the poor lived under circumstances of great squalor. The city did not have anything like a modern fire department, however, so that when fires broke out among the crowded wooden structures, large parts of the city would vanish in flame.

Crassus organized a fire department of his own, hastened them out to any structure that was on fire and bargained with the owner. After he had bought the property for virtually nothing — and only then — he put the fire out. Often he was able to buy neighboring property, too, since that would also burn if Crassus sat by and did nothing. In this way, he came to own a large part of the real estate in Rome.

Nevertheless, he was a reasonably competent soldier, and when sent against Spartacus, he managed to defeat him in two engagements. In the second of these in 71 B.C., Spartacus met his death and his army was virtually destroyed. Pompey returned from Spain at this point and managed to get in on the act. He and Crassus wiped up the straggling remnants of the rebels and again Pompey got more credit than he deserved.

So viciously and cruelly were the captured slaves punished that Rome was never to experience another serious slave insurrection.

Pompey got along well with Crassus at that time. Crassus's wealth did not suffice to make him socially acceptable to the Senatorial aristocrats and he was forced to turn to the people, before whom he began to pose as a philanthropist. He lent money without interest, made it a practice to speak in defense of individuals who were brought before the courts without being able to afford a lawyer, and so on.

As for Pompey, the senate had grown increasingly suspicious of him and his successes. He was too young and too popular with his troops for the senate to feel safe with him. Pompey realized this and he, therefore, began to turn against the senate.

The senate was very shortsighted in all this, for once Pompey and Crassus joined forces they were able to campaign for the consulate in 70 B.C. and win. As consuls, they promptly set about weakening the senate. They restored the powers of the tribunes and censors, so that only eight years after the death

of Sulla all his work had been undone — and at the hands of
two of his own particular favorites whom the senate had fool-
ishly antagonized.

Pompey and Crassus also set about reforming the law courts,
which Sulla had left in the senate's hands alone, and which continued to be notoriously corrupt.

A particularly disgusting example of this involved a Roman
politician named Gaius Verres (ver'eez). Verres was an unscrupulous and unprincipled man whose only real object in life
was to steal. He was originally pro-Marius, but he switched to
Sulla when he realized that Sulla was going to win. Sulla pardoned him for the robberies he had already committed and
placed him in Asia on the staff of the governor of that province
in 80 B.C. Both stole shamelessly from the helpless provincials,
but when they were placed on trial in Rome, Verres calmly
turned states' evidence against the governor and got off scot-
free.

Eventually, in 74 B.C., he was made governor of Sicily, where
he proceeded to enrich himself further. It was, of course, customary for governors to enrich themselves by illegal means.
Then, when their term of office was over and the provincials
brought suit against them to the senate, it was customary for
the senate to turn a blind eye to it all. Each senator was waiting his own chance to make a killing, or had already done so.

The plundering, however, had to be within reason, and
Verres knew nothing of reason. He broke all records for villainy.
His robberies were beyond belief, and he even stole from the
city of Rome itself, holding back money paid him for the grain
ships that carried food from Sicily to Rome.

At this time there was rising to prominence in Rome, however, another new man, Marcus Tullius Cicero.

Cicero, born in 106 B.C., was not a fighter, but was rather
sickly in his youth and was an intellectual. He served in the
ranks as a young man during the Social War; that was his only
taste of military life and not much of one. During the civil war,

his sympathies had been with Sulla, but he managed to avoid fighting. Instead, he concentrated on an education, travelling all over the cultured East in order to sit at the feet of great teachers. On returning to Rome in 77 B.C., he married Terentia, a rich woman with a temper who henpecked him (for he was not a fighter at home, either).

Cicero was naturally gifted as a writer and a speaker. In the East he had learned oratory, and he became the greatest orator in Roman history. Only he can be mentioned in the same breath with Demosthenes, the great Greek orator who lived two centuries before him. Where it was a question of talking, Cicero could fight strongly, attack energetically, and win.

In those days, the legal decisions reached by courts did not always depend on the evidence. Often the judges (and the people) were swayed by the oratory of the opposing lawyers, who might deliberately seek to rouse prejudice and emotion on behalf of their clients. Cicero did quite well at this, thanks to his oratorical genius, and he rapidly became a most sought-after lawyer.

Cicero had served in Sicily in 75 B.C., and since he was an honest man, the Sicilians trusted him. When Verres left his post in Sicily in 70 B.C., it was naturally to Cicero that the Sicilians turned for redress. They pled with him to defend them in a lawsuit against Verres.

Cicero took the case gladly, although Verres was supported by almost the entire senatorial aristocracy. (Fortunately, the judge in charge happened to be one of the few honest senators.) For months, the senators tried every trick in the book to get Verres off on one technicality or another. They found a skillful lawyer to defend him, they tried to substitute a dummy prosecutor in place of Cicero, to delay the trial in order to obtain a new judge. All they succeeded in doing was to get more and more publicity for the trial, while Cicero skillfully blocked all their maneuvers.

Finally, Cicero began to present his evidence against Verres, and the case was so overwhelmingly against the master thief that there was no contest. Verres ran away to Massilia and was condemned in his absence. (However, he kept much of his stolen goods and lived in comfort for another quarter of a century.)

The Verres case helped keep down the level of dishonesty in the provinces a bit, but its chief result was that it was the making of Cicero. It also helped reduce the reputation of the senate, so that Pompey and Crassus had no trouble in putting through their program of reforming the law courts the year after the trial.

## POMPEY CLEARS THE EAST

Pompey was now a great popular favorite. He had been victorious in Sicily, Italy, and Spain; he had broken with the aristocracy and proven himself a successful champion of the people and of reform. What other problems were there for him to solve?

To be sure, the East was still in turmoil thanks to the tireless Mithradates. At the moment, though, Lucullus was taking care of that, winning victories in Pontus and Armenia (see page 168). There was, however, trouble closer to home.

When Rome weakened the last important commercial Greek city, Rhodes, she removed a valuable policeman against pirates. Now the whole Mediterranean was rotten with them, much more so than in the old days of Illyrian piracy nearly two centuries before (see page 84).

It was almost impossible for honest ships to make their way safely from one part of the Roman realm to another without paying tribute or being destroyed. The very grain shipments to Rome were interfered with, so that the price of food in that city was rising steadily. What's more, the pirates raided towns here and there, kidnapping men, women, and children and selling them to slave dealers who were careful not to ask too many questions. The coasts of Italy itself were not immune from their cruel activity. (Ironically, the pirates themselves were often escaped slaves who turned to piracy as the only way of remaining at liberty.)

Rome's involvement in wars against allies, against slaves, and against herself had made it difficult for her to take firm action against the pirates. In 74 B.C. she had annexed the Greek city of Cyrene (sy-ree'nee) on the African coast west of Egypt. For over two centuries, Cyrene had been part of Ptolemaic Egypt. Toward the end it had become a pirate hangout, but Rome's takeover put an end to that.

Other pirate centers remained. One was on the island of Crete northeast of Cyrene and another was on Cilicia (sih-lish'-ee-uh), a section of the southeastern coast of Asia Minor.

In 68 B.C., Quintus Caecilius Metellus Pius (the son of the Metellus Numidicus who had successfully fought Jugurtha) took to the sea against the pirates. He had been one of Sulla's most successful generals, and success did not entirely fail him now either, for he conquered Crete, and that island became a Roman province in 67 B.C. The pirates still held Cilicia, however.

In 67 B.C., therefore, Pompey himself was called to the task. He was put in charge of the entire Mediterranean coast to a distance of fifty miles inland for three years and told to use that time for destroying the pirates. So great was Roman confidence in Pompey that food prices fell as soon as news of his appointment was made public.

Nor did he disappoint Rome. He took his measures with the utmost vigor. In no time at all, he had cleared the western Mediterranean of pirates; then sailing east, he defeated the pirate fleet off Cilicia and managed to get them to surrender by promises of pardon and easy treatment. The whole business had taken him only three months.

If Pompey had been popular before, he was Rome's sweetheart now. It was clear that Lucullus, thanks to the mutiny of his army, was no longer of much use against Mithradates, and so Pompey was appointed to replace him. Pompey marched into the interior of Asia Minor where, as it turned out, Lucullus had done all the hard work but where Pompey was again to get all the credit. Pompey easily defeated Mithradates, who again back-pedalled eastward toward hopes of safety with Tigranes of Armenia. This time Tigranes had had enough. He avoided further trouble by refusing entry to Mithradates and agreeing to accept the domination of Rome.

Mithradates fled north of the Black Sea where Pompey chose not to follow him. For a while, Mithradates considered the wild possibility of collecting a large horde of barbarians and invading Italy itself, but the few followers remaining to him began to rebel against his useless wars with Rome. When his own son moved into the opposition, Mithradates finally gave up and, in 63 B.C., killed himself and ended his long reign of fifty-seven years.

Meanwhile, Pompey was clearing the east. Pontus became a Roman province in 64 B.C., and Cilicia became another that same year. Virtually the entire Asia Minor coast was now Roman. In the interior there were still a few regions such as Cappadocia and Galatia which remained under the nominal control of native rulers. They were, however, firmly in the Roman grip and within thirty or forty years were also to become provinces.

With affairs in Asia Minor settled, Pompey turned south and marched along the eastern coast of the Mediterranean. There he found a last remnant of the Seleucid Empire which, under Antiochus III, a century and a quarter before, had dared challenge Rome. Now it was reduced to a petty realm that included

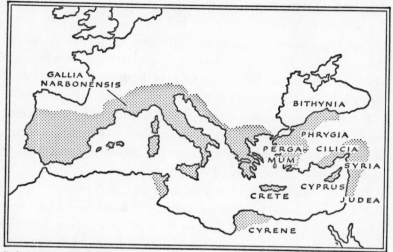

End of Mithradatic Wars — 64 B.C.

only the region in Syria around its capital, Antioch (an'tee-ok).

For a century, Seleucid history had consisted almost entirely of struggles between various contenders for an increasingly worthless throne. The possessor of the throne at the moment was Antiochus XIII, who had been placed there four years earlier by Lucullus.

Pompey now decided to end the entire useless mess. He unseated Antiochus and annexed his realm to Rome as the Province of Syria.

South of Syria was the land of Judea. A century before, Judea had revolted against the Seleucid Empire and had gained its independence under a line of rulers known as the Maccabees (mak'uh-beez). Judea prospered under them at first, but eventually its history, too, came to be largely that of the quarrels among different members of the ruling family.

When Pompey arrived, two brothers of the Maccabee family were fighting a civil war. One was Hyrcanus II (her-kay'nus) and the other Aristobulus (uh-ris"toh-byoo'lus) — both Jews despite their Greek-sounding names. Each brother tried to win the all-powerful Roman to his side.

Pompey demanded that all fortresses in Judea be surrendered to him. This was denied him, and Jerusalem refused to allow him to enter. For three months Pompey laid siege to it, and then the always stiff-necked Jews reluctantly gave in.

Pompey took the city and, out of curiosity, entered the Holy of Holies of the Temple at Jerusalem — the most sacred chamber of the Temple which only the High Priest might enter and then only at the Day of Atonement.

No doubt many Jews must have expected Pompey to die on the spot as a result of divine displeasure, but he emerged completely unharmed. Nevertheless, it is an interesting fact that from that point on, from the time of his violation of the Temple, Pompey's successes came to an end. The rest of his life was one long frustrating failure.

In 63 B.C. Pompey put an end to the line of the Maccabees as kings, but allowed Hyrcanus to keep the post of High Priest. As the real power in Judea (under Roman supervision) Pompey established Antipater (an-tip′uh-ter), who was not a Jew by birth but an Idumaean; that is, a native of the region south of Judea. Antipater remained a loyal ally of Rome, and from this time on, Judea remained under firm Roman control.

Pompey was now on top of the world. In 61 B.C., at the age of forty-five, he returned to Italy and received the most magnificent triumph Rome had seen up to that time. The senate was in terror lest he use his army to set himself up as dictator of Rome after Sulla's fashion, but Pompey did not have Sulla's temperament. Instead, he disbanded his army and took his place in Rome as a private citizen.

Undoubtedly, Pompey assumed that he would now dominate Rome through the sheer magic of his name without requiring the support of a single soldier. If so, he was wrong. Scipio Africanus could not control Rome just through the magic of his defeat of Hannibal; nor could Marius through the magic of his defeat of the Cimbri and Teutones. Pompey was not to succeed either. To control Rome required great shrewdness, a cool head, a sharp sense of chicanery — and an army.

Pompey had none of these things.

# 9

# THE TRIUMVIRATE

## THE CONSPIRACY OF CATILINE

During Pompey's absence in Asia, Crassus was riding high as the leader of the popular party. He had as his henchman that charming but extravagant aristocrat Gaius Julius Caesar, who had once stood up to Sulla himself and had gotten away with it (see page 165).

Caesar, who was born in 102 B.C., came of one of the oldest and most noble families in Rome, and one would have supposed he would be firmly on the side of the senatorial conservatives. He was born, however, in the year of Marius' great victory over the barbarians; his aunt had married Marius, and he himself had married the daughter of Marius' associate, Cinna. Caesar apparently built up a strong emotional attachment to the memory of Marius and this brought him over to the side of the popular party.

Prudently, after his set-to with Sulla, in which he lost property and position even though he saved his life, he did not press his luck. He left Italy to serve in the Roman armies fighting in Asia Minor and did not return till after Sulla was safely dead. Then, like Cicero, he made himself well-known as an orator before the law courts. In fact, in oratorical ability, he eventually made himself second only to Cicero.

In 76 B.C., he set sail for the island of Rhodes in order to study oratory further under the best Greek teachers. On the way, he was captured by pirates who held him for ransom. They demanded something like $100,000 in modern money. While the money was being scraped up by friends and relatives, Caesar charmed his captors (he charmed everyone). They apparently had a pleasant time together and in the course of friendly conversation, the pirates asked Caesar what he would do once he was free. Caesar said calmly that he would return with a fleet, capture and execute those who were now holding him for ransom.

The pirates laughed at the joke. Nevertheless, when Caesar's ransom arrived and he was set free, he proceeded to collect ships, return, capture the pirates, and have them executed — as he had promised. The gay young aristocrat was no one to trifle with.

After a short stay in Rhodes, Caesar went to Asia Minor again and served against Mithradates. Then he returned to Rome and decided to enter politics in a big way. He got himself elected to a variety of offices by buying popularity. He poured out his inherited wealth like water, let no one leave him empty-handed, sponsored huge games for the populace, and charmed everyone with his lavish, gay way of life.

What's more, he championed the cause of the dead Marius, whose memory was still held in honor by many of the people. Sulla had removed the statue of Marius and the trophies in his honor that had stood in the Capitol. In 68 B.C., however, when Caesar's aunt (the widow of Marius) died, Caesar boldly arranged to include a bust of Marius in the funeral procession. Then, in 65 B.C. he had the statue and trophies of Marius restored to the Capitol. The senate was horrified but dared not act because of the roar of delight from the multitude.

Caesar's unbelievable extravagance wiped out his own fortune completely and put him millions of dollars in debt. That ought to have destroyed him but it didn't. Crassus realized the usefulness of a fellow like Caesar — such an orator, such a darling of the people, and having such a constant need for money. If Crassus supplied that money, he could count on Caesar's charm, wit and popularity on his own side, and Caesar could continue being extravagant.

The popular party attracted a number of people who for one reason or another wanted to see Roman society overturned and some kind of revolution set in motion. It wasn't always out of idealism or out of sympathy for the poor and oppressed. Sometimes, those who wanted an overturn, wanted it only so that they might gain power, wealth, or revenge.

An example of such a self-seeking revolutionary was a debt-ridden nobleman, Lucius Sergius Catilina, commonly known in English as Catiline (kat'ih-line). Like Caesar, he was of an aristocratic family and, like Caesar, he had ruined himself by extravagance. Unlike Caesar, however, he lacked charm and the gift of success.

The only descriptions we have of Catiline are those of his enemies and, undoubtedly, they are greatly exaggerated. Still, if even a portion of the tales told about him are true, he was a horrible person, cruel, vicious and even murderous. He had been a henchman of Sulla and a member of the conservative party. Yet when his financial situation seemed to hit bottom, he had no hesitation in turning violently against the conservatives in order to improve his situation.

It seemed to him that the only way he could get out of debt was to have himself elected consul. To bring this about, he courted the popular party by favoring their program of dividing up land among the landless and of looting the provinces for the benefit of Rome.

Crassus supported him as he supported Caesar, but Catiline failed to win the consulship. He then began to plot a much more desperate scheme, that of assassinating the consuls and plundering the city itself. (At least this was what his enemies claimed he was plotting.) It is doubtful how far Crassus and Caesar went in continuing to support Catiline in this sinister scheme. It seems unlikely that Crassus should want Rome overturned and looted when he himself was the richest possible source of loot. Perhaps they were not aware of Catiline's most extreme plans; or perhaps Catiline's plans weren't quite as radical as his enemies made them out to be.

In any case, the conservatives later claimed that Crassus and Caesar were deeply involved in the conspiracy; and most historians seem to think they were.

Definitely against Catiline was the leader of the senatorial conservatives, Marcus Porcius Cato, great-grandson and namesake of old Cato the Censor. (This new Cato is sometimes called "Cato the Younger" and sometimes "Cato of Utica," from the place where he eventually died.)

Cato the Younger was a model of rigid virtue. He had served in Asia under Lucullus, whose stern discipline he greatly admired. Cato deliberately conducted his life along the lines of the stories that were told of the ancient Romans. Since he was always very ostentatious about his virtue, he annoyed other people; since he never made allowance for the human weaknesses of others, he angered them; and since he never compromised, he always went down to defeat in the end. (Later generations, who didn't have to deal with him, have greatly admired his rigid honesty and his unbending devotion to his principles.)

Also against Catiline was Cicero, who belonged to neither the senatorial nor the popular party. Cicero was, on the whole, a kindly man, noble and honest, with high principles. Cicero had Cato's honesty without his priggishness. Cicero was not, however, a very strong man. He was often undecided as to what action he ought to take in particular cases and this indecision sometimes made him look like a coward.

Now, however, Cicero acted with the greatest decision of his career. He ran for the consulship for 63 B.C. against Catiline and was elected. As consul, Cicero proceeded to take action. One of the conspirators was indiscreet and specific knowledge of some of the plans of the conspiracy came to Cicero's ear, including a plot to assassinate Cicero himself. Diligently, he gathered further evidence. Furthermore, he took action against a possible military uprising. He had the walls of Rome manned, the citizens armed, and then he called a meeting of the Senate.

Catiline had the nerve to appear at the meeting, for he was, after all, a senator. Cicero rose and poured forth the most eloquent and effective speech of his life, reciting to Catiline's face all his plans, all his actions, all his intentions. As he spoke those senators who happened to be sitting near Catiline moved away, leaving the conspirator sitting alone, surrounded by empty seats.

The day was carried by Cicero's passionate words and Catiline, not daring to remain in Rome, escaped by night and fled to the army his associates had been raising. He was now in open rebellion against Rome, the people of which were roused to fury by a second eloquent speech by Cicero, delivered in the Roman Forum.

Cicero next uncovered evidence that Catiline's friends within Rome were dickering with representatives of the still-unconquered tribes of central and northern Gaul. The plan was, supposedly, to have the Gauls attack the Roman borders, while Catiline struck at the heart.

The conspirators within the city were at once seized and the problem arose as to what to do with them. By Roman law, they had to be tried, but Cicero wanted them executed out of hand ("lynched," we would say today). He was afraid that in case of an appeal to the law, they might escape through the use of influence and corruption.

Crassus prudently kept out of the way, knowing the rumors about his own connection with the conspiracy. Caesar, about whom the same rumors were current, was bolder. He made a firm speech urging that the conspirators be tried and not lynched. So persuasive was he that for a while it looked as though law would win out over lynching.

But then Cato the Younger rose and spoke so effectively that opinion shifted again and the conspirators were executed without trial.

A Roman army met Catiline's army 200 miles north of Rome and Catiline was defeated. He took what seemed to him the only way out and committed suicide in 62 B.C.

The end of the conspiracy of Catiline brought Cicero to the height of his political career. For a brief moment, he was the acknowledged savior of Rome or, as Cato's flattery put it, "the father of his country."

## THREE-MAN RULE

Cicero, who was a vain man, probably felt that his life should now be one long round of glory, but that was not to be. For one thing, Pompey was coming home; Pompey the unconquerable general who had placed the entire East at the feet of Rome; who had demolished the pirates, ended the stubborn threat of Mithradates, brought Armenia to its knees and wiped up Syria and Judea with a wave of his hand.

Pompey received a magnificent triumph and then, in complete confidence that he would be refused nothing even though he had disbanded his army, he asked the Senate to ratify all his acts in the East. He asked them to ratify in one great vote all the peace treaties he had made, the provinces he had absorbed and the kings he had placed on thrones or taken off. He asked them also to distribute land among his soldiers. He fully expected the senate to vote one tremendous "Yes" to everything.

They did not. Pompey, like Cicero, found that last year's glory did not move this year's men. To Pompey's humiliation and surprise, his reward for disbanding his army was the loss of power. Some senators were suspicious of him, others jealous. Cato demanded that every last one of Pompey's acts be separately discussed. Lucullus (whom Pompey had replaced and whose hard work had merely served to increase Pompey's laurels) was particularly bitter. He attacked Pompey's acts unsparingly. Crassus had grown envious of Pompey, so that the popular party was also against the general.

While the political pot boiled, Caesar was absent. Uncertain of Pompey's intentions and quite aware that the conspiracy of Catiline had left him tainted, he had left for Spain before the general's return. In Spain, Caesar defeated some rebellious tribes in the western reaches of the province, thus accomplishing two things. First, he gathered enough wealth by one means or another to pay off his debts to Crassus and others; second, he gained the beginnings of a military reputation.

When he returned to Italy in 60 B.C., he found the situation made to order for him. Pompey, frustrated and angry, was ready for almost anything to get his revenge on the senatorial conservatives — provided only that someone else would tell him what to do. Caesar was only too ready to serve as his adviser.

Caesar suggested they join forces: Pompey the great general and Caesar the accomplished orator. All they lacked was money and that Crassus could supply. Let him join also. Pompey and Crassus were on bad terms, to be sure, but Caesar was sure he could smooth that over, and he did.

All three therefore agreed to act together in one another's

interest. Thus was formed the *First Triumvirate* (a word coming from a Latin phrase meaning "three men").

Caesar was right. With Crassus's money, Pompey's military reputation, and Caesar's own political ability, the three ran Rome. Cicero, despite his moment of glory against Catiline, found himself forgotten, while Cato and his conservative group found themselves powerless.

Caesar was easily elected consul for 59 B.C., and as consul he loyally supported the interests of the other members of the triumvirate. The other consul was a conservative and tried to interfere, but Caesar (as Sulla had once predicted) was a more determined man and a less easily confused one than Marius. He simply drove the other consul out of the Forum and forced him to remain a prisoner in his own house. He then served his term as virtually the sole consul. He saw to it that all Pompey's acts in the East were ratified and he arranged to have Pompey's soldiers get land assignments in Italy.

The one man with courage to stand against Caesar, despite any threat of imprisonment or death, was Cato. Caesar therefore had him assigned as governor of the distant island of Cyprus, and off he had to go.

Cicero, another opponent, was less courageous than Cato. He could be intimidated, and for that purpose Caesar turned a vicious man loose upon the great orator.

The man was Publius Clodius (kloh′dee-us), a completely unprincipled aristocrat, conceited, willful, and self-indulgent. He was constantly making trouble and, usually, managed to have the trouble recoil upon himself. He had served under Lucullus (his brother-in-law) in Asia Minor but had won no military distinction.

He first attracted serious attention in 62 B.C. when, as a kind of foolish joke, he interfered with certain religious rites that were proceeding in Caesar's house. Only women were allowed to attend, but Clodius disguised himself in women's clothing and invaded the rites. He was detected by Caesar's mother and had to stand trial for sacrilege. He was acquitted, thanks to his lavish use of bribery.

There were rumors that Clodius had managed this joke in poor taste through an understanding he had had with Caesar's second wife, Pompeia. (Clodius, after all, was a handsome villain, so much so that he received the nickname Pulcher — "good-looking.") Caesar declared his wife to be innocent of any wrong-doing, but divorced her anyway, since even the suspicion of wrong-doing was unbearable for Caesar. He is quoted as saying "Caesar's wife must be above suspicion." This remark has become famous as representing an extreme demand of rigid virtue.

During Clodius's trial, Cicero acted firmly for the prosecution. His bitter sarcasm against Clodius roused the latter's undying hatred. In 59 B.C. Clodius had himself adopted into a plebeian family, abandoning his aristocracy in order that he might qualify as tribune.

Clodius was elected tribune and, in order to discredit Cicero, seized upon the lynching of the Catilinian conspirators five years before. By executing them without trial, he maintained, Cicero had broken the law and should be executed. Cicero pleaded that the city had been in danger and that, far from being blamed, he should be praised for his quick action.

If Cicero had been as bold as Caesar he might have carried his point, but his courage failed him. Clodius had, in his pay, a gang of toughs who were engaged to harass poor Cicero. Cicero could not as much as travel from his house to the senate chamber without having his servants attacked and put in danger of death.

Cicero gave up. He left voluntarily for exile in Epirus, very depressed and sorry for himself. In his absence, Clodius had his property confiscated.

Caesar had thus handled all the powerful men of Rome. Two of them, Pompey and Crassus, he had tied firmly to himself. Two more, Cato and Cicero, he had driven away. Now he was free to carry out the next step, which was to gain military glory for himself. Once he had that, he could rule alone.

For the purpose, his eyes rested on Gaul. Southern Gaul was a Roman province, but to the north were wide reaches of un-conquered territory which, it seemed to him, he ought to be able to handle.

In this, he might have seemed to others to be overoptimistic. He was a middle-aged man by now, forty-four years old. So far he had had very little experience in battle; some action in Asia Minor and a little more in Spain, but nothing very much. He had rather lived a life of ease and luxury which should have made him completely unfit to soldier in the wild barbar-ian regions of northern Gaul.

However, Caesar was a most remarkable man and well he knew it. He felt he could do anything he set his mind to, and certainly his life story seems to prove he could.

In 58 B.C., he had himself assigned the provinces of Cisalpine and Transalpine Gaul for the unprecedented period of five years. Before he left, he tried to make certain that in his ab-sence Pompey would not decide to become an enemy. He did this by arranging to have his lovely young daughter Julia marry Pompey. Caesar himself married, as his third wife, Calpurnia, a daughter of one of Pompey's friends.

GAUL

Caesar took his station in southern Gaul and waited for his chance for military glory. He had not long to wait. The Rhine River divided the tribes of Gaul in the west from German-speaking tribes in the east, and the latter were on the move.

One of the German tribal chieftains, Ariovistus (ar"ee-oh-vis'tus), crossed the Rhine in 60 B.C. and conquered large areas of Gaul. In 58 B.C., the Gallic tribe of the Helvetii (hel-vee'shee-igh) determined to get out of the way of Ariovistus by leaving its home (in modern Switzerland) and migrating to the shores of the Atlantic. The Helvetii asked Caesar for permission to travel peacefully through Roman territory.

Caesar took the attitude that an invasion by nearly 400,000 wild Gauls could not be allowed. By quick marches and daring tactics, he defeated the Helvetii and virtually wiped them out at a battle near the modern Autun, a hundred miles west of Switzerland. The luxurious man of pleasure showed himself quite capable of living hard and dangerously and of handling men with great sureness and competence.

The Gallic tribes now asked Caesar for help against Ariovistus. This was exactly what Caesar wanted. He sent messages to Ariovistus in a deliberately arrogant tone, forcing Ariovistus to be arrogant in return. In no time at all, they were exchanging threats. Caesar marched northward and in a battle near the modern Besançon, a hundred miles northeast of Autun, defeated Ariovistus and drove him back across the Rhine. Caesar played the role of the protector and patron of the tribes of central Gaul from then on.

Caesar was satisfied with the results of his summer of campaigning and during the winter retired to Cisalpine Gaul. In fact, he did this in each succeeding winter that the Gallic War lasted, since in that way he could remain in close touch with the situation in Rome.

This annual retirement from Gaul made the task of conquering the area difficult. Whatever Caesar's victories in the summer (and his generalship continued to be brilliant) the stubborn Gauls always broke loose in one area or another during the winter, when Caesar was absent.

In 57 B.C. Caesar fought in northern Gaul and forced the submission of almost the whole area. In 56 B.C. the tribes of what is now Brittany, the northwestern corner of Gaul, rose and Caesar crushed them and sold them wholesale into slavery.

In 55 B.C., there was a new invasion of Germans from across the Rhine. Caesar went to meet them and held a conference with them in the territory of what is now Belgium. In an act of bad faith, he seized the German leaders. He then attacked the German hordes who were unprepared for battle, since they were under the illusion that there was a truce in force while their leaders conferred with Caesar.

Having wiped out the German army, Caesar bridged the Rhine and led his army a small way into Germany. He did not intend to try to conquer the land. He merely wanted to display Roman power and keep the Germans quiet.

Caesar next made an even more daring move. Help had reached the Gallic rebels from the island of Britain lying to the north of Gaul (an island which in this way first enters the current of history). Caesar felt a demonstration in that direction would be helpful. In the late summer of 55 B.C., he made a short thrust across the channel into what is now Kent, at the southwestern tip of Britain. There was some skirmishing and the Romans left.

The next year (having had his assignment to Gaul renewed for five more years) Caesar made a more serious attempt in this direction. His army landed in Britain again and was countered by the natives under Cassivelaunus (kas″ih-veh-loh′nus). Caesar penetrated far inland with five legions, crossing the Thames River and defeating Cassivelaunus about twenty miles north of the stream. Cassivelaunus was forced to agree to the payment of an annual tribute, and Caesar then returned to Gaul.

Actually, nothing much was accomplished by this expedition into Britain, except for the dramatic exhibition of Roman power farther north than ever before. Cassivelaunus never paid his tribute and no additional Roman soldiers appeared in Britain for another century.

In 53 B.C., Caesar made another gesture across the Rhine, and then in 52 B.C. the tribes of central Gaul, tired of Roman rule and of the hardships involved in being protected by Cae-

sar, flared into dangerous revolt yet again, this time under Vercingetorix (ver″sin-jet′oh-riks). Caesar, caught flat-footed in
Cisalpine Gaul, had to hasten to the scene at breakneck speed,
slipping past Vercingetorix's army to join his own. Then, after
particularly hard fighting and some dangerous repulses, Caesar
finally crushed this last revolt. By 50 B.C., all Gaul was quiet.
Caesar declared it a Roman province, and from thenceforward
for nearly five hundred years it was to remain a valuable part
of the Roman dominion.

Caesar had his military glory, for all Rome rang with his
dramatic exploits. To make sure they did, Caesar wrote a book,
*Commentaries on the Gallic Wars*, in clear and polished prose.
He spoke of himself in the third person and managed to put
across a feeling of objectivity and impartiality, but no one could
read the book without feeling the force of Caesar's genius. And,
of course, that was exactly what Caesar intended.

PARTHIA

The eight years that Caesar spent in Gaul were busy ones
in Rome too. As soon as Caesar had left for Gaul, the senatorial
conservatives began to make headway. For one thing, Cato
came back from his governorship of Cyprus, bringing with him
a large quantity of money that he had gathered legally and
that he deposited in the city treasury without filching any of it.
(He was the only Roman who wouldn't have filched it, and the
populace knew it.)

Cato at once began to oppose the triumvirate and Caesar in
particular. When Caesar, in 55 B.C., had captured the German
leaders and destroyed their forces by treachery, Cato rose to
denounce him as soon as the news reached Rome. He even
suggested that Roman honor would not be cleared until Caesar

was handed over to the Germans. However, the Roman people were willing to overlook treachery as long as it was practiced on the enemy.

Furthermore, Clodius had gone too far in his persecution of Cicero. Cicero's tearful letters from abroad roused sympathy, as did the fact that Clodius had burnt down Cicero's villa and had persecuted Cicero's wife and children.

The friends of Cicero in the senate began to maneuver to have him brought back from exile. With the help of Pompey (who had always been friendly to Cicero) this was done, and in 57 B.C. Cicero was back in Rome.

Next the senate moved to neutralize the power of Clodius. Clodius had won great popularity with the poor by supervising the distribution of free grain, but his chief strength lay in his gang of bullies, drawn from among the gladiators.

The senate fought fire with fire. One of the tribunes most active in forcing the recall of Cicero was Titus Annius Milo Papinianus, who was married to a daughter of Sulla. This Milo organized a gang of gladiators of his own, and from then on Rome was made hideous by the continuous fighting of these rival gangs. Ordinary citizens cowered in fear as these groups (for all the world like modern gangsters) took over the city.

Finally, in 52 B.C., the two gangs happened to meet unexpectedly, with Milo and Clodius at their heads. In the "rumble" that followed, Clodius was killed.

This was the signal for virtual anarchy in Rome. The followers of Clodius howled in rage. Milo was brought to trial, and Cicero, naturally, defended him. The wild mob and the hostile soldiers lining the Forum scared poor Cicero into voicelessness. He could deliver only a weak mumble of a speech. Milo was convicted and sent into exile.

Still, with Clodius gone, the situation had improved for the conservatives. They had long since recognized their mistake in humiliating Pompey upon his return from Asia and had repented of it. They had come to realize that there had been no reason to treat Pompey in that manner, since he was not the kind of man who could have taken over Rome. If he had been kept friendly to the senate, he might have been used by the conservatives against Caesar, who (the senators now realized) was indeed just the kind of man who could take over Rome.

Perhaps it was not too late. Pompey had been watching Caesar's triumphs in Gaul and had turned a bright green with envy. It was, after all, Pompey who was supposed to be the great general, not Caesar.

Caesar was perfectly aware that his successes would rouse the envy of Pompey, and of Crassus, too, and that he would have to try to appease his two associates. In 56 B.C. Caesar met with Pompey and Crassus in Luca — the modern Lucca — at the southern boundary of Cisalpine Gaul.

It was arranged that Pompey and Crassus would be consuls for 55 B.C. Furthermore, Pompey and Crassus could have some military glory for themselves if they wished. Caesar would take Gaul for five more years, but Pompey could have Spain and Crassus could have Syria.

This suited Crassus well. Where Pompey had gained great glory in Asia and Caesar was gaining great glory in Gaul, Crassus had only a victory over slaves to boast of. Crassus felt he now had a chance to show what he could really do. Furthermore, the rich and gorgeous East was exactly where he could most easily increase his already enormous wealth. There was no specific provision in the agreement that Crassus was to make war, but it was perfectly understood that he was going east to engage in a military triumph.

As for Pompey, the new agreement suited him well, too. He did not go to Spain, where conditions were quiet, but sent lieutenants instead. He remained in Rome, where he could keep at the center of things. If anything happened to either Crassus or Caesar, or both, Pompey imagined he would be ready to seize the advantage.

While he was alone in Rome, with the other two triumvirs

gone, he was also a sitting duck for the scheming conservatives. The new agreement, and his love for Caesar's daughter, kept Pompey loyal to Caesar for a while. Unfortunately, Julia died in 54 B.C. at the age of about thirty and the strongest bond between two of the triumvirs was gone.

And then came dramatic news from the East —

Crassus had sailed eastward only after considerable opposition. The senate did not want to see the third of the triumvirate also become a military hero. Then, too, many of the more superstitious Romans felt that it would be unlucky to engage in war without provocation. Throughout their history the Romans had always waited for some excuse, however flimsy, before making war, and Crassus was not going to wait for one. There were even attempts to stop Crassus's departure by force, but they failed, and Crassus set forth.

At the time Crassus left, the Romans already controlled all those sections of Asia that were Greek in language and culture — Asia Minor and Syria.

Stretching eastward beyond those lands were vast tracts that had once belonged to the Persian Empire and that had been conquered by Alexander the Great. For a century and a half after Alexander's death, those areas had remained under the gradually weakening control of the Seleucid Empire, but Greek culture had never struck permanent roots out there.

About 250 B.C., the native tribesmen of the region southeast of the Caspian Sea revolted against the Seleucids and set up a kingdom which, after some ups and downs, finally took control of the territory making up modern Iran. By 140 B.C. they had conquered Mesopotamia (the modern Iraq) from the Seleucids and confined that shrinking Empire to Syria.

The eastern kingdom — called Parthia, a form of the word "Persia" — stretched out further eastward in 130 B.C., to take over the region now included in Afghanistan and to stretch its borders to India itself. In the west, Mithradates of Pontus and Tigranes of Armenia put a stop to Parthian expansion, but with the defeat of those monarchs by Rome that western wall had been badly weakened.

Parthia had thus become a major power and a threat to Rome. Indeed, in 64 B.C. the Parthian monarch, Phraates II (frah-ay'-teez), defeated Tigranes, who had just become a Roman ally. However, Pompey, who was then in Syria, sent ambassadors to settle the matter and save the Armenian king.

After the death of Phraates, two sons contested the throne and one of them, Orodes (oh-roh'deez), had just won a final victory and established himself as the Parthian king, when Crassus arrived. Crassus intended to take advantage of the confusion resulting from this Parthian civil war to conquer the land. There are even hints that his view extended farther to include fabled India, which lay beyond Parthia.

In 54 B.C. Crassus raided Mesopotamia and met with little resistance. He left garrisons in some of the chief places and returned to Syria to plan the main expedition in the following year. In the spring of 53 B.C., he led seven legions across the Euphrates River, penetrating over a hundred miles inland from the Mediterranean.

It was his intention to follow the course of the river to Ctesiphon (tes'ih-fon), the Parthian capital. However, Crassus was guided by an Arabian chieftain, who, apparently, was secretly in the pay of the Parthians.

Crassus let himself be persuaded by the Arab to strike still farther eastward, away from the river and into desert regions. The Parthian army was waiting near Carrhae (kar'ee), a city whose older name was Haran — where the Biblical patriarch, Abraham, had lived for some years during his migration from Ur of the Chaldees to Canaan.

The Parthian army was strong in cavalry, who were particularly skillful in the use of the bow. They would come raiding in on thundering hooves, doing as much damage as they could, then veer off in flight. And as the opposing army then lunged forward in pursuit, each Parthian horseman would rise in his saddle and send an arrow speeding backward over his shoulder. The unprepared enemy would often be thrown into confusion by this sudden and unexpected blow. It is for that reason that the phrase "Parthian shot" has come to mean any damaging last-minute blow, either in word or deed.

Crassus lacked the ability to adjust his strategy to meet the requirements of the situation. Pompey might have; Caesar certainly would have; but Crassus could not. He fought the battle according to the strict Roman rules of war, as though he were fighting Spartacus' army of rebelling slaves again.

Crassus's son led the Roman cavalry in an attempt to drive off the Parthians, but failed and was killed. A party of mocking Parthians came swooping down toward the main Roman army, but not to fight — not at that moment. At the end of one spear was the head of Crassus's son.

It had a chilling effect on the army, although Crassus rose to unexpected heights of Roman bravery by crying out to the army, "Be not disheartened. This is my loss, not yours!"

But it was the army's loss, too, for they were gradually being cut to pieces, and when Crassus tried to negotiate a truce, the Parthians killed him, and what was left of the army had to fight its way back to Syria.

There is a story that the head of Crassus was brought to the Parthian king who ordered molten gold to be poured into the mouth. "Here," he said, "you have been greedy for this all your life. Eat it now." (This sounds as though it were made up by the Roman historians to point a moral.)

The Romans did not know it at the time, of course, but the defeat of Crassus at Carrhae marked a turning point in their history. Until then, Roman defeats, even great ones at the hands of men such as Pyrrhus, Hannibal and Mithradates, had always been avenged. The Roman enemies were eventually defeated in their turn and, in the end, their homelands — Epirus, Carthage, Pontus — were absorbed into the Roman dominion.

Not so in the case of Parthia. The Romans were to defeat them on a number of occasions, but they were never to conquer the land. Parthia remained the permanent eastern limit against which Roman expansion came to a halt. It is interesting then that the Battle of Carrhae (53 B.C.) took place in 700 A.U.C., just seven centuries after the founding of Rome.

# 10

# CAESAR

## THE SECOND CIVIL WAR

The destruction of Crassus and his army in 53 B.C., left Pompey and Caesar alone. Caesar, however, was still in Gaul and about to face the most serious Gallic uprising of all. Pompey, on the other hand, was in Rome and making the most of it.

He did nothing to try to stop the increasing anarchy in the streets, perhaps because he was waiting for the time to be ripe for him to step in as dictator. If so, that time came after the gangland-style killing of Clodius. In the disorders that followed, the senate called in Pompey as sole consul in 52 B.C.

Under Pompey, order was restored and the senate set about persuading him to serve as their protection against the redoubtable Caesar. Pompey was easily persuaded by now. He had married a new wife, the daughter of one of the chiefs of the senatorial conservatives and he proceeded to make his father-in-law his fellow consul. This openly placed him on the side of the senate and the break with Caesar was final.

The next step was to reduce Caesar to harmlessness. If he could be removed from office, he could be prosecuted for something or other. (Any Roman general or governor could be prosecuted for something — and usually he was guilty of the charge, whatever it was.) Caesar could see what was coming, however, and managed to arrange matters so that he would keep his province through 49 B.C. and then immediately take over as consul, with no time in between in which he would be out of office and available for prosecution.

Pompey then made use of the Parthian disaster as a device with which to destroy Caesar. The war with Parthia was obviously a serious one and the senate decreed, in 50 B.C., that each of the commanders give up a legion for use in that war. Pompey had, at an earlier time, lent Caesar one of the legions under Pompey's control. He now demanded it back from Caesar as his own contribution to the Parthian war, and a second, in addition, to serve as Caesar's contribution.

Fortunately, Gaul had now been conquered and Caesar could afford to part with two legions. Stifling his resentment, he did so. The senate took this for weakness, and Pompey assured them that even though the army assigned to him was in Spain, they had nothing to fear from Caesar. "I have but to stamp my foot upon the ground," he said, "and legions will rise up to support us."

The conservatives were heartened, therefore, to take the final step. On January 7, 49 B.C., the senate issued an order that unless Caesar disbanded his army altogether and entered Rome as a private citizen (as Pompey had once done) he would be declared an outlaw.

Of course, when Pompey had given up his army, there was no enemy band waiting in Rome to have him exiled or, possibly, executed. Caesar well knew he could not disband his army. Yet what was the alternative?

Fortunately for Caesar he had strong partisans in Rome, as well as enemies. One of these friends of Caesar was Marcus Antonius, better known in English as Mark Antony. He had been born about 83 B.C. His father had died while he was quite young, and he was brought up by a foster-father who was later ordered to be executed by Cicero as one of the conspirators of Catiline. As a result, Mark Antony nourished an undying hatred for Cicero. In 54 B.C., he joined Caesar (to whom he was related on his mother's side) in Gaul and became one of the most loyal of the pro-Caesar group. He returned to Rome in 52 B.C. and in 49 B.C. was serving as tribune.

As tribune, Mark Antony now took the action most calculated to help Caesar. He and his fellow tribune, having opposed the outlawing action, claimed that they were in danger of their lives and fled to Caesar's camp in Cisalpine Gaul.

That gave Caesar his perfect excuse. The tribunes were calling upon Caesar to protect them against death at the hand of the senators. Surely Caesar was bound to take action to protect the tribunes, the sacred representatives of the people. The senate might call it treason, but Caesar knew the common people would consider it the right action.

On January 10, Caesar made his decision. That night he crossed the Rubicon River, which divided his province of Cisalpine Gaul from Italy, and by that action he started the Second Civil War. (The first had been between Marius and Sulla.) Ever since, the phrase "crossing the Rubicon" has been used to apply to any action that forces some crucial decision. As Caesar crossed, he is supposed to have muttered, "The die is cast" — another phrase now used for the same purpose.

It was time, then, for Pompey to stamp his feet and get his legions, but he had fooled himself and the senate badly. He was no longer the conqueror of the East and the darling of the

Romans. He hadn't been that for a long time. His stay in Rome
for a dozen years, during which time he had been consistently
outsmarted by Caesar, and outbid for popularity by the handsome and unscrupulous Clodius, had left him a back number.

When Caesar and his grim legions, fresh from their victories
in Gaul, hastened southward, Pompey found his own soldiers
deserting and joining the charming Caesar. There was nothing
for him to do but retreat quickly — run at top speed was more
like it — with Caesar chasing after.

By a hair, Pompey managed to make it across the staits to
Greece, and with him went the aristocracy of Rome, including
most of the senators.

Within three months of having crossed the Rubicon, Caesar
was in control of all of Italy. It was necessary for him now to
sweep up the Pompeian armies overseas. He hastened to Spain
where at Ilerda (ih-lur'duh), the modern Lerida, he met the
legions who were under senatorial control.

There Caesar maneuvered like a ballet dancer, keeping the
Pompeians off-balance and finally cutting them off from their
water supply. The two armies fraternized — after all, why
should Roman fight Roman? — and in no time at all, Caesar
had done better than destroy an enemy. He made friends and
doubled his own forces. Hastening home, he accepted the surrender of Massilia on the southern coast of Gaul. Western Europe was clear.

In Africa things did not go so well. There the Pompeian
forces under Juba, king of Numidia, managed to win out over
Caesar's representatives. (Caesar was not there personally.)

But Africa would have to wait for the moment. Caesar had
himself elected consul for 48 B.C. and made ready to attack the
Pompeian forces in their stronghold in Greece, where Pompey
himself was to be found. Ignoring the fact that Pompey had
managed to gather a large army, and also a fleet, Caesar crossed
over from the Italian heel straight into the port of Dyrrhachium
(dih-ray'kee-um) — the modern Durres, chief port of Albania.

Dyrrhachium was under the control of the Pompeians, and Caesar placed it under siege. Here, however, he made a mistake. At any rate, Pompey's fleet showed up, the town gave no signs of surrendering, and Caesar, finding his army pushed back and cut off from its base, realized that his one course was to disengage.

In fact, if Pompey had taken firm action and attacked Caesar's besieging army more briskly, he might have won then and there. He did not, however. He was slow, where Caesar was always prompt and decisive. Caesar tore away and moved farther into Greece.

Again Pompey lost a chance. With Caesar disappearing into Greece, Pompey would have done well to descend like lightning upon Italy itself. Unfortunately for him, he (and even more so the young aristocrats that filled his army) was breathing fire and slaughter against Caesar personally. Pompey wanted to meet Caesar and defeat him in order to show the world which one of them was the great general.

Pompey therefore left Cato at Dyrrhachium with some of the army, and with the main forces, pursued Caesar. He caught up with him at the town of Pharsalus (fahr-say'lus) in Thessaly, on June 29, 48 B.C.

Pompey's army still outnumbered Caesar's by better than two to one, and Pompey was confident of victory. He might have starved Caesar into submission, but he wanted the glory of a battle fought and won, and the senatorial group with him wanted it even more.

Pompey was counting on his cavalry in particular; a cavalry consisting of gallant young Roman aristocrats. Sure enough, at the start of the battle, Pompey's cavalry charged round the end of Caesar's army and might well have wreaked havoc from the rear and cost Caesar the battle. Caesar, however, had foreseen this and had placed some picked men to meet them with instructions not to throw their lances but to use them to poke directly at the faces of the horsemen. He estimated that the

aristocrats would not stand up to the danger of being disfig-
ured, and he was right. The cavalry broke.

Moreover, Caesar's hardened infantry attacked the enemy's
superior numbers and broke through. Pompey had not yet lost,
but he was used only to victories over weak foes and had no
training in having to change apparent defeat into victory
(something Caesar had had to do a number of times). Pompey
fled, and with that, the army collapsed and Caesar had the
complete victory.

In this way, it was indeed decided who was the great general, but the decision was not as Pompey had expected it would
be.

EGYPT

With the loss of the battle, Pompey's forces all over Greece
and Asia Minor melted away, as officers hastened to join the
side of the winner. Pompey, left helpless, had to get away
quickly and escape to some area not ruled by Rome. Only
when he was off Roman soil altogether would he feel safe.

There was but one such area in the eastern Mediterranean
and that was Egypt.

Egypt was the last remaining Macedonian kingdom. In it,
the line of the Ptolemies still ruled, chiefly because they had
formed an alliance with Rome immediately after the time of
Pyrrhus and had maintained that alliance ever since. At no
time did the Ptolemies give Rome cause to be offended.

From 323 B.C. to 221 B.C. the first three Ptolemies, who were
capable men, kept Egypt strong and well-governed. After that,
however, came a series of rulers who were either children, or
incapable, or both. The land remained rich, for the Nile River
was a guarantee that there were always good harvests, but
government grew weak and inefficient.

On several occasions, the Romans stepped in to prevent part or all of Egypt from falling into the hands of the more capable Seleucids, until the Seleucid Empire itself weakened to the point where it was no longer a threat. Rome eventually annexed some of Egypt's outlying territories, such as Cyrene and the island of Cyprus, but even in 48 B.C. Egypt remained essentially intact. Its large and populous capital, Alexandria, rivaled Rome in size, and was far its superior in culture and science.

Of course, the Egyptian rulers were nothing more than Roman puppets and Pompey expected good treatment, since a recent Ptolemy had received particular favors at his hand. This was Ptolemy XI, commonly called Auletes (oh-lee′teez) meaning "flute-player," since that seems to have been his only talent.

Ptolemy Auletes had been claiming the throne ever since 80 B.C., but he needed Roman backing. He finally managed to supply enough Romans with large enough bribes to receive the necessary support in 59 B.C. He had spent so much money, however, that he had to raise the taxes. The enraged populace promptly kicked him off the throne, and in 58 B.C. he was in Rome trying to get the Romans to restore him.

In the end, he managed to get Pompey's aid (with the help of huge bribes to some of Pompey's lieutenants) and was restored to the throne in 55 B.C. For this reason, Pompey felt the Egyptian royal house ought to be indebted to him.

To be sure, Ptolemy Auletes had died in 51 B.C., but his young son was on the throne as Ptolemy XII, and Auletes in his will had left the young king under the guardianship of the Roman senate, which then assigned the task to Pompey. The boy-king of Egypt was therefore Pompey's ward and ought, reasoned Pompey, to greet his guardian joyfully. Pompey sailed for Egypt, expecting to be able to collect troops and money there and to make use of Egypt as a base from which to rebuild his fortunes in Rome.

But Egypt was itself in chaos at the time. The young king was only thirteen years old, and by his father's will he ruled together with his twenty-one-year-old sister, Cleopatra. Of course, the king was too young to rule, and a courtier named Pothinus (poh-thy'nus) was the power behind the throne.

Pothinus found himself at odds with Cleopatra who, although a woman and young, was the ablest of all the later Ptolemies. Intending to seize control of Egypt, Cleopatra fled the capital and assembled an army, so that Egypt was in the middle of a civil war herself when Pompey's ship appeared off Alexandria.

Pothinus was now in quite a pickle. He needed Roman help against Cleopatra, but how could he get that Roman help safely when he didn't know which Roman general was going to be the one who would survive in the end? If he refused to let Pompey land, Pompey might find refuge elsewhere and someday come back to visit slaughter on Egypt out of revenge. On the other hand, if he let Pompey land, Caesar might follow and, if he won, *he* would visit slaughter on Egypt.

The wily Pothinus thought of a way out. A boat was sent to Pompey's ship. Pompey was greeted with great gladness and asked to come personally to shore, where all sorts of people waited for him. Then, when Pompey stepped ashore (and while his wife and son watched from the ship) he was stabbed and killed.

Pompey was dead now, so he could never take revenge against Egypt. Caesar would be grateful for the death of his enemy, so he would not have cause for revenge against Egypt. Therefore, Pothinus reasoned, Egypt was safe.

But meanwhile Caesar was chasing after Pompey. He did not want to leave him at large to serve as a center for new armies and more fighting. In addition, he needed money and Egypt was an excellent place to get it. With only 4,000 men he arrived at Alexandria only a few days after Pompey's death.

Quickly, the Egyptians trotted out Pompey's head in order to show their loyalty to Caesar and earn his gratitude. To their surprise Caesar was upset at the sight of the head of his one-time associate and son-in-law, killed by treachery after a life which — until his violation of the temple at Jerusalem — had been filled with such glory.

After this, Caesar might well have collected some money and left, but Pothinus felt that as long as Caesar was there he might as well see to it that Ptolemy XII was firmly placed on the throne and that the rebellion of his sister, Cleopatra, be brought to an end.

Caesar might have gone along with this, after exacting the customary payment, not caring which Ptolemy ruled in Egypt.

Here, however, the intelligence of Cleopatra interposed itself. She had an advantage that Pothinus did not have, for she was young and beautiful. If she could only talk to Caesar she was sure she could persuade him to see her side of the story. She set sail from Syria (her temporary headquarters), landed in Alexandria, and managed to have a large carpet delivered to Caesar. Pothinus's forces saw no reason to stop the delivery, for they did not know that wrapped in the carpet was Cleopatra herself.

Her guess was perfectly correct, too. Once Caesar had had a good heart-to-heart talk with the beautiful girl, he decided she was a fine person and would make an excellent queen. He therefore ordered the original arrangement to be restored, with Cleopatra and her young brother serving as joint monarchs.

This did not at all suit Pothinus. Pothinus knew that Egypt couldn't possibly win a war against Rome, but it might win a war against Caesar. Caesar was present with only a tiny force and he could be overwhelmed by the large Egyptian army. Once Caesar was dead, the anti-Caesar faction in Rome could seize control and surely they would then have only praise and gratitude for Pothinus.

He therefore stirred up a rebellion against Caesar, and for three months Caesar maintained himself only by personal bravery and by the skill with which he handled his few troops. But Pothinus was not helped by the Alexandrian War he had fomented, for Caesar had him seized and executed. In the course of this small war, the famous library of Alexandria was badly damaged.

Finally, however, reinforcements reached Caesar and the Egyptians were defeated in battle. In the flight that followed, the young Ptolemy XII tried to escape on a barge on the Nile River. The barge was too heavily loaded, and it sank. That was the end of him.

Caesar could now settle affairs in Egypt. He had grown friendlier and friendlier with Cleopatra and was determined to keep her on the throne. However, a queen had to have some sort of male associate, and for that purpose Caesar made use of Ptolemy XII's (and Cleopatra's) younger brother. He was only ten years old at the time he was made joint king with Cleopatra under the title of Ptolemy XIII.

It was high time, too, that the settlement was made, for affairs were dragging Caesar elsewhere. New disorders were breaking out in Asia Minor.

North of the Black Sea there still lived Pharnaces (fahr'nuh-seez), the son of Mithradates of Pontus, Rome's old enemy. Pharnaces had rebelled against his father in 63 B.C., causing the old man to kill himself. He had then submitted to Pompey, who allowed him to retain rule over the regions north of the Black Sea (the modern peninsula of Crimea.)

Pharnaces remained loyal to Pompey during the years that followed, but could not resist taking advantage of the civil war by invading Pontus in an effort to regain his family's lost dominions. In the process, he defeated a Roman army under one of Caesar's underlings.

Caesar marched into Asia Minor in 47 B.C. and met Pharnaces at Zela (zee'luh), a town on the western border of Pontus. The battle was brief and one-sided. Pharnaces' men broke and fled and that was the end of that. It was the last gasp of Pontus, and Caesar sent a brief message to Rome, clearly indicating the rapidity of the victory: "Veni, vidi, vici" ("I came, I saw, I conquered").

Following the campaign against Pharnaces, Caesar finally returned to Rome after an absence of more than a year.

He had not left Rome unattended, of course. Mark Antony (Caesar's second in command at the battle of Pharsalus) had been sent back to Rome while Caesar himself went on to Egypt. Mark Antony kept Rome safe enough, though he lacked Caesar's ability and was far too rash to keep things going smoothly, especially when rumors began to spread that Caesar had died in Egypt. The best Mark Antony could do was use his soldiers to slaughter some of the Roman citizenry when things got too unruly.

Caesar's return, however, meant a sure hand at the controls once more. To the surprise of many, he didn't follow the usual technique of executing many men and rewarding his followers with their property. Instead, he practiced mildness and in that way won over the hearts of many who had opposed him.

Cicero was a case in point. He had had a long-standing friendship with Pompey, but in the months during which the conflict between Caesar and Pompey was gathering steam, Cicero could not make up his mind what to do.

In the end, however, he left Italy with Pompey's forces, displaying thereby such uncertainty and timidity that he was a drag on Pompey rather than a help. After the battle of Pharsalus, he had had enough and returned to Italy.

Caesar might have had Cicero executed; no one would have been surprised and it would have fitted the times. After all, Cicero had lent Pompey money and the influence of his name. What's more, Antony, who hated Cicero, undoubtedly tried to sway Caesar in the direction of strong action.

Nevertheless, Caesar treated Cicero with kindness and

showed him every respect. In return, Cicero displayed no open hostility to Caesar or his policies.

Yet Caesar's mildness caused him some trouble. One of his legions rebelled because they had been promised all kinds of rewards which weren't coming through. (Perhaps they had expected enrichment as a result of executions they could see were not coming to pass.) They marched to Rome to press their demands personally.

Caesar approached the rebelling legion alone and unattended, as though daring them to do him violence. They watched this man who had led them safely through so many dangers, and for a moment there was breathless silence.

Then Caesar said, with contempt, "You are discharged, citizens."

At hearing the term "citizens," the military pride of the legion was touched. They begged to be restored to Caesar's favor and the title of soldier, and were willing to be punished if only they might be kept in the army. (It was a sad mark of the decline in the Roman way of life that the once-proud term of "citizen" had become an insult.)

Nor were Caesar's military labors done. Although Pompey was defeated and dead, the Pompeian party still had an army at Dyrrhachium, with Cato at their head. They still had a considerable supply of money, and they had a fleet. Moreover they had defeated Caesar's troops in Africa so that they had a land base from which to operate.

Cato took his force to Africa and joined them with those of Juba of Numidia. Before long, the equivalent of ten legions were concentrated at Utica, a town fifteen miles northwest of the spot where Carthage had once existed. Juba had brought with him 120 elephants, and Gnaeus Pompeius, Pompey's eldest son, brought the fleet. It was a respectable force, and the Pompeians had a decent chance of turning the tide.

Nevertheless, once again they lost their best chance through delay. They might have taken advantage of Caesar's entrapment in Alexandria and his absence in Asia Minor; they might have mounted an invasion of Italy. Unfortunately for itself, the African army spent most of its time waiting for its leaders to finish squabbling among themselves, since of them all, only Cato was in it for anything more than personal power.

The army was still in Africa when Caesar finally sailed to attack it. The opposing forces met at Thapsus about 100 miles south of Utica, on February 4, 46 B.C. Many of Caesar's men were recruits and he wasn't certain of their steadiness. He therefore tried to hold them back, seeking to wage battle only at the best possible moment. However, his troops would not be restrained but roared into action without any word from him, and carried all before them. The enemy elephants, stung by arrows, fled back through their own ranks, spreading additional confusion. It was a complete victory for Caesar.

When the remnants of the defeated army returned to Utica, Cato tried to persuade them to reorganize for the defense of the city, but there was no heart left in them. Cato therefore arranged to have the ships of the navy carry them to Spain. His family and friends expected he would follow, but he had given up at last and that night he committed suicide.

Juba also committed suicide, and the kingdom of Numidia, which had once been ruled over by Massinissa and by Jugurtha, came to an end. The eastern portion was annexed to Rome as part of the Province of Africa and the western portion was added to Mauretania, a nominally independent kingdom which had remained allied to Caesar.

Caesar returned to Rome again, more powerful than ever. After Pharsalus, he had been made consul for a five year term and each year he was elected dictator, too. Now, after Thapsus, he was made dictator for a ten year term.

In July 46 B.C., Caesar celebrated four successive triumphs in Rome on four successive days in honor of his victories over the Gauls, the Egyptians, the Pontines and the Numidians.

After that, it was time for one last battle, for the Pompeians still fought on in Spain under Gnaeus Pompeius. Caesar took his legions to Spain and on March 15, 45 B.C., a battle took place at Munda. The Pompeians fought remarkably well, and Caesar's forces were driven back. For a time indeed, Caesar must have thought that years of victory were going to be brought to ruin in one last battle, as in the case of Hannibal. So desperate was he that he seized a shield and sword himself, rushed into the battle, shouting to his retreating men, "Are you going to let your general be delivered up to the enemy?"

Stung into action, they lunged forward once more and carried the day. The last Pompeian army was wiped out. Gnaeus Pompeius escaped from the field of battle, but was pursued, caught, and killed.

Caesar remained in Spain some months, reorganizing the country, then returned to Rome and in October of 45 B.C. celebrated one last triumph. He was appointed dictator for life, and there was no question but that he intended at some convenient time to make himself king.

Most of the period during which Caesar was supreme in Rome saw him engaged in warfare against his enemies. He was in Rome, however, from June to September of 46 B.C. and from October 45 B.C. to March 44 B.C., a total of eight months altogether. During that time, he worked feverishly on the reorganization and reform of the government.

Caesar had the vision to see that Rome's wide realm could not be ruled by the city of Rome itself. He increased the senate to 900 members and included many men from the provinces among the new senators. This weakened the conservatives, since the senate no longer represented merely the narrow interests of a tightly-bound oligarchy. But it strengthened the Roman realm generally, since the provinces were given some voice in the government. Caesar tried to help the provinces in another way, too, by reforming the system of taxation.

Caesar was the first to spread Roman citizenship beyond Italy itself. All of Cisalpine Gaul was awarded the citizenship and so were a number of cities in Gaul itself and in Spain. Caesar was especially considerate of scholars, who were given a chance to gain the citizenship whatever their place of origin, and he planned to grant citizenship to the Sicilians, though time ran out for him before he could carry that through.

He began the reconstruction of Carthage and Corinth, the two cities destroyed by Rome a century before, populating the former with Romans, the latter with Greeks.

He tried to reorganize and make more efficient the system by which free grain was distributed to qualified citizens. He tried to encourage marriage and children by granting mothers permission to wear additional ornaments and granting fathers tax-relief. He opened Rome's first public library; he had huge plans (which he did not live to carry through) for mapping the whole Roman realm, for draining marshes and improving harbors, for reorganizing the law codes, and so on.

His most enduring reform was that of the calendar. Until 46 B.C. the Roman calendar had been governed by the moon by a system that, according to legend, dated back to Numa Pompilius. Twelve lunar months (counting a month as extending 29½ days from new moon to new moon) make up only 354 days. Each lunar year falls 11 days behind the solar year of a little over 365 days, so that the months gradually fall out of their proper seasons.

In order to allow planting, harvest, and other agricultural activities to fall in the same month every year, it was necessary to insert an additional month into the year every once in a while. The Babylonians had invented a complicated system for this that worked quite well and that had been adopted by the Greeks and the Jews.

The Romans did not adopt this system. Instead, they put the control of the calendar in the hands of the Pontifex Maximus (the High Priest; and we still call the Pope the "Pontiff," by the way) who was usually a politician. He could very easily put an extra month in whenever he wanted a long year to keep his own friends in power, or leave it out when he wanted a short year because his enemies were in power.

By 46 B.C., therefore, the Roman calendar was in a state of confusion. It was eighty days behind the sun. The winter months were falling in autumn, the autumn months in summer, and so on.

In Egypt, Caesar had observed the workings of a much better calendar, and something like it was what he wanted. He sought the help of an Egyptian astronomer, Sosigenes (soh-sij'uh-neez) and established the new calendar. First he let 46 B.C. continue for 445 days, adding two months at the end, in order to let the Roman calendar catch up to the sun. (This was the longest year in civilized history and is sometimes referred to as "the Year of Confusion." It should be called "the Last Year of Confusion.")

Beginning with January 1, 45 B.C., the year was given 12 months of 30 or 31 days each (except for February, which the Romans considered an unlucky month and which ended with only 28 days). The total length of the year was 365 days, and the phases of the moon were ignored.

To be sure the actual length of the year is close to 365¼ days. To prevent the calendar from falling a day behind the sun every four years, a "leap year" was established every four years, a year in which an extra day was added as February 29, so that the leap year is 366 days long.

Caesar also altered the date on which the year began, changing it from the traditional March 1 to January 1, for it was on the latter day that the Roman magistrates had always taken office. This change made nonsense out of the names of some of the months. September, October, November, and December contain the Latin words for "seven," "eight," "nine," and "ten" in their names, since they are the seventh, eighth, ninth, and tenth months, respectively, when March begins the year. Under the present system, September is the ninth month, not the seventh, and the others are equally displaced. However, no one seems to mind.

This calendar, called the Julian Calendar in honor of Julius Caesar, has survived ever since with only minor modifications. In addition, the month known to the Romans as "Quintilis" had its name changed to "Julius" in honor of Caesar (it was his birth month), and it is known to us as July.

## THE ASSASSINATION

If we consider what Caesar was trying to do, we can't help but be on his side. After all, a drastic reorganization of Roman government had to be made. The Roman system of government was originally designed to run a small city; it was failing badly when it came to be applied to an area of nearly the size of the United States.

The Roman system had certain elements of democracy, for there were elections for various offices. However, only those present in Rome could vote, and a great deal of the power was in the hands of the senate, which represented the interests of only a narrow class of society.

We might feel it was a pity that the Romans never developed a system of representative government, in which different areas could vote for people who would travel to Rome and represent their interests in a senate of the whole realm. We must, however, remember that this was a time when the fastest means of communication was that of riding a horse. To gather representatives from various parts of the Roman dominions and to keep them informed of the problems and opinions at home would have been an impossible task. In fact, our form of democracy didn't become truly practical for large countries until modern times.

The choice in Roman times was not between monarchy and democracy, therefore, but between efficient and honest government as opposed to inefficient and dishonest government. From the time of the Gracchi onward, Roman government under the senate had become increasingly inefficient and dishonest. What's more, the opposition to the senate consisted very often of conniving or scoundrelly politicians, and both sides made use of mobs in attempting to gain control.

Under the conditions of the time, an efficient and honest government could best be brought about by some one person in charge who was himself efficient and honest and who had sufficient energy and ability to dominate other men and keep them efficient and honest, too — or replace them. (Someone with the power of a strong American president, in other words.)

Julius Caesar wasn't ideal for the purpose; no man would have been ideal; but he was one of the most capable men in history and no man in Rome at that time could have done better. There were times in his life when he showed himself to be wasteful or dishonest or treacherous or cruel; but he could also be keen and efficient, mild and forgiving. Above all, he seemed to want to see Rome well-governed, and for that he needed to establish himself in firm power. He saw no other way.

Since he was dictator for life, he did have complete power, but he wanted to be king. There was some sense to that, too. As merely the dictator, his death would be the sign for a new struggle for power; whereas if he were king, he might be succeeded by a son or by some other relative as a matter of course and there would be continued peace. (Of course, the history of the other kingdoms of the time showed that virtually every one of them was riddled with civil war between members of the ruling family, but one could hope this wouldn't be the case among a people so used to being governed by law as the Romans.)

However, the Romans had a horror of the position of king that dated back to the time of the Tarquins. Every Roman child was educated in ancient Roman history, and the story of the Tarquins and the glorious establishment of the Republic produced a permanent bias against kings in his mind. In addition to that, the history of Rome showed that the Republic had triumphed over one eastern kingdom after another. Obviously then, a republican form of government was better than a monarchy.

Secret opposition to Caesar therefore grew after his return from Spain. Some of the opposition came from members of the old senatorial party who saw in Caesar's reforms the destruction of the old system which they felt had made Rome great. Some came from people who dreaded the establishment of a monarch. Some came from people who were jealous of Caesar personally and who resented the fact that someone who had once been just another politician should now be revered and almost worshipped. Indeed, divine honors were beginning to be paid to Caesar, and those who resented a man becoming a king resented his becoming a god even more.

Among those who conspired against Caesar was Marcus Junius Brutus, born about 85 B.C. He was a nephew of Cato the Younger, and he had accompanied Cato to Cyprus when Cato had been forced out of the city by Caesar and Pompey. In Cyprus, Brutus's character didn't show up in a very good light, for he extorted money from the provincials in a most heartless fashion.

It was natural, perhaps, for Cato's nephew to be on the side of Pompey. He accompanied Cato and Pompey to Greece and fought on Pompey's side at the battle of Pharsalus. Brutus was taken prisoner there, but Caesar pardoned and liberated him.

Indeed, before Caesar left for Africa to fight the forces under Cato, he placed Brutus in charge of Cisalpine Gaul. While

Cato committed suicide rather than submit to Caesar, Cato's nephew was doing a good job for Caesar in the Po Valley.

After Caesar returned from Spain, Brutus married his cousin, Porcia, the daughter of Cato, and was appointed by Caesar to high office in Rome itself. He then joined the conspiracy against Caesar, presumably because he was afraid Caesar might make himself king.

It is customary to consider Brutus a high-minded patriot, largely because of Shakespeare's flattering portrait of him in his play *Julius Caesar*. There he is called "the noblest Roman of them all" (meaning of all the rest of the conspirators), for he alone was supposed to have entered into the conspiracy only out of idealism. It would be more impressive, however, if his idealism had shown up a little sooner and if he hadn't accepted pardons and honors at Caesar's hands up to the very last moment.

Another conspirator was Gaius Cassius Longinus. Cassius had accompanied Crassus to Parthia and after the disastrous defeat at Carrhae had brought the remnants of the army back to Syria. Then, when the Parthians invaded Syria in their turn, Cassius defeated them and turned them back.

Cassius sided with Pompey, was in command of a squadron of Pompey's fleet, and won some victories, too. After the battle of Pharsalus, he reconsidered. He went to Asia Minor and, meeting Caesar there on the occasion of the war against Pharnaces, threw himself on the conqueror's mercy. Caesar pardoned him and let him serve under him.

It was apparently Cassius who was the leading spirit in the conspiracy. He had married Junia, the sister of Brutus, and through her approached Brutus and persuaded him to join the conspiracy.

Other conspirators included Decimus Junius Brutus, who had been one of Caesar's generals in Gaul, and who had served as governor of Gaul for a period. Caesar even made him one of his heirs. Still another was Lucius Cornelius Cinna, son and namesake of Marius's co-consul (see page 163) and brother of Caesar's first wife.

By February 44 B.C. (709 A.U.C.), the conspirators felt they had to make haste. Already, Caesar was conducting certain experiments to see how the notion of monarchy might sit with the Roman people. At a certain holiday celebration on February 15, Mark Antony, Caesar's faithful friend, offered him a diadem, or linen headband, which in the East was the symbol of monarchy. At the shocked silence that followed, Caesar pushed it aside and said, "I am not king, but Caesar," and tumultuous applause followed. The try at monarchy had failed.

Nevertheless, the conspirators were certain Caesar would try again — and soon. He was arranging to ship the legions across the Adriatic, perhaps for a campaign against the Parthians. Before Caesar left, he would be sure to have himself declared king, and once he joined his army he would be surrounded by devoted soldiers and it might then prove impossible to kill him.

The senate was convened for March 15 (the "ides of March" on the Roman calendar), and on that day Caesar intended to announce himself king, everyone was certain. All sorts of stories have grown up about the ides of March: that there had been prophetic warnings to Caesar against that day; that his wife, Calpurnia, had bad dreams and begged him not to go, and so on.

Caesar supposedly spent the morning uncertain whether to be swayed by superstition or not, until Decimus Brutus was sent to visit him. Decimus Brutus pointed out how Caesar's prestige would sink if he stayed home, and Caesar, knowing the importance of "face," made up his mind to go.

On his way to the senate house, someone placed a message in his hand telling him of the conspiracy, but Caesar had no chance to look at it. He held it in his hand as he entered the senate.

The conspirators, all of whom were friends of Caesar and

well known to him, managed to surround him as he approached the senate and were all about him when he took his chair at the foot of the statue of Pompey (of all people). Mark Antony, who might have defended Caesar, had deliberately been called aside by one of the conspirators and engaged in conversation. (Some had favored killing him, too, but Marcus Brutus had opposed that as needless bloodshed.)

Caesar was alone, then, when suddenly knives were out. The unarmed Caesar tried desperately to struggle against the savage mass attack until he recognized Marcus Junius Brutus, a particular favorite of his, among the attackers.

"Et tu, Brute?" ("You too, Brutus?") he choked out, and gave up. He was stabbed twenty-three times, and then the dictator of Rome lay dead in a pool of blood at the base of the statue of Pompey.

# 11

# THE END OF THE REPUBLIC

## CAESAR'S HEIR

With Caesar dead, Brutus jumped up, waving his blood-stained knife, and called out to the senators that he had saved Rome from a tyrant. He called on Cicero particularly to take the lead in reorganizing the government.

The city was in a state of paralysis, however, each man expecting nothing but horror and bloodshed to follow. Caesar's backers were too stunned to take immediate action; even Mark Antony sneaked off into hiding.

But when night came, affairs began to move. There were a legion of troops under the command of one of Caesar's loyal generals, Marcus Aemilius Lepidus, son and namesake of the general who had been defeated by Pompey thirty-three years before (see page 170). These troops were brought into Rome, so that the conspirators had to move cautiously.

Meanwhile, Mark Antony had recovered his wits sufficiently to lay his hands on the treasures that Caesar had put aside for the military campaign he had been planning, and to persuade Calpurnia to let him have Caesar's papers.

As for the assassins, they labored to win over Cicero, who decided to go along with them. They then (with one eye on Lepidus's troops) negotiated with Mark Antony, who also seemed to agree to go along with them. Apparently, the danger of civil war was averted.

It was agreed to arrange a compromise. The senate was to ratify all of Caesar's actions so that his reforms would remain. It was also agreed to let Caesar's will, sight unseen, be considered valid. In return, the chief conspirators were assigned provinces that would give them power and take them out of Rome.

After that, there seemed no reason not to allow Caesar a public funeral. Marcus Brutus (against the advice of some of the other conspirators) felt it would be a harmless gesture that would conciliate and console Caesar's admirers.

At the funeral, Mark Antony rose to make an oration. He recited Caesar's great deeds and read Caesar's will, in which his gardens were donated to the use of the public and in which every Roman citizen received a donation worth perhaps $25 in modern money. This example of magnanimity stirred the people deeply.

Mark Antony went on to describe the wounds Caesar had received as reward for all his greatness and generosity, and in no time at all, the audience was clamoring for revenge against the conspirators. Those present who were friends of the conspirators grew anxious and sought safety. Mark Antony was, for the moment, master of Rome.

But coming to Rome was a new personality, a nineteen-year-old youth named Gaius Octavius.

Gaius Octavius was the grandson of Julia, the sister of Julius Caesar, and was therefore the grand-nephew of the dictator.

He was born in 63 B.C., the year of the conspiracy of Catiline. Caesar had no children of his own and Octavius was his logical heir.

Octavius was a sickly youth and was obviously unsuited for war. Nor was his great-uncle anxious to push him into warfare; he needed him alive as an heir. Therefore, when Caesar was making ready to leave on his Parthian campaign, he ordered Octavius to Apollonia, a town south of Dyrrhachium, where he might complete his studies.

He was there when the news of Caesar's assassination reached him and he left immediately for Italy. He had been named as heir in Caesar's will, and that will had been ratified by the senate. Octavius had every intention of demanding that which he felt was coming to him, even though his immediate family thought he would be thrown into dangerous political waters and urged him not to do so.

The arrival of Octavius was distasteful to Mark Antony who considered himself the actual heir in terms of power. He did not wish to share that power with a sickly boy. By the terms of Caesar's will, Octavius had been adopted as Caesar's son, but Mark Antony prevented the ratification of that item by the senate. Nevertheless, Octavius adopted the name Gaius Julius Caesar Octavianus and is commonly known, in English, as Octavian thereafter.

Mark Antony did not have it all his own way, either. Many of the troops were on the side of Octavian if only for the sake of Caesar's name. What's more, Cicero, a sworn enemy of Mark Antony, sided with Octavian (whom he hoped to make use of for his own purposes) and made a series of effective and powerful orations against Mark Antony.

Mark Antony decided it was time to gain popularity through military victories. One by one, the conspirators had left Rome and gone to their respective provinces. Marcus Brutus was in Greece, Cassius in Asia Minor, and Decimus Brutus in Cisalpine Gaul. Decimus Brutus was closest to Rome, and Mark

Antony therefore marked him out as victim. Lepidus had been
sent to Spain to take care of the remnant of Pompeians still to
be found there, but Mark Antony was confident he could take
care of Decimus Brutus alone. He forced the senate to reassign
Cisalpine Gaul to himself and marched northward. Thus began
the Third Civil War.

As soon as Mark Antony left, however, the senate was persuaded by Cicero and the young Octavian to declare Mark
Antony a public enemy, and to send an army against him. This
army was commanded by the two consuls and included Octavian in a secondary command. (Octavian was thus fighting on
behalf of Decimus Brutus, his great-uncle's assassin, and
against Mark Antony, his great-uncle's most loyal associate.
This, however, was only a first step in Octavian's far-sighted
plans. What no one had yet realized was that Caesar's heir,
though no general, was every bit as clever a politician as Caesar
himself had been.)

Decimus Brutus had fortified himself in Mutina (myoo'tih-
nuh), the modern Modena, and could not be dislodged. Mark
Antony, with one enemy inside the city and another outside,
was defeated and, in April 43 B.C., had to lead his army in
retreat across the Alps to southern Gaul where Lepidus was
now stationed, having marched back from Spain.

Everything broke well for Octavian. Not only was Mark Antony deprived of any chance of military glory, but the two Roman consuls died in battle leaving Octavian in command of
the army. He returned to Rome and, with the troops at his back,
had no difficulty in persuading the senate to ratify his position
as Caesar's adopted son and to elect him consul.

Now that he was in effective control of Rome, he could finally
take action against the conspirators. He forced the senate to
declare against the conspirators, and in September he was again
in Cisalpine Gaul, but this time to take Decimus Brutus. He
accomplished what Mark Antony could not. Brutus's soldiers

deserted in droves, so that the conspirator was forced to flee. He was taken in flight, however, and executed.

## THE SECOND TRIUMVIRATE

Meanwhile, Marcus Brutus in Greece and Cassius in Asia Minor were gathering men and money (Cassius was particularly brutal in extorting money out of the helpless provincials) and were quickly becoming formidable. If Octavian and Antony continued to fight each other, both might lose.

Lepidus therefore labored to bring Caesar's old friend and Caesar's heir together. All met in Bononia, the modern Bologna, and agreed to divide the Roman dominions among themselves. In this way, on November 27, 43 B.C., the Second Triumvirate was established, including Mark Antony, Octavian, and Lepidus.

Octavian, by entering into the agreement, had deserted the senate, which was rendered powerless again. In particular, Cicero, who had staked everything on Octavian's backing the orator's eloquent attacks on Antony, could now see that death was certain.

Antony as part of the price for entering the triumvirate demanded the execution of Cicero, and Octavian agreed. Indeed, all three set up a system of proscriptions as in Sulla's day almost forty years earlier. Numerous well-to-do individuals were executed and their property confiscated.

Cicero tried to escape and leave Italy, but contrary winds drove his ship back to shore. Before he could try again, the soldiers sent to kill him had arrived. He refused to allow his men to offer resistance, for that would have been useless. He met his death alone, and bravely.

Oddly enough, Mark Antony also listed Cicero's old enemy, Verres (see page 174), for execution. Verres was still living in comfortable exile in Massilia. Greedy to the end, he refused to surrender some art treasures that the equally greedy Mark Antony desired. Verres paid for this with his worthless life.

With the Second Triumvirate formed, with Italy held firmly and the senatorial party cowed by terror, it was time to face Brutus and Cassius. The army of the triumvirs moved into Greece to meet them. (Octavian fell ill at Dyrrhachium and had to be carried on a litter to the site of the battle.)

The battle was fought at Philippi (fih-lip′igh) in eastern Macedonia, about ten miles north of the Aegean Sea. (Philippi had been first developed and fortified by King Philip of Macedon, the father of Alexander the Great, three centuries earlier, and had been named in his honor.)

The conspirators would have done well to delay, for Antony and Octavian were poorly supplied and might have been starved into retreat or defeat. Cassius advised this, but Brutus could not stand the suspense and wanted the matter decided. In October 42 B.C., a battle was fought in which Brutus had considerable success against Octavian's forces. Cassius did not do as well, however, and killed himself in unreasoning despair over a battle that was actually no worse than a draw.

Brutus was extremely depressed at this news and some weeks later forced a second battle in which he was beaten by superior numbers. He, in turn, committed suicide.

The triumvirs now ruled Rome and perhaps felt it would be best for everyone if they separated. Lepidus received the west and Antony the east, while Octavian was to stay in Rome.

In a way, Antony may have seemed to have the best of matters. The east, despite its continual looting by Roman governors and the demands placed upon it by a long line of Roman generals, could still be squeezed a little and Antony looked forward to loot. In midsummer of 41 B.C., he arrived at Tarsus on the

southern coast of Asia Minor and there he took up the matter
of Egypt, still the richest nation in all the Mediterranean world.

Egypt seemed ripe for the plucking. Since Caesar had placed
Cleopatra and her younger brother in joint possession of the
throne, there had been quiet in Egypt — no wars and no up-
risings.* In 44 B.C. when her younger brother reached his four-
teenth birthday and demanded an active part of the royal
duties, Cleopatra settled matters very neatly by having him
poisoned. After that, she ruled alone.

In the months after the assassination, Cleopatra maintained
a careful neutrality, waiting to see how matters would turn out.
It seemed to Antony, though, that she had been a little
too neutral and that for not having supported the triumvirs
actively she might as well be made to pay heavily. He ordered
the queen of Egypt to attend him at Tarsus, therefore.

Cleopatra came in the royal barge with every intention of
persuading Mark Antony of the rightness of her side of
the story as, seven years before, she had persuaded Caesar of
the same thing. Cleopatra was twenty-eight now and apparently more beautiful than ever.

After some time together, Mark Antony decided that she certainly didn't deserve to be made to pay tribute. Instead, he
decided to return the visit and go to Alexandria with her.
There he had a pleasant time of it, relaxing in the queen's
charming company and forgetting all about the problems of
war and politics.

Back in Italy, Octavian might have been glad to have been
able to do the same. Antony's wife Fulvia (who had been married to Clodius earlier in her life, and who was a rather furious
shrew) was particularly enraged at the situation. She saw quite

---

* There are stories that Caesar took Cleopatra back to Rome
with him and that she stayed there till his assassination, but this
is based on very flimsy evidence and is very unlikely to be true.
It is much more likely that she stayed in Egypt where she belonged.

well that if Octavian was at Rome, it would be he who would finally rule the entire realm. Nor did she approve of Antony's relaxed holiday in Alexandria with Cleopatra.

Fulvia therefore persuaded Lucius Antonius (Mark Antony's brother), who happened to be consul that year, to raise an army and march against Octavian. In that way she hoped to weaken Octavian and to force Mark Antony to take action against him, if only to protect his wife and brother.

Octavian, not much of a soldier, entrusted his army to Marcus Vipsanius Agrippa (uh-grip'uh), a man of obscure family who was Octavian's age and who had studied with Octavian at Apollonia. Agrippa drove the rebels northward to Perusia (peh-roo'shuh), the modern Perugia, and forced their surrender in 40 B.C.

Mark Antony was moving to the support of his family, but it was all over too quickly, and when Fulvia fled to Greece and died there almost immediately, that really ended it.

It seemed best, though, to renew the triumvirate and to straighten out the problems that had arisen. The triumvirs therefore met in southern Italy and made a new division of the Roman dominion. Mark Antony kept the east, but Octavian took Italy, Gaul, and Spain. Lepidus, odd man out, had to be satisfied with Africa.

To cement the union, a marriage was agreed upon. Just as Caesar's lovely daughter Julia had married Pompey in order to keep him in the family, so now Octavian's lovely sister, Octavia, was handed over to Mark Antony.

For the moment all seemed well and happy. Octavian and Antony went their separate ways.

For Octavian, at least, troubles continued, however. There was the problem of a new Pompey; Sextus Pompeius, the younger son of the old general. Sextus had accompanied his father to Egypt after the battle of Pharsalus and had been in the ship at sea from which he watched his father struck down on the shore. He had also been at the battle of Munda, after which his older brother had been killed, while he himself went safely into hiding, emerging only after Caesar had left Spain.

Slowly, Sextus built up a following and, during the disorders that followed Caesar's assassination, he collected ships and grew strong at sea. In essence, he was a most successful pirate. He seized Sicily, and that put him in a strong position, for Rome depended for its food supply on Sicilian grain. It meant he had a noose around Rome's neck, a noose he could tighten whenever he chose. Furthermore, if any grain shipments were brought in, say, from Egypt, the ships of Sextus Pompeius could stop them.

Hunger and discontent at Rome forced the triumvirs to come to some sort of arrangement with Sextus. They met with him at Misenum (my-see'num), a promontory northwest of the Bay of Naples, in 39 B.C. and it was agreed to let him have Sicily, Sardinia, Corsica, and the southern part of Greece. It was quite a concession, particularly for Octavian, but he was buying time.

By 36 B.C. Octavian had with difficulty organized a fleet of his own, which he placed under the command of Agrippa. He then found a pretext for war with Sextus and sent Agrippa's fleet after him. Agrippa suffered losses in storm and battle but finally trapped Sextus near the strait between Sicily and Italy. In the naval battle that followed, Agrippa won a complete victory. Sextus got away and managed to land in Asia Minor, but that did him no good. He was captured there by Antony's soldiers in 35 B.C., and was executed.

Meanwhile, Lepidus, in cooperation with Octavian against Sextus, had landed troops in Sicily. It occurred to Lepidus, who was rather chafed at the puny nature of his own share of the triumvirate, that he might as well keep Sicily for himself. However, his troops deserted to Octavian, who consequently relieved Lepidus of all responsibility and retired him to a quiet life in Rome.

By 36 B.C., then, Octavian had the entire west in a firm grip. Fulvia was dead, Sextus Pompeius was dead, Lepidus was harmless. Only Mark Antony remained to dispute mastery with him, and Mark Antony seemed in no mood to dispute anything with anyone.

## ANTONY AND CLEOPATRA

Mark Antony's marriage to Octavia had really done no good, since Mark Antony did not, apparently, care for her. As soon as possible, he was back in Alexandria with Cleopatra, a situation that suited him much better.

While he had been away from Egypt, there had been considerable trouble with the Parthians. This was brought about through the actions of a Roman traitor, Quintus Labienus (lab''ih-ee'nus). He was the son of a general who had served with Caesar in Gaul but had then switched to the side of Pompey and was killed in action at the battle of Munda. The younger Labienus remained a die-hard in opposition to Caesar and joined the army of Brutus and Cassius. Even after the battle of Philippi, he refused to submit and retired instead to the Parthians.

Orodes, whose armies had defeated Crassus, was still king of Parthia. He had kept clear of the Roman civil wars for the most part, perfectly content to let Rome tear herself apart without running any risks himself.

Labienus, however, persuaded him to take advantage of the anti-triumvir sentiment that Labienus maintained was present in Syria and Asia Minor. Orodes therefore placed a Parthian army at his disposal, and it turned out that Labienus had not exaggerated. In 40 B.C. the Parthians, with Labienus at their head, moved westward, and in short order almost all of Syria and

Asia Minor was occupied, various Roman garrisons joining the Roman renegade.

These Roman defeats took place in Mark Antony's part of the Roman realm, and he had to take counter-action. For the purpose, Mark Antony made use of Publius Ventidius Bassus (ventih'dee-us). In early life, Ventidius had been a poor man who made a living renting mules and carriages. He rose to become a general serving under Caesar in Gaul. Unlike Labienus's father, he remained loyal to Caesar during the war with Pompey and then sided with Mark Antony after the assassination of Caesar.

In 39 B.C., Ventidius moved into Asia Minor and the enemy retreated before him. He fought a battle in the eastern portion of that peninsula, won a victory and forced the Parthians to abandon their conquests.

The next year the Parthians tried again, and Ventidius met them again in Syria and defeated them even more strikingly. The date of this second battle is placed by the ancient historians on June 9, 38 B.C., the fifteenth anniversary of the defeat of Crassus. Orodes died that year, too, as though to mark the passing of Parthia's peak of power. Nevertheless, although the Romans may have felt they had avenged Crassus, they had merely held their own. Parthia was prevented from annexing Roman territory but, on the other hand, its own territory remained intact — and continued to remain so.

In 37 B.C., Mark Antony returned to the east and was not entirely pleased with Ventidius' victories. He would rather have had the glory of them himself. He relieved Ventidius and sent him back to Rome for a triumph, then prepared to attack Parthia in person (after spending some time in Alexandria first).

Antony's campaign, begun in 36 B.C., was a failure. He did not defeat the Parthians. On the contrary, he was forced to retreat with heavy losses when he tried to invade Parthia. All he could salvage was a victory the next year over the Armenians, a much weaker adversary. He returned to Alexandria with his military reputation much damaged, at the very time that Octavian was reaching heights of power in the west.

Octavian felt the time had now come, at last, for the crushing of his one remaining rival. He was making himself increasingly popular in Rome, for he reduced brigandage in Italy, restored quiet and prosperity, carried on building programs in Rome itself, and generally showed himself a wise and prudent ruler. In 38 B.C. he had married Livia, a sagacious Roman matron who advised him well through a long life together, and who made a very respectable contrast to Antony's foreign queen.

To the Roman people, it seemed that Antony had abandoned all thought of his position as Roman ruler in the east and was content to spend all his time holidaying with Cleopatra. Reports reaching Rome described him as wearing Greek clothes, and devoted only to pleasing the Egyptian queen. He was ready, so went the story, to turn all of Rome over to her, or as much of Rome as he could manage.

Undoubtedly, the reports were exaggerated, and it suited Octavian to have them exaggerated. Octavian procured Antony's letters to Cleopatra and his will and used them as evidence that Antony was indeed ready to abandon Rome to her. (Perhaps they were forgeries, for Octavian was unscrupulous enough to use false documents if it suited his purpose, but they may have been real, too, for Antony was foolish enough to put such things in writing.)

In 32 B.C. Antony divorced Octavia, and that made it seem as though he were preparing to make Cleopatra his legal wife. That was the last straw. Octavian had been carefully building up a hatred and fear of the Egyptian queen among the Roman populace, and now he maneuvered the senate into declaring war upon her.

Mark Antony recognized that the war was really against him, and he endeavored to rouse himself from his three-year holiday. He collected ships, moved into Greece, set up headquarters in the western regions of that country, and prepared to invade Epirus and then, eventually, Italy.

But Octavian's fleet, under Agrippa, appeared also in the waters west of Greece. After endless maneuverings and preparations, Cleopatra urged Antony to force a naval battle. Antony's ships were twice as numerous as Octavian's and were larger besides. If Antony won the naval battle, Cleopatra pointed out, his army was more numerous than that of Octavian's and final victory was sure to be his.

The battle took place on September 2, 31 B.C., off Actium (ak'shee-um), a promontory on the coast of southern Epirus, and proved to be the climax of what might be termed the Fourth Civil War.

At first, Octavian's ships could make little impression on Antony's large vessels, and the battle seemed to be a useless one between maneuverability and power. Finally, though, Agrippa maneuvered Antony into stretching his line so that Agrippa's ships could dart through the openings that resulted, making straight for Cleopatra's fleet of sixty ships that lay behind the line.

According to the story, Cleopatra, in a panic, ordered her ships to retreat and sail off. When Antony was made aware that Cleopatra and her ships were leaving the scene of battle, he proceeded to the most foolish act of a career which included a large number of foolish acts. He got into a small vessel, abandoning his loyal ships and men (who might still have won victory) and sailed after the cowardly queen.

His fleet did its best, but without its commander the heart was out of it, and before evening had come the fleet was destroyed. Octavian founded the city of Nicopolis (nih-kop'oh-lis), or "city of victory," near the site of the battle, a city that was in future to become the capital of Epirus. He then returned to Rome for the inevitable triumph.

Meanwhile, Antony and Cleopatra had scuttled to Alexandria. There was nothing for them to do but to wait for Octavian to find the time to go to Egypt after them. This happened in July 30 B.C.

Octavian appeared from the east, from the direction of Judea. Antony tried to resist but it was no use. On August 1, Octavian entered Alexandria and Mark Antony committed suicide.

That left Cleopatra. She still had her beauty and charm, and she hoped to use it on Octavian as she had used it on Caesar and Antony. She was thirty-nine now but that was not too old, perhaps.

She therefore asked to see him, and there was an interview that seemed to go well. Octavian was gentle, but obviously unmoved by her. He was neither Caesar nor Antony, and nothing ever distracted him from his purposes. Cleopatra saw that and realized that if he was speaking softly to her now, it was only that he might seize her and carry her back to Rome to grace a triumph. She would be forced to walk in chains behind Octavian's chariot.

There was left but one way of escape from that ultimate humiliation. She pretended complete submission, but when, later on, Octavian's messengers arrived to order her to accompany them, they found her dead. Octavian had foreseen such a possibility and had had all cutting utensils and other instruments of death removed from Cleopatra's apartments — but she had somehow managed to commit suicide. In that way, she tricked Octavian out of the last bit of victory.

The tradition arose that she had made use of a poisonous snake (an asp) that had been smuggled to her in a basket of figs, and that is perhaps the most dramatic and best-known incident of her entire glamorous career. However, no one knows if that is really true, and it is very likely that no one will ever know.

Egypt was made a Roman province in that year and became virtually the personal property of Octavian. Thus came to an end the last Macedonian kingdom and the last Macedonian monarch three centuries after the death of Alexander the Great.

Octavian had now reached the heights. It had been just a hundred years since the attempted reforms of Tiberius Gracchus, and a century of chaotic politics and four separate civil wars had come to an end. Great names had flashed through that century: Marius, Sulla, Pompey, Caesar, Mark Antony, but now only one remained, Octavian.

There was no further enemy, no opposition to be feared. Octavian was absolute ruler of all the Roman world in 30 B.C. On January 11, 29 B.C. (724 A.U.C.), the temple of Janus was closed for the first time in two hundred years. It was peace at last.

Rome, despite all the turbulence of the last century, had become a center of culture as well as of military power.

Cicero himself had been the greatest and most successful example of that culture. More of his work survives than of any other Roman writer, and it has been much more admired than that of any other. We have fifty-seven of his orations in complete form and know of eighty others which have not survived in full. These orations are bitter and often display what would now be considered poor taste, but it was not customary in those times to treat enemies with what is now known as sportsmanship and fair play. Their style is considered perfect; no other writer can match the ease of flow and mastery of the Latin language that was Cicero's. For two thousand years, now, he has been considered the model of all that is admirable in the language.

Cicero also wrote on rhetoric and on philosophy, not so much contributing anything deep of his own, as making known the Greek work on the subject to the Romans and doing so delightfully. In addition, nearly a thousand of his letters survive; letters in which he discusses frankly all the issues of the day.

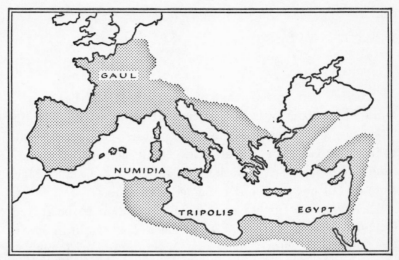

End of Republic — 29 B.C.

In fact, he is so frank (apparently without thought of publication) that he reveals his own weaknesses; his vanity, his eagerness for praise and flattery, his timidity, his capacity for self-pity and so on.

On the whole, though, Cicero manages to be the most attractive and human Roman of them all; honest and humane without being priggish; timid but capable of rising to courage on occasion.

Second to Cicero as a prose writer of the period is Caesar himself, whose commentaries on the war in Gaul survive and are studied in school to this day. The opening sentence — "All Gaul is divided into three parts" — has become almost a catch phrase. It is written with all the virtue of a soldier; clear, simple and straightforward, without unnecessary ornament. Unfortunately, his orations do not survive, which is a pity, for they were much admired in his time.

Among the Roman poets of the period, two names are preeminent. One of them is Titus Lucretius Carus, born about 95

B.C. His fame rests on his long poem "De Natura Rerum" ("On the Nature of Things") published in 56 B.C. In it, Lucretius describes the universe according to the philosophy of the Greek thinker Epicurus (ep-ih-kyoo'rus), who had lived two and a half centuries earlier. This philosophy included the view that everything is composed of tiny, indivisible particles, which the Greeks called "atoms." It developed a rational, materialistic, almost atheistic view of the universe.

Of all the ancient writings we know, Lucretius's poem most nearly represents the philosophic viewpoint of modern science. It was lost and nearly forgotten in later centuries, but in 1417 a single manuscript was discovered. Soon after the invention of printing, the poem was set in type and numerous copies were made, so that it grew popular, and undoubtedly had an important influence on the development of thought leading to modern views of the universe.

Much less weighty, but much more beautiful, were the lyrics of Gaius Valerius Catullus (ka-tul'us). About 116 pieces of his verse survive out of a much greater number that he wrote. Some of them would be considered indecent today, but many others are touching and delicate. Many of them are addressed to "Lesbia," who is thought to represent none other than Clodia (the sister of the infamous Clodius), with whom Catullus was hopelessly and uselessly in love. In Catullus, the flexibility of Greek poetry was introduced into Latin.

Several Roman historians of note flourished in the period, too. One of these was Gaius Crispus Sallustius, usually known in English as Sallust (sal'ust). He was one of the followers of Clodius, and then of Caesar. Caesar left him as governor of Numidia after the destruction of Cato's army and he was accused of enriching himself by illegal means. The matter was never brought to trial, but Sallust, who had been poor before his African tour of duty, was rich afterward, which is good enough circumstantial evidence of his guilt. He wrote an account of the conspiracy of Catiline and another history (perhaps influenced by his stay in Africa) about the war against Jugurtha. Both of these have survived. He also wrote a general history of Rome, but only fragments of this remain in existence.

Cornelius Nepos, a friend of Cicero and Catullus, wrote a series of biographies of noted Greeks and Romans.

Marcus Terentius Varro's long life of ninety years spanned virtually the entire period of troubles (from 116 B.C. to 27 B.C.). He fought for Pompey but made submission to Caesar and was pardoned. He wrote prolifically and, according to report, was the author of nearly 600 volumes. Only two of his books survive, however. One of them is part of a book on the Latin language and the other, written when Varro was eighty, is a book on agriculture, perhaps the most important book on the subject surviving from ancient times.

It is not to be supposed, though, that culture can flourish only in times of war and insurrection. With the coming of Octavian's peace, a new and even greater period of culture was to break upon Rome.

Indeed, centuries of peace were now to descend upon the entire Mediterranean area after centuries of war, the longest period of continued peace the western world was ever to know either before or after. It was to be called the Pax Romana ("Roman peace").

It came, however, at a price, for the Roman Republic which had advanced through five hundred years of continuous war, from a backward village to world rule, was no more. Instead, the word of one man, Octavian, was law.

In 27 B.C., Octavian received the name of Augustus, meaning "of good omen," a sort of good-luck name by which he has been known to history ever since.

Like his grand-uncle, he allowed his birth month to be renamed in his honor. What had been "Sextilis" in the days of the Republic now became "Augustus" or, as it is known to us, "August."

Augustus always claimed it was his intention to "restore the

Republic." He never assumed the title of king, and he lived up to all the forms of the Republic. However, he concentrated all the offices in his own person, and he was the *Imperator*, meaning "Leader."

This word has come down to us as "Emperor." Augustus was therefore the first of a long line of Roman Emperors, and the realm over which he and his successors ruled was the Roman Empire.

The tale of that Empire, of its glories, its miseries, and of the influence it has had on human history to this very day, I will tell in another book.

# TABLE OF DATES

NOTE: B.C. *represents the number of years before the birth of Christ;* A.U.C. *represents the number of years after the founding of Rome.*

| B.C. | A.U.C. | | B.C. | A.U.C. | |
|------|--------|--|------|--------|--|
| 1000 | | Villanovans enter Italy | 534 | 219 | Assassination of Servius Tullius; Tarquinius Superbus seventh king |
| 900 | | Etruscans enter Italy | | | |
| 814 | | Carthage founded | | | |
| 753 | 1 | Rome founded; Romulus first king | 509 | 244 | Exile of Tarquinius Superbus; Roman Republic founded |
| 734 | 19 | Syracuse founded | | | |
| 716 | 37 | Death of Romulus; Numa Pompilius second king | 508 | 245 | Lars Porsenna attacks Rome; Horatius at the bridge |
| 707 | 46 | Tarentum founded | 496 | 257 | Battle of Lake Regillus |
| 673 | 80 | Death of Numa Pompilius; Tullus Hostilius third king | 494 | 259 | Plebeians secede from Rome; tribunate established |
| 667 | 86 | Battle between Horatii and Curiatii | 491 | 262 | Coriolanus leads army against Rome |
| 665 | 88 | Alba Longa destroyed | 474 | 279 | Greeks defeat Etruscans at Cumae |
| 641 | 112 | Death of Tullus Hostilius; Ancus Martius fourth king | 458 | 295 | Dictatorship of Cincinnatus |
| 616 | 137 | Death of Ancus Martius; Tarquinius Priscus fifth king | 450 | 303 | Establishment of Twelve Tables |
| 578 | 175 | Assassination of Tarquinius Priscus; Servius Tullius sixth king | 445 | 308 | Intermarriage of patricians and plebeians allowed |
| | | | 421 | 332 | Quaestorship open to plebeians |
| 540 | 213 | Etruscans defeat Greeks at Alalia | 396 | 357 | Camillus takes Veii after ten year siege |

| B.C. | A.U.C. | | B.C. | A.U.C. | |
|------|--------|--|------|--------|--|
| 391 | 362 | Camillus exiled | 304 | 449 | End of Second Samnite War |
| 390 | 363 | Gauls defeat Rome at Allia River, take city; capitol saved by Manlius | 298 | 455 | Third Samnite War begins |
| 384 | 369 | Manlius executed | 295 | 458 | Fabius Maximus defeats Gauls at Sentinum |
| 367 | 386 | Licinio-Sextian laws open consulate to plebeians | 290 | 463 | End of Third Samnite War |
| 365 | 388 | Death of Camillus | 289 | 464 | Death of Agathocles |
| 354 | 399 | Latin League established under Roman domination | 281 | 472 | Tarentum appeals to Pyrrhus for help against Rome |
| 351 | 402 | Censorship opened to plebeians | 280 | 473 | Pyrrhus defeats Rome at Heraclea |
| 343 | 410 | First Samnite War | 279 | 474 | Pyrrhus defeats Rome at Ausculum |
| 340 | 413 | Latin War | 275 | 478 | Rome defeats Pyrrhus at Beneventum |
| 338 | 415 | Philip II of Macedon establishes domination over Greeks | 272 | 481 | Rome takes Tarentum; death of Pyrrhus in Greece |
| 334 | 419 | Gauls make peace with Rome; Alexander the Great invades Persia | 270 | 483 | Rome completes conquest of Magna Graecia; Hiero II becomes king of Syracuse; birth of Hamilcar Barca |
| 332 | 421 | Alexander of Epirus comes to aid of Tarentum | 269 | 484 | Fourth Samnite War |
| 326 | 427 | Death of Alexander of Epirus; Second Samnite War begins | 264 | 489 | First Punic War begins |
| 323 | 430 | Death of Alexander the Great | 263 | 490 | Rome invades Sicily |
| 321 | 432 | Samnites defeat Rome at the Caudine Forks | 260 | 493 | Rome wins naval victory over Carthage |
| 318 | 435 | Birth of Pyrrhus | 256 | 497 | Romans under Regulus invade Africa |
| 312 | 441 | Building of the Appian Way | 255 | 498 | Regulus defeated and captured |
| 310 | 443 | Agathocles of Syracuse invades Africa | 248 | 505 | Hamilcar Barca rises to Carthaginian command |
| 308 | 445 | Fabius Maximus defeats Etruscans | 247 | 506 | Birth of Hannibal |

| B.C. | A.U.C. | | B.C. | A.U.C. | |
|---|---|---|---|---|---|
| 241 | 512 | End of First Punic War; Sicily becomes Roman province | 210 | 543 | Scipio the Elder takes command in Spain |
| 236 | 517 | Hamilcar Barca establishes Carthaginian power in Spain | 207 | 546 | Romans defeat Hasdrubal at Lake Metaurus |
| 234 | 519 | Birth of Cato the Elder | 206 | 547 | Scipio defeats Carthaginians at Ilipa in Spain |
| 231 | 522 | Sardinia and Corsica become Roman province | 205 | 548 | End of First Macedonian War |
| 229 | 524 | Illyrian war | 202 | 551 | Scipio defeats Hannibal at Zama in Africa |
| 228 | 525 | Death of Hamilcar Barca | | | |
| 223 | 530 | Antiochus III becomes Seleucid king | 201 | 552 | End of Second Punic War |
| 222 | 531 | Flaminius defeats Gauls; Rome dominates all of Italy to the Alps | 200 | 553 | Second Macedonian War begins |
| | | | 197 | 556 | Flamininus defeats Macedonians at Cynoscephalae; Spain organized into Roman provinces |
| 221 | 532 | Hannibal takes over command in Spain; Philip V becomes king of Macedonia | 196 | 557 | End of Second Macedonian War; "liberation" of Greece; Hannibal flees to Asia |
| 220 | 533 | Flaminius constructs Flaminian way | | | |
| 219 | 534 | Second Punic War begins; Rome annexes Corcyra | | | |
| 218 | 535 | Hannibal crosses Alps; defeats Romans at Trebia | 192 | 561 | Syrian War (with Antiochus) begins |
| | | | 191 | 562 | Romans defeat Antiochus at Thermopylae |
| 217 | 536 | Hannibal defeats Romans at Lake Trasimenus | 190 | 563 | Romans defeat Antiochus at Magnesia; first appearance of Romans in Asia |
| 216 | 537 | Hannibal defeats Romans at Cannae | | | |
| 215 | 538 | First Macedonian War begins | 189 | 564 | End of Syrian War |
| 212 | 541 | Marcellus conquers Syracuse | 187 | 566 | Death of Antiochus III |
| | | | 184 | 569 | Cato the Elder becomes censor |
| 211 | 542 | Hannibal at the gates of Rome | 183 | 570 | Death of Hannibal |

| B.C. | A.U.C. | |
|---|---|---|
| | | and of Scipio the Elder |
| 179 | 574 | Death of Philip V |
| 172 | 581 | Third Macedonian War begins |
| 168 | 585 | Romans defeat Macedonians at Pydna and end Third Macedonian War; Polybius and a thousand Greek hostages carried off |
| 167 | 586 | Roman citizens freed of direct taxation |
| 163 | 590 | Birth of Tiberius Gracchus |
| 155 | 598 | Birth of Marius |
| 153 | 600 | Birth of Gaius Gracchus |
| 151 | 602 | Scipio the Younger pacifies Spain; Polybius and other Greek hostages freed |
| 149 | 604 | Third Carthaginian War begins |
| 148 | 605 | Fourth Macedonian War |
| 146 | 607 | Carthage destroyed; Corinth sacked; Macedonia becomes Roman province |
| 138 | 615 | Birth of Sulla |
| 135 | 618 | First Servile War (in Sicily) |
| 133 | 620 | Scipio defeats Spanish tribesmen at Numantia; Pergamum annexed as Province of Asia; Tiberius Gracchus becomes tribune |
| 132 | 621 | Assassination of Tiberius Gracchus |

| B.C. | A.U.C. | |
|---|---|---|
| 129 | 624 | Death of Scipio the Younger |
| 125 | 628 | Romans conquer southern Gaul |
| 123 | 630 | Gaius Gracchus becomes tribune |
| 121 | 632 | Assassination of Gaius Gracchus; southern Gaul organized as Roman province; Mithradates VI becomes king of Pontus |
| 115 | 638 | Birth of Crassus |
| 113 | 640 | Cimbri invade Gaul |
| 111 | 642 | Jugurthine War begins |
| 107 | 646 | Marius elected consul for first time |
| 106 | 647 | Birth of Pompey; Birth of Cicero |
| 105 | 648 | Marius defeats Jugurtha |
| 104 | 649 | Death of Jugurtha |
| 103 | 650 | Second Servile War (in Sicily); Teutones join Cimbri |
| 102 | 651 | Marius destroys Teutones; Birth of Julius Caesar |
| 101 | 652 | Marius destroys Cimbri |
| 100 | 653 | Marius forced to kill the tribune, Saturninus; loses political power |
| 95 | 658 | Birth of Cato the Younger |
| 91 | 662 | Assassination of the tribune, Drusus; Social War begins |
| 89 | 664 | Sulla defeats Italian rebels |
| 88 | 665 | End of Social War; |

| B.C. | A.U.C. | | B.C. | A.U.C. | |
|---|---|---|---|---|---|
| | | First Mithradatic War begins; First Civil War breaks out in Rome as Sulla drives Marius from the city. | 69 | 684 | Lucullus defeats Tigranes of Armenia; Birth of Cleopatra |
| | | | 67 | 686 | Crete becomes Roman province; Pompey clears Mediterranean of piracy |
| 86 | 667 | Sulla sacks Athens; Marius seizes control of Rome, then dies | 66 | 687 | Lucullus recalled to Rome and replaced by Pompey |
| 85 | 668 | Birth of Brutus | | | |
| 84 | 669 | End of First Mithradatic War | 64 | 689 | Pompey in East; Pontus, Cilicia, Syria and Judea become Roman provinces; Conspiracy of Catiline |
| 83 | 670 | Birth of Mark Antony | | | |
| 82 | 671 | Sulla defeats Marian army at Colline Gate | | | |
| 81 | 672 | Sulla becomes dictator of Rome; Second Mithradatic War | 63 | 690 | Cicero becomes consul and attacks Catiline; Death of Mithradates; Octavian born |
| 79 | 674 | Sulla resigns dictatorship | | | |
| 78 | 675 | Death of Sulla | 62 | 691 | Death of Catiline |
| 76 | 677 | Caesar captured by pirates | 61 | 692 | Pompey returns to Rome |
| 74 | 679 | Bithynia and Cyrene become Roman provinces; Third Mithradatic War; Verres governor of Sicily | 60 | 693 | Establishment of First Triumvirate |
| | | | 58 | 695 | Clodius becomes tribune; Cicero driven into exile; Caesar begins Gallic War |
| 73 | 680 | Lucullus defeats Mithradates; Spartacus leads Third Servile War against Rome | 55 | 698 | Caesar invades Germany and Britain |
| | | | 53 | 700 | Crassus dies at Battle of Carrhae against Parthians |
| 72 | 681 | Pompey defeats Marian forces in Spain | 52 | 701 | Death of Clodius; Pompey sole consul |
| 71 | 682 | Crassus defeats slave army; death of Spartacus | 51 | 702 | Caesar completes conquest of Gaul; Pompey turns against him |
| 70 | 683 | Cicero prosecutes Verres | | | |

| B.C. | A.U.C. | |
|---|---|---|
| 49 | 704 | Caesar crosses Rubicon; Second Civil War begins |
| 48 | 705 | Caesar defeats Pompey at Pharsalus; Pompey assassinated in Egypt; Caesar follows and meets Cleopatra |
| 47 | 706 | Caesar defeats Pharnaces of Pontus at Zela |
| 46 | 707 | Caesar returns to Rome in supreme power; defeats Pompeian army at Thapsus in Africa; suicide of Cato the Younger |
| 45 | 708 | Caesar defeats Pompeian army at Munda in Spain; reforms the calendar |
| 44 | 709 | Assassination of Caesar by Brutus, Cassius and others |
| 43 | 710 | Third Civil War begins; Second Triumvirate formed; murder of Cicero |
| 42 | 711 | Octavian and Mark Antony defeat Brutus and Cassius at Philippi; suicide of Brutus and Cassius |
| 41 | 712 | Antony meets Cleopatra |
| 38 | 715 | Ventidius defeats Parthians |
| 36 | 717 | Octavian defeats Sextus Pompeius, controls west |
| 32 | 721 | Fourth Civil War |
| 31 | 722 | Octavian defeats Mark Antony and Cleopatra at Actium |
| 30 | 723 | Suicide of Mark Antony and Cleopatra |
| 29 | 724 | Octavian in sole control of all Roman dominion; end of Roman Republic |
| 27 | 726 | Octavian receives name of Augustus |

# INDEX

Abraham, 198
Achaean League, 112–114; and Rome, 118, 124; destruction of, 130–131
Actium, battle of, 235
Aediles, 30
Aeneas, 8, 22
Aequians, 36
Aetolian League, 112–114; and Antiochus III, 119–120
Africa, Province of, 129
Agathocles, 61–62, 71
Agrigentum, battle of, 77
Agrippa, Marcus Vipsanius, 230–231; at the battle of Actium, 235
Alalia, battle of, 21
Alba Longa, 7; Latium and, 9–10; destruction of, 15–16
Alexander I of Epirus, 45; and Tarentum, 50
Alexander III (the Great) of Macedon, 50; successors of, 65–66
Alexandria, 207; library of, 210
Alexandrian War, 209–210
Allia River, battle of, 38
Alps, 92
Ancus Martius, 16–19
Andriscus, 130
Antigonus II of Macedon, 85
Antioch, 179
Antiochus III of Seleucid Empire, 116–117; war with Rome, 119–121; death of, 132

Antiochus IV of Seleucid Empire, 132
Antiochus XIII of Seleucid Empire, 179
Antipater, 180
Antonius, Lucius, 230
Antony, Mark. See Marcus Antonius
Appian Way, 55
Appius Claudius, 29
Appius Claudius Caecus, 53–55; and Pyrrhus, 69
Appius Claudius Caudex, 76
Appius Claudius Crassus, 33
Apulia, 51
Aquae Sextiae (Aix), 145; battle of, 150
Aquilonia, battle of, 60
Archimedes, 101–102
Ariovistus, 191–192
Aristobulus, 179
Armenia, 160, 168; and Mark Antony, 233–234
Ascanius, 9
Asia, Province of, 132
Asia Minor, 4; after Alexander the Great, 66, 116; and Mithradates VI, 158–161
Assyria, 12
Athens, 44–45, 49; and Rome, 116; sack of, 163
Attalus I of Pergamum, 116
Attalus III of Pergamum, 131–132
August, 240
Augustus, 240–241
Ausculum, battle of, 70
Aventine Hill, 10, 17

Balearic Islands, 74–75
Barcino (Barcelona), 89
Beneventum, battle of, 71
Bithynia, 121, 158; and Mithradates VI, 160; becomes Roman province, 167
Bocchus, 148
Bononia (Bologna), 227

Brennus, 40

Britain, 193

Brutus, Decimus Junius, 220; after assassination of Caesar, 226–227; death of, 227.

Brutus, Lucius Junius, 23; death of, 25

Brutus, Marcus Junius, 219; after assassination of Caesar, 223–224, 227–228; death of, 228

Caelian Hill, 15

Caesar, Gaius Julius, 165; connection with Marius, 182–184; and the pirates, 183; and Crassus, 184; and conspiracy of Catiline, 187; and Pompey, 188–189; as consul, 189; and Clodius, 189–190; in Gaul, 191–194; in Germany, 193; in Britain, 193; as author, 194; faces opposition of Pompey, 201–202; and Mark Antony, 203; at Rubicon River, 203; in control of Italy, 204; in Greece, 204–206; defeats Pompey, 205–206; in Egypt, 208–210; in Asia Minor, 210; returns to Rome, 211; in Africa, 213; as dictator, 213ff.; Roman citizenship and, 214–215; calendar reorganization, 215–216; and the kingship, 218–219; conspiracy against, 219–222; assassination of, 221–222; writings of, 238

Caesar, Lucius Julius, 155–156

Calendar, Roman, 38, 215–216

Calends, 38

Calpurnia, 191, 221, 224

Calvinus, Sextius, 145

Camillus, Marcus Furius, 37; and the Gauls, 40; and the plebeians, 41–42; military innovations of, 56

Campania, 34–35, 46

Cannae, battle of, 97–98

Capitol, 19; Gauls and, 39

Capitoline Hill, 12–13

Cappadocia, 199

Capua, 35; and Hannibal, 99, 102–103

Carrhae, battle of, 198–200

Carthage, 6; Aeneas and, 8–9; Etruscans and, 21; Agathocles and, 61; alliance with Rome, 70; growth of, 74–75; explorations by, 75; in Sicily, 75; wars with Rome, 76ff.; civil war in, 83; in Spain, 89; Hannibal and, 104; defeat at Zama, 108; after the battle of Zama, 127; destruction of, 129

Carthago Nova (Cartagena), 89

Cassius Longinus, Gaius, 220; after the assassination of Caesar, 227–228; death of, 228

Cassivelaunus, 193

Catilina, Lucius Sergius (Catiline), 184–187

Cato, Marcus Porcius (I), 125–126; and Carthage, 127–128

Cato, Marcus Porcius (II), 185; and conspiracy of Catiline, 187; and Pompey, 188; exile to Cyprus, 189; return from Cyprus, 194; in Africa, 212–213; death of, 213

Cato of Utica. See Cato, Marcus Porcius (II)

Cato the Younger. See Cato, Marcus Porcius (II)

Catullus, Gaius Valerius, 239

Caudine Forks, battle of, 52

Caudium, 51

Celts, 144

Censor, 54

Census, 54

Cicero, Marcus Tullius, 174; as orator, 175; and Verres case,

175–176; and conspiracy of
Catiline, 185–186; and Clodius,
189–190; exile of, 190; returns
from exile, 195; at trial of Milo,
195; and Mark Antony, 203; and
Caesar, 211; and Caesar's as-
sassin's, 223; death of, 227; writ-
ings of, 237–238
Cilicia, 177
Cimbri, 148, 150
Cincinnati, 37
Cincinnatus, Lucius Quinctius, 36
Cineas, 68
Cinna, Lucius Cornelius (I), 163–
164
Cinna, Lucius Cornelius (II), 220–
221
Circus Maximus, 19
Cisalpine Gaul, 35; conquered by
Rome, 85–86
Citizens, Roman, 136
Civil War, First, 162–165; Second,
203–206; Third, 226–228;
Fourth, 234–236
Cleopatra, 208; and Caesar, 208–
210; in Rome, 229n; and Mark
Antony, 229ff.; at the battle of
Actium, 235; death of, 236
Claudius Pulcher, Publius, 81
Cloaca Maxima, 19
Clodius, Publius, 189–190; death
of, 195
Clusium, 27
Colchis, 160
Collatinus, Tarquinius, 23
Colline Gate, battle of, 164
Consuls, 25
Corcyra, 85
Corfinium, 155
Corinth, 131
Coriolanus, 31
Corioli, 31, 32
Cornelia, 139, 143
Cornelius Nepos, 240

Corsica, 21; annexed by Rome, 84
Crassus, Marcus Licinius, 172;
wealth of, 172; and Pompey,
173–174, 188–189; and Caesar,
184; and conspiracy of Catiline,
187; and the invasion of Parthia,
196–199; death of, 199
Crete, 177
Crimea, 160
Ctesiphon, 198
Cumae, 22, 34
Curiatii, 16
Cynoscephalae, battle of, 117–118
Cyprus, 189
Cyrene, 177

Dating, 10–12
Decemvirs, 32
Decius Mus, Publius (I), 47
Decius Mus, Publius (II), 59
Decius Mus, Publius (III), 70
Delos, 124
Dictator, 36
Dido, 8
Dionysius, 45
Dionysius Exiguus, 11
Drepanum, battle of, 81
Drusus, Marcus Livius, 153–154
Duilius Nepos, Gaius, 78
Dyrrhachium, 204–205

Ebro River, 90
Ecnomus, battle of, 79
Egypt, 12; Ptolemaic, 66; and
Rome; 115–116; and Caesar,
206–210; becomes a Roman
province, 236
Elephants, Pyrrhus and, 67–68;
Hannibal and, 92; at the battle
of Zama, 108; at the battle of
Cynoscephalae, 117; at the bat-
tle of Thapsus, 213
Empire, Roman, 241
Enna, 138

Ennius, Quintus, 115
Epicurus, 239
Epirus, 45, 66; ravaged by Romans, 123
Equites, 153
Esquiline Hill, 20
Etruria, 3
Etruscans 3–4; civilization of, 3–5; domination over Rome, 17–23; at height of power, 21; decline of, 34; Gauls and, 35; conquered by Rome, 57–58
Eumenes II of Pergamum, 119, 122
Eunus, 137

Fabius Maximus Rullianus, Quintus (I), 57–59
Fabius Maximus Rullianus, Quintus (II), 95–97
Fabricius, Gaius, 69
Fasces, 33
Flaccus, Marcus Fulvius, 144
Flaminian Way, 86
Flamininus, Titus Quinctius, 117–119; and Hannibal, 121
Flaminius, Gaius, 85–86; and Hannibal, 95
Forum, 19
Fregellae, 51
Fulvia, 229–230

Galatia, 159
Gallia Narbonensis, 145
Gaul, Transalpine, 144–145; Caesar in, 191–194
Gauls, 35; capture Rome, 38–40; peace with Rome, 47–48; defeated by Rome, 58–59; in Macedon, 70; and Hannibal, 92; in Asia Minor, 159
Gelon, 34
Germany, 191
Gladiatorial War, 171–173
Gladiators, 19, 171

Gracchi, 138ff.
Gracchus, Gaius Sempronius, 138; as tribune, 142–143; death of, 143
Gracchus, Tiberius Sempronius, 138; as tribune, 139–141; death of, 141
Greece, 12
Greeks, Etruscans and, 21, 34; internecine struggles, 45; and Rome, 85; and Philip V of Macedon, 112–114; liberation by Rome, 114–118

Hamilcar Barca, 81–82; and Carthaginian civil war, 83; in Spain, 87–89
Hannibal, 90; takes Saguntum, 90; enters Italy, 91–93; defeats Romans, 93–98; in Magna Graecia, 103; at the gate of Rome, 103; returns to Africa, 107; and Antiochus III of Seleucid Empire, 119–121; death of, 121
Haran, 198
Hasdrubal (I), 89
Hasdrubal (II), 100; invades Italy, 104; death of, 105
Hellenistic kingdoms, 66
Helvetii, 192
Heraclea, battle of, 68
Herod, 11
Hiero II of Syracuse, 76, 99
Hieronymus, 99
Horatia, 16
Horatii, 15–16
Horatius Cocles, Publius, 27
Hyrcanus II of Judea, 179

Ides, 38
Ilerda, battle of, 204
Ilipa, battle of, 106
Illyria, 84–85
Illyrian War, 85

Imperator, 241
Israel, 12
Italy, prehistoric, 2–5; Roman conquest of, 44ff.; Roman government over, 72–73; and Punic wars, 99; Romanization of, 111; Roman citizenship in, 142–143, 152, 154, 156; revolt of, 155–156

Janiculum Hill, 27
Janus, 14; temple of, 14–15
Jeroboam II, 12
Jerusalem, 180
Jesus Christ, 11
Jews, 132
Juba of Numidia, 204; death of, 213
Judea, 179–180
Jugurtha of Numidia, 145–148; death of, 148
Jugurthine War, 146–148
Julia, 191, 197
Julian Calendar, 216
July, 217
Junia, 220
Jupiter, temple of, 19

Labienus, Quintus, 232
Lake Regillus, battle of, 28
Lake Trasimenus, battle of, 95
Latin League, 7, 20–21, 42–43
Latinus, 9
Latin War, 47
Latius, 7
Legion, 56
Lepidus, Marcus Aemilius (I), 170
Lepidus, Marcus Aemilius (II), 223; and Second Triumvirate, 227; retirement of, 231
Licinio-Sextian laws, 42
Licinius, Gaius, 42
Lictors, 32
Lilybaeum, 75, 77
Livia, 234

Lucania, 51
Lucilius, Gaius, 125
Lucretius, Titus Carus, 238–239
Lucullus, Lucius Licinius, 167–169; and Pompey, 188
Lusitania, 131

Maccabees, 132, 179
Macedon, 45–46; domination of Greece, 49; after Alexander the Great, 66; and Hannibal, 99–100; and Rome, 112–118; end of monarchy, 123; becomes Roman province, 130
Macedonian War, First, 114; Second, 117–118; Third, 123; Fourth, 130
Magna Graecia, 6; Etruscans and, 34; Rome and, 60ff.
Magnesia, battle of, 120
Mago (I), 74
Mago (II), 94
Mamertines, 71, 76
Maniples, 56–57
Manlius, Marcus, 39–41
Marcellus, Marcus Claudius, 100–102
Marcius, Gaius (Coriolanus), 31
Marcus Antonius (Mark Antony), 203, 211; Caesar's kingship and, 221; and assassination of Caesar, 222; after the assassination of Caesar, 224; and Octavian, 225–226; and Decimus Brutus, 226; and Second Triumvirate, 227ff.; and Cleopatra, 229ff., and Parthia, 232–234; in Armenia, 233–234; at the battle of Actium, 235; death of, 236
Marius, Gaius, 147; in Numidia, 147–148; and the barbarian menace, 149–150; eclipse of, 152; and Social War, 155–156; and

the First Civil War, 161–162; in exile, 162; death of, 164

Mark Antony. *See* Marcus Antonius

Massilia, 144

Massinissa, 107–109; after the battle of Zama, 127–128

Mauretania, 148, 213

Menenius Agrippa, 29–30

Messana, 76

Metaurus River, battle of, 105

Metellus, Quintus Caecilius (I), 130

Metellus, Quintus Caecilius (II), 146–147, 151

Metellus Pius, Quintus Caecilius, 177

Milo Papianus, Titus Annius, 195

Mithradates I of Pontus, 159

Mithradates V of Pontus, 159

Mithradates VI of Pontus, 159; and Rome, 160–161; defeat of, 163; after Sulla, 166–168; death of, 178

Mithradatic War, First, 161; Second, 166; Third, 167–168

Months, Roman, 216–217

Mucius, Gaius, 27

Mummius, Lucius, 131

Munda, battle of, 214

Mutina (Modena), 226

Mylae, battle of, 78

Nabis of Sparta, 118–119

Names, Roman, 16n, 18n

Narbo Martius (Narbonne), 145

Neapolis (Naples), 105

Nebuchadrezzar, 74

Nero, Gaius Claudius, 105

Nicomedes III of Bithynia, 167

Nicopolis, 235

Nola, 101

Nones, 38

Numantia, 131

Numa Pompilius, 14–16

Numidia, 107, 204; under Jugurtha, 145–148

Octavia, 230, 234

Octavianus, Gaius Julius Caesar (Octavian), 224; and Mark Antony, 225–226; and Decimus Brutus, 226–227; and Second Triumvirate, 227ff.; marriage of, 234; final victory of, 236

Octavius, Gaius. *See* Octavianus

Octavius, Marcus, 140

Oligarchy, 28

Olympian Games, 12

Orodes of Parthia, 198; death of, 233

Palatine Hill, 9–10

Pandosia, 50

Panormus (Palermo), 75

Papirius Cursor, Lucius, 53, 58

Parthia, 197–200, 232–234

Patricians, 17; plebeian struggle against, 28–33

Paulus, Lucius Aemilius (I), 97

Paulus, Lucius Aemilius (II), 123–124

Pax Romana, 240

Pergamum, 116; becomes Roman province, 131–132

Perseus of Macedon, 122–123

Persian Empire, 44

Perusia (Perugia), 230

Phalanx, 46, 57, 123

Pharnaces, 210

Pharsalus, battle of, 205–206

Philip II of Macedon, 45–46, 49

Philip V of Macedon, 112–118; and Hannibal, 114; after Cynoscephalae, 122

Philippi, battle of, 228

Phoenicians, 6, 74

Phraates II of Parthia, 198

Piracy, 84–85, 176–177

Plautus, Titus Maccius, 115
Plebeians, 17; struggle for power, 28–33, 41–42; secession of, 29–30
Polybius, 124; release of, 126; at destruction of Carthage, 129–130
Pompeia, 190
Pompeius, Gnaeus (Pompey), 169; and Sulla, 169–170; in Spain, 170–171; and Crassus, 173–174; and pirates, 176–177; in Judea, 180; returns to Rome, 180–181, 187; reconciliation with Senate, 195–196; as sole consul, 201–202; flight from Italy, 204; flight to Egypt, 206; death of, 208
Pompeius, Gnaeus (II), 212
Pompeius, Sextus, 230–231
Pontifex Maximus, 215
Pontus, 158–162; becomes Roman province, 178
Porcia, 220
Porsenna, Lars, 27–28
Portus Magonis (Port Mahon), 75
Pothinus, 208; death of, 209
Praetor, 24
Praetorian guard, 149
Proletariat, 136
Provence, 145
Provinces, Roman, 82–83
Prusias II of Bithynia, 121
Ptolemy I of Egypt, 66
Ptolemy II of Egypt, 116
Ptolemy IV of Egypt, 115
Ptolemy V of Egypt, 115
Ptolemy XI of Egypt, 207
Ptolemy XII of Egypt, 207; death of, 210
Ptolemy XIII of Egypt, 210
Punic War, First, 76–82; Second, 91ff.; Third, 128–129
Pydna, battle of, 123
Pyrrhic victory, 70

Pyrrhus, 66; in Italy, 67–72; in Sicily, 71, 75; death of, 72

Quaestors, 25
Quintilis, 217
Quirinal Hill, 12
Quirinus, 12, 14

Regulus, Marcus Atilius, 79–81
Remus, 10
Rhegium, 72
Rhodes, 116, 124
Roman Empire, 241
Roman Republic, founding of, 23; government of, 24–25; end of, 240–241
Rome, Etruscan borrowings by, 4; founding of, 7–10; kings of, 12ff.; gods of, 14; Greek influence over, 14; Latium and, 15–16; dominated by Etruscans, 17–23; engineering feats of, 19; end of kingdom, 23; Etruscan assault on, 25–28; government of, 30–31, 54; laws of, 32; defeats Veii, 37; Gauls and, 38–40; calendar of, 38, 215–216; Samnites and, 49ff.; roads of, 55; military techniques of, 55–57; Magna Graecia and, 62ff.; Pyrrhus and, 65ff.; alliance with Carthage, 70; conquers Magna Graecia, 72; Syracuse and, 76; Carthage and, 76ff.; builds navy, 77–78; provinces of, 82–83; piracy and, 84–85; Illyria and, 84–85; Greeks and, 85; Hannibal and, 90ff.; conquers Syracuse, 101–102; Spain and, 109–111; Macedon and, 112–118; Greek culture and, 114–115, 124–125; literature of, 115, 125; Seleucid Empire and, 119–121; Pergamum and, 131–132; after period of conquest, 134ff.;

slaves in, 135–138; internal troubles of, 134ff., 151ff.; citizens of, 136; Jugurtha and, 145–148; barbarian invasions and, 148–150; generals and, 149; taxation in, 152; Mithradates VI and, 161ff.; civil wars in, 162; Armenia and, 168; gladiators in, 171; Senatorial corruption in, 175; oratory in, 175; pirates and, 176–177; end of republic of, 240–241

Romulus, 10, 12–14

Rubicon River, 72, 203

Sabines, 13

Saguntum, 90

Sallustius, Gaius Crispus (Sallust), 239

Samnites, 34–35; wars with Rome, 46ff.; conquered by Rome, 60

Samnite War, First, 46–47; Second, 51–58; Third, 59–60; Fourth, 72; Fifth, 155

Samnium, 35

Sardinia, 21; annexed by Rome, 83–84

Saturninus, Lucius Appuleius, 151–152

Scipio, Publius Cornelius, 92–94

Scipio Aemilianus, Publius Cornelius, 124–126; in Spain, 126, 131; and destruction of Carthage, 128–129; death of, 141

Scipio Africanus, Publius Cornelius, in Spain, 100, 105–107; in Africa, 107–108; in Asia, 120; death of, 122

Scipio Asiaticus, Lucius Cornelius, 120–121, 125

Scipio the Younger. See Scipio Aemilianus

Seleucid Empire, 66; at peak of power, 116; decline of, 132–133; absorbed by Rome, 178–179

Seleucus, 66

Sempronia, 139

Sempronius Longus, Tiberius, 93

Senate, 17; corruption of, 153; Marius and, 164; Sulla and, 165–166

Sentinum, battle of, 59

Sertorius, Quintus, 170–171

Servian Wall, 20

Servile War, First, 138; Second, 150; Third, 171–173

Servius Tullius, 20–21

Sextilis, 240

Sextius, Lucius, 42

Sibyl, Cumaean, 22

Sibylline books, 22

Sicily, 6, 45; annexed by Rome, 82; slave rebellion in, 137–138; under Verres, 174

Slaves, 135; rebellion of, 137–138, 150, 171–173

Social War, 155–156

Sosigenes, 216

Spain, Carthage in, 89; during Second Punic War, 100; taken by Rome, 106–107; becomes Roman province, 110–111; Roman wars in, 126, 131, 170–171

Sparta, 45; and the Achaean League, 114; final defeat of, 118–119

Spartacus, 171–173

SPQR, 42

Sulla, Lucius Cornelius, 147–148; and Social War, 156; and First Civil War, 161–162; in Greece, 162–163; in Asia Minor, 163; returns to Italy, 164; as dictator, 165; proscriptions under, 165; death of, 166

Sulpicius Rufus, Publius, 161–162

Syracuse, 7; Etruscans and, 34; under Dionysius, 45; Agathocles and, 61–62; Rome and, 76; joins

Carthage, 99; conquered by Rome, 101–102

Syria, province of, 179

Syrian War, 120

Taras, 6

Tarentum, 6; Samnites and, 50; Agathocles and, 61–62; Rome and, 62–63; Pyrrhus and, 67–68; conquered by Rome, 72; Hannibal and, 103

Tarpeia, 13

Tarpeian Rock, 13

Tarquinii, 18

Tarquinius Priscus, Lucius, 18; assassination of, 20

Tarquinius Sextus, 22–23

Tarquinius Superbus, Lucius (Tarquin), 21ff.; Cumaean sibyl and, 22; fall of, 23; final defeat of, 28

Tarsus, 229

Tauromenium (Taormina), 138

Temple of Jerusalem, 180

Terentia, 175

Terentius Afer, Publius (Terence), 125

Teutones, 149

Thapsus, battle of, 213

Thebes, 45, 49

Thermopylae, battle of, 120

Thrace, 171

Thurii, 62

Ticinus River, battle of, 93

Tigranes of Armenia, 168, 178, 197

Transalpine Gaul, 35

Trebia River, battle of, 93–94

Tribune, 30

Trinacria, 6

Triumph, 20

Triumvirate, First, 189ff.; Second, 227ff.

Trojan War, 8

Tullus Hostilius, 15–16

Twelve Tables, 32

Tyrrhenian Sea, 3

Utica, 212

Varro, Gaius Terentius, 97–98

Varro, Marcus Terentius, 240

Veii, 37

Ventidius Bassus, Publius, 233

Vercellae, battle of, 150

Vercingetorix, 194

Verres, Gaius, 174–176; death of, 228

Veto, 30

Villanovans, 3

Viminal Hill, 20

Virginia, 33

Viriathus, 131

Volscians, 22, 31, 35

Washington, George, 37

Xanthippus, 79

Zama, battle of, 107–108

Zela, battle of, 210